**Fodor's** InFo

# SAVANNAH

T0016309

# Welcome to Savannah

You may find it especially easy to get acquainted with the "Hostess City," as it is known to those smitten by its hospitality and charm. Some people come just to eat at its amazing restaurants, but with an eclectic array of shops, bars, museums, and monuments to experience, you'll find plenty to occupy your time. As you plan your upcoming travels to Savannah, please confirm that places are still open and let us know when we need to make updates by emailing us at editors@fodors.com.

## TOP REASONS TO GO

★ **Winsome architecture:** Savannah has no shortage of architectural or historical marvels.

★ *Midnight in the Garden of Good and Evil:* John Berendt's famous 1994 book still draws travelers.

★ **Famous Southern restaurants:** Savannah's elegant restaurants serve exquisite Southern cuisine.

★ **Historic inns and bed-and-breakfasts:** A unique pleasure is the opportunity to stay in a historic home.

★ **Savannah by night:** Barhopping and ghost tours are fun nocturnal activities.

# Contents

## MAPS

Chapter 1

# EXPERIENCE
# SAVANNAH

# 16 ULTIMATE EXPERIENCES

Savannah offers terrific experiences that should be on every traveler's list. Here are Fodor's top picks for a memorable trip.

ELIZA WILHELMIN
THE DEVOTED WIFE O
THOMAS N THEUS
DIED FEBRUARY 21 18

## 1 Relax in a Cemetery

The dead and the living share the beautiful, slightly spooky green spaces of Revolutionary War–era Colonial Cemetery, the famous Bonaventure. *(Ch. 6)*

## 2 Take a Pedicab Ride

Hop in one of these bicycle-wheeled vehicles from Savannah Pedicab or Royal Bike Taxi, powered by charming humans who are full of local intel and travel the entire historic district for tips. *(Ch. 3)*

## 3 Shop for Antiques

With almost 300 years of history here, antiquing is practically an art form. Peruse old historic mansions-turned-shops and wondrous warehouses to find the perfect piece of furniture or knickknack to take home. *(Ch. 3)*

# 4 Sip Local Brews

Fill a pint glass with unique IPAs, pilsners, sours, and other hopped-up suds from a bevy of fine breweries. *(Ch. 3)*

# 5 Sit in a Square

Cultivate Savannah's favorite pastime on a bench in a square or park chatting with your favorite folks or a new friend among the beauty of the azaleas, camellias, and magnolias. *(Ch. 3)*

# 6 Dig Deeper into History

A major port for the Transatlantic slave trade, Savannah preserves a slew of important African American historic locations, including Underground Railroad stops and the Civil Rights Museum. *(Ch. 1, 3)*

# 7 Eat Local Shrimp

Whether you like 'em barbecued, boiled, baked, stir-fried, or over grits, ask for plump, sweet wild Georgia shrimp caught in the nets of local fishing fleets, á la *Forrest Gump*. *(Ch. 3, 7)*

# 8 Visit the Beach

Just a 25-minute drive from downtown lie the beaches of Tybee Island, where you can catch sunrays and surf, build sand castles, and watch ships glide into the horizon. *(Ch. 7)*

# 9 Take a Dolphin Cruise

Take a boat tour to commune with the friendly mammals who feed on shrimp and other goodies in local marshes—they are most active at sunrise and sunset. *(Ch. 7)*

# 10 Mercer Williams House

The historic former home of Jim Williams, who was the central figure in John Berendt's *Midnight in the Garden of Good and Evil*, is now a museum. *(Ch. 3)*

# 11 Explore Modern Art

A dynamic arts community supports a revolving roll of fascinating contemporary exhibits at the Jepson Center for the Arts and SCAD MOA. *(Ch. 3)*

## 12 Walk Up Bull Street

This Spanish-moss draped boulevard runs for two miles, passing by squares and shops, Forsyth Park, the Victorian District, and the heart of the Starland District. *(Ch. 3, 4, 5)*

## 13 Salute the Girl Scouts

Thousands of girls in green make the pilgrimage every year to the Juliette Gordon Low Birthplace, the First Girl Scout Headquarters, and the new national corporate offices. *(Ch. 3)*

## 14 Explore Military History

If historic battlegrounds are your thing, strap on your combat boots to explore Revolutionary and Civil War history at Fort Pulaski, Old Fort Jackson, and Tricentennial Park. *(Ch. 3, 6)*

# 15 Hunt for Ghosts

Savannah may be one of the most haunted cities in America. Check out hallowed places like the Eliza Thompson House, 17Hundred90, The Pirates' House, and of course, Bonaventure Cemetery. *(Ch. 1, 3, 6)*

# 16 Look for a Flying Dinosaur

Turn your head upward inside the lobby at Plant Riverside, where a real, chromed skeleton of *Amphicoelias fragillimus* flies above other ancient fossils and sparkling geodes. *(Ch. 3)*

# WHAT'S WHERE

**1 The Historic District.** This area is home to the city's historic squares as well as many of its finest hotels, restaurants, and shopping.

**2 The Victorian District and Eastside.** The Victorian District is where you'll find gorgeous homes that date to the 1800s.

**3 The Starland District, Thomas Square, and Midtown.** The Starland District and Thomas Square have funky shops and great restaurants. Midtown is home to historic Grayson Stadium.

**4 The Moon River District.** Twenty minutes south of the Historic District toward the marsh, this area includes the Sandfly, Isle of Hope, and Skidaway Island neighborhoods.

**5 The Islands and Thunderbolt.** About 15 minutes east of the Historic District, this area includes Wilmington and Whitemarsh Islands as well as the town of Thunderbolt.

**6 Tybee Island.** A barrier island 18 miles east of Savannah, Tybee is a quirky beach town with kitschy shops, interesting restaurants, and outdoor activities.

**7 Southside, Gateway, and Greater Savannah.** Southside (anything south of Derenne Avenue) is far from downtown. Gateway is right off of I–95 and home to the Coastal Georgia Botanical Gardens.

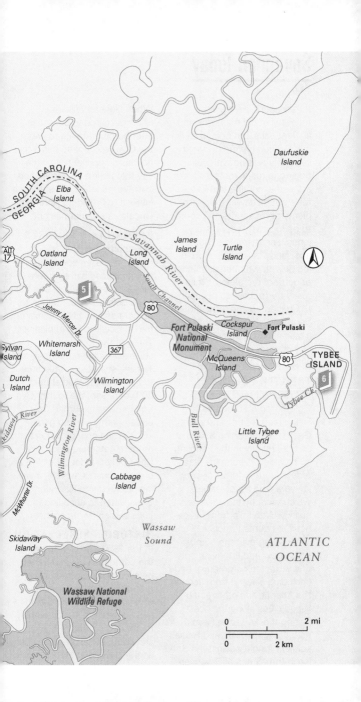

# Savannah Today

It may seem like a sleepy town full of old mansions and ancient oaks, but behind Savannah's venerable moss curtain lies a city pulsing with cutting-edge restaurants, modern art, and a nightlife that keeps folks out 'til dawn. There are plenty of museums and house tours to satisfy your history jones, and the golden marshes and sandy beaches surrounding downtown offer all manner of outdoor recreation. While many try to draw comparisons to Charleston and other storied Southern cities, Savannah has a fascinating past, contemporary culture, and dynamic vibe all its own.

## THE 13TH COLONY

In 1733, General James Oglethorpe claimed this inland bluff for England's King George, establishing Savannah as the first city in the fledgling 13th colony. Among his first orders were to forbid slavery, lawyers, and liquor—all of which went by the wayside quickly. With help from Indigenous residents Tomochichi and Mary Musgrove, the outpost soon grew into a thriving port that attracted commercial trade (including slavery) from across the Atlantic and other established cities along the coast. During the American Revolution, French, Polish, and Haitian soldiers fought against the British in the "Siege of Savannah."

When General William T. Sherman came to Savannah after burning Atlanta to win the Civil War, legend has it that he was so enchanted by the city that he left its homes and businesses intact, presenting it instead to President Abraham Lincoln as a Christmas gift.

## SAVANNAH'S SQUARES

Oglethorpe's unique layout of green spaces surrounded by residences has endured through the centuries, and the city's downtown continues to be heralded as a lasting example of excellent urban planning. Three of the four original squares—Johnson, Wright, and Telfair—still exist in the same footprint as they did almost 300 years ago; the fourth, Ellis Square, was exhumed from underneath a parking garage in 2005 and now provides a modern gathering place near City Market. Today 22 of the 24 original squares survive, inviting passersby to sit under the trees, listen to sparkling fountains and enjoy the scenery.

## HISTORIC PRESERVATION

In the 1950s, after witnessing the demolition of yet another beloved historic structure, a group of Savannah women organized the Historic Savannah Foundation, which went on to save dozens of homes and commercial buildings such as the Davenport House and

Kennedy Pharmacy. Forty years later, the Savannah College of Art & Design pioneered a historic preservation degree program, which has restored many downtown structures into stunning, functional spaces as part of the SCAD campus. These and ongoing efforts to shore up and revamp Savannah's antebellum and Victorian-era edifices contribute significantly to the city's value as a place to visit and live.

## TOURISM AND THE "TO GO" CUP

While Savannah has always been a historically popular vacation destination, from rural farmers looking for fun in the big city or millionaires racing fancy cars around the track across the river, there is no doubt that John Berendt's 1994 bestselling book *Midnight in the Garden of Good and Evil* created an international buzz around the Hostess City that has resulted in a tourism boom that's kept on booming. These days Savannah welcomes more than 14 million visitors a year to its cobblestone streets, many of whom come to explore its charms and take advantage of the generous "cocktails to go" policy (unlike most American cities, Savannah allows people to walk around the city with alcoholic beverages as long as they're in a plastic cup).

## PORT OF SAVANNAH

If you stand on River Street for any time at all, chances are you'll come face-to-stern with one of the biggest ships you've ever seen. Often stacked ten stories high with colorful containers, these massive ships deliver goods from around the globe to the Port of Savannah, the second-largest and fastest-growing seaport on the East Coast. The carriers must travel 18 miles from the open ocean and sail under the Talmadge Bridge to reach the port's massive cranes, where they are unloaded onto a revolving fleet of trucks that distribute them throughout the southeast. Tugboats guide the giants up and down the channel, and to accomodate the increasing size of the ships, the river must be constantly dredged.

## Savannah Historic Essentials

**TYBEE ISLAND LIGHTHOUSE**
Georgia's oldest and, at 145 feet, tallest lighthouse has stood since 1736, offering incomparable coastal views to those who brave its 178 steps.

**TRICENTENNIAL PARK**
Three centuries of history are encompassed in this grand brick complex, including Revolutionary War battlegrounds and the Central of Georgia Railroad Roundhouse.

**FIRST AFRICAN BAPTIST CHURCH**
The oldest Black church in North America has operated continuously since 1773, providing solace to parishioners and serving as a stop on the Underground Railroad.

**BONAVENTURE CEMETERY**
Famous for its exquisite statuary and famous residents like songwriter Johnny Mercer, poet Conrad Aiken, and Little Gracie Watson, this 160-acre parcel provides quietude and river views.

**FLANNERY O'CONNOR CHILDHOOD HOME**
Southern Gothic's literary grand dame lived in this three-story house on Lafayette Square until she was ten (when her family decamped to Milledgeville, Georgia to live at Andalusia Farm), experiencing her first brush with fame when she taught a chicken to walk backwards.

**JULIETTE GORDON LOW BIRTHPLACE**
Built in the 1820s, this beautifully preserved house museum is where the founder of the Girl Scouts began her worldwide movement in the parlor. It was designated Savannah's first historic landmark in 1965.

**RALPH MARK GILBERT CIVIL RIGHTS MUSEUM**
Follow Savannah's African American history from its tragic inception to its thriving business districts to its peaceful protests of the 1960s.

**CONGREGATION MICKVE ISRAEL**
Home to the third-oldest Jewish congregation in the U.S., the Gothic synagogue on Monterey Square offers tours of its sanctuary and museum, which houses one of the oldest Torah scrolls in North America.

**OWENS-THOMAS HOUSE & SLAVE QUARTERS**
Under the auspices of Telfair Museums, tours of this 1819 Regency mansion and its gardens explore the household's fraught relationship between the home's owners and enslaved people against the backdrop of beautiful restoration.

**CATHEDRAL BASILICA OF ST. JOHN THE BAPTIST**
The double spires, stained-glass windows and procession of carved saints make this Roman Catholic church on Lafayette Square a destination for the religious and non-religious alike.

## Don't-Miss Dishes

### SHRIMP N' GRITS
Savannah's iconic meal of wild-caught Georgia shrimp over a bowl of creamy corn grits gets superstar treatment at Cotton & Rye, where it's served in its own cast-iron pan.

### WHOLE FISH
Whether it's crispy scored flounder, lip-smacking mackerel, or lemony redfish, you can't go wrong with anything prepared fresh off the line with its head on at The Grey.

### CHICKEN FINGERS
Even if you consider finger food too pedestrian, these crispy, juicy delights ubiquitous to kiddie menus everywhere were actually invented at Spanky's River Street and deserve a dip in your favorite sauce.

### CUBAN SANDWICH
Soft bread, delicious ham, and homemade pickle pressed to perfection make up this signature street-fare snack.

### RACK OF RIBS
Slow-smoked for hours in a parking lot and slathered with secret sauce, the best braised bones in town come from Tricks BBQ in the Starland District.

### MEAT & THREE
Sisters of the New South offers up platters of pork chops, oxtails, or fried chicken surrounded by sweet potatoes, okra, collard greens, red beans, or yellow rice—the hard part is having to choose just three.

### RED VELVET CAKE TRUFFLE
Every confection at Chocolat by Adam Turoni is a delectable dream, but these flavors in particular put the South in your mouth in the sweetest possible way. A full selection of delicious treats are available at two impeccably decorated downtown locations.

### BISCUITS & GRAVY
There's a reason why there's always a long line at Mrs. Wilkes' Boarding House, where folks sit together family-style to dig into traditional Southern staples. Best y'all mind your manners!

Pizzeria Vittoria Napoletana at Starland Yard

### BAKED CHEESE SANDWICH

You don't have to be a vegetarian to fall in love with this heralded favorite from Brighter Day Natural Foods, stuffed with tomatoes, sprouts, and special sauce on whole-grain bread.

### LA DIAVIOLA PIZZA

This spicy pie full of olives and garlic at Pizzeria Vittoria Napoletana inside Starland Yard might have you swearing that you ended up in Naples instead of Savannah; get extra chilies if you dare.

## Drinks with a View

**A-J'S DOCKSIDE**
Grab a beer and squeeze yourself into a spot at this popular Tybee stronghold to watch the sun set behind Little Tybee. If you decide to stay for dinner, there's a full menu that includes fresh seafood, steaks, chicken fingers, sandwiches, and salads.

**ROCKS ON THE ROOF**
The bar on top of The Bohemian hotel offers a look at the ships passing to and from the port—and a chance to win a round of Tequila Verditas every evening as part of the "Hail and Farewell Challenge."

**PERCH**
Escape the sidewalk hubbub in this aerie in the oak trees on top of Local 11ten with its delightful wine list and small bites. Enjoy the views of Forsyth Park during happy hour or until the sun goes down.

**THE PEREGIN**
Atop Perry Lane Hotel awaits glorious bridge views and the finest rosé slushies in all the land. The crafted shaken and stirred cocktails are just as good, especially when paired with some tacos or a burger.

**TOP DECK**
Enjoy the fresh breezes, sweeping vistas, and the formidable whiskey and scotch list found at the pinnacle of the Cotton Sail Hotel. Pair your cocktail with a flatbread or slider.

Electric Moon Skytop Lounge at Plant Riverside

### ELECTRIC MOON SKYTOP LOUNGE
You can see for miles from the roof of Plant Riverside, but the real spectacle is in your glass: try a Short Circuit craft cocktail in a flashing lightbulb cup. Stay for a shrimp corn dog or jerk chicken wings.

### THE WYLD
Listen to the water lap at the dock as you make your way through a Painkiller or three and some fresh seafood; the luckiest folks get here by boat or kayak.

### THE LOST SQUARE
High above the riverfront at the Apex of the Alida Hotel sits an elegant outdoor spot boasting a creative cocktail menu that rotates with the seasons. Add some charcuterie or marinated olives.

### FANNIE'S ON THE BEACH
You can't miss the candy pink building on Tybee Island's south end; climb to the third floor for generous pours and unbroken views of the Atlantic Ocean. There's a full menu of seafood and sandwiches, too.

### BAR JULIAN
Gain new perspective from the top of the Thompson, where three sides look out onto the newly constructed Eastern Wharf with views of the Savannah River, Talmadge Bridge, and the finest sunsets in town.

# Savannah with Kids

Touring historic homes and visiting museums might be fascinating for grown-ups, but let's face it, children don't always share that sentiment. Good thing Savannah offers plenty of hands-on adventures to keep little minds occupied while showcasing the city's history, cultural arts, and ecology.

## IN THE HISTORIC DISTRICT

One good bet for kids of all ages is **Tricentennial Park**, which includes the **Savannah Children's Museum** and its epic outdoor playground built in the ruins of an old woodshed, and the **Georgia State Railroad Museum**, where families can explore the old roundhouse tracks and catch a ride on an antique train engine during warmer months. This spot is close to most of the downtown hotels and an excellent open zone to let travel-fevered kids run off some steam. Afterward, head over to the **Pirates' House** where they can explore the old dungeon and practice their best "arrrgh" with the servers.

For a dose of culture, families flock to the **Children's Art Museum** (CAM) inside the **Jepson Center for the Arts**, featuring interactive exhibits about painting and architecture. If making art is your family jam, check out **Henny Penny Café** on Bull Street where kids can take a drop-in painting lesson while parents enjoy lattes and pastries. The Girl Scouts were launched in Savannah over a hundred years ago, and even if you've never taken the oath you can tour the **First Headquarters**, the **Juliette Gordon Low Birthplace**, and the new national offices with its souvenir gift shop featuring a few flavor of its famous cookies, even in the off season.

If it's warm outside, hit the sidewalk fountains at **Ellis Square**, where jets of water shoot up in the middle of the park (be sure to bring a towel and a change of clothes; this is a wet activity). A few blocks south, the skies are wide open at **Forsyth Park**, where two playgrounds, a fragrant garden, and green fields perfect for tossing a Frisbee or football invite everyone to play outside. For snacks and services at the park, the restored historic fort in the middle offers public restrooms, the **Collins Quarter Café**, and a visitor information kiosk. For older kids who want their own scene, the **Sentient Bean** coffee shop on the south end of the park is one of the city's few all-ages venues.

## ELSEWHERE IN SAVANNAH

When it comes to entertaining children, you can't go wrong with the beach: Enjoying **Tybee Island** can be as simple as bringing a blanket to relax on North Beach while the kids make sand castles and chase the surf, or rent bicycles or kayaks to explore farther. Kid-friendly eats can be found at **Huc-A-Poos** and **Bubba Gumbo's**, and ice cream on the **Tybee Island Pier & Pavilion** is a summer tradition. An immersive experience under live oaks, **The Crab Shack** is a kid favorite for several reasons: excellent hush puppies; tables that have holes in the middle where diners push their spent seafood platters instead of clearing the table; and dozens of baby alligators kept in their own habitat for safe up-close viewing—and feeding!

To hang out with more indigenous wildlife, make the drive to **The Oatland Island Wildlife Center**, a few miles east of downtown Savannah. This outdoor zoo features large exhibits housing bald eagles, owls, cougars, bobcats, foxes and an incredible glass compound where visitors can come nose-to-nose with a family of wolves, all while traversing through the woods and marsh along a wooden walkway. Don't forget the sunscreen and the bug spray!

Speaking of bugs, the **Savannah Bee Co.** flagship store on Wilmington Island is a fun place to bring kids to see the indoor hive or even suit up in beekeeper gear to watch the bees in action; of course, honey tastings make a visit even sweeter. For those who like to play soldier, the costumed interpreters at **Old Fort Jackson** reenact historic battles—and set off actual cannons! Farther out on the islands, **Fort Pulaski** is an almost 300-year-old fort that still holds up to kids and adults alike scrambling all over its archways and turrets.

# What to Watch and Read

### MIDNIGHT IN THE GARDEN OF GOOD AND EVIL

This was John Berendt's account of Jim Williams's salacious murder trial in the early 1990s; the equally influential 1997 film version directed by Clint Eastwood introduced viewers to many now-familiar locations.

### SAVANNAH SIDEWAYS

A cheerful outsider and award-winning local columnist Jessica Leigh Lebos compiles adventures and observations of her adopted hometown, shining new light on usual haunts. Available at E. Shaver Booksellers and The Book Lady.

### SAVANNAH

Set after the Civil War and featuring plenty of historical locations, this well-received 2013 film starring Chiwetel Ejiofor and Jim Caviezel follows the friendship between a duck hunter and a former slave.

### BLACK, WHITE, AND THE GREY

The story of how New York venture capitalist Johno Morisano teamed up with African American chef Mashama Bailey to open the most talked-about restaurant in the country.

### PRINCE OF TIDES

While it's set in South Carolina, this classic family drama by Pat Conroy describes the beauty and charm of the Lowcountry. Barbra Streisand's film was shot in and around Beaufort.

### SAVANNAH BLUES

Chick lit fans everywhere have fallen in love with this romantic mystery series by Mary Kay Andrews featuring the art of antiquing, Tybee Island–style.

### DREAMS OF THE IMMORTAL CITY SAVANNAH

A collection of thoughtful essays by Aberjhani examine Savannah history and culture through a lens that is pure poetry.

### THE DIRT ON JANE

Dig into this "anti-memoir" by beloved columnist and renegade gardener Jane Fishman.

### SOUTHERN CHARM: SAVANNAH

If Bravo-style reality TV is your thing, tag along with this gang of Savannah socialites for wild parties, relationship woes, and fabulous water views.

### UNDERGROUND

This critically acclaimed historical drama on OWN Network returned several of Savannah's squares back to the 1800s to tell the characters' heroic escape story.

# Chapter 2

# TRAVEL SMART

Updated by
Jessica Leigh Lebos

**★ CAPITAL:**
Atlanta

**♦ POPULATION:**
147,088

**💬 LANGUAGE:**
English

**$ CURRENCY:**
U.S. dollar

**☎ AREA CODE:**
912

**⚠ EMERGENCIES:**
911

**🚗 DRIVING:**
On the right

**⚡ ELECTRICITY:**
120–220 v/60 cycles;
plugs have two or
three rectangular
prongs

**🕑 TIME:**
EST (same as New
York City)

**✈ AIRPORT:**
SAV/HHI

**🌐 WEB
RESOURCES:**
savannahga.gov
visitsavannah.com

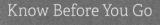

# Know Before You Go

## WEAR YOUR WALKING SHOES

Savannah was founded in 1733 and built for walking. River Street and Factor's Walk were built from the ballast stones of old ships, and navigating them can be challenging, especially if you've partaken in a few drinks. Watch those high heels! If your time is limited, walk up Bull Street from Bay Street to Forsyth Park—you'll cross through centuries of history and impressive periods of architecture.

## SWEET TEA MEANS

The local non-alcoholic beverage of choice in the South is pekoe tea brewed strong, sweetened, and served over ice: expect a cool, refreshing drink with enough sugar in it to rot your teeth immediately out of your head. However, most restaurants also brew "unsweet tea." Try ordering a "half and half" to reduce the sweetness. If you like a bit of tartness in your tea, order unsweet tea with already sweetened lemonade, otherwise known as an "Arnold Palmer," named after the famous golfer.

## WATCH THE WEATHER

There's a saying in Savannah: "If you don't like the weather, wait ten minutes and something else will show up." Spring and fall are mostly glorious with balmy temperatures and cool breezes. The camellia trees bloom from December through February, followed by the famous azalea bushes bursting out in pinks, reds, and corals. The sweet-smelling, white magnolia flowers come out in May, showering the city in yellow pollen. Humidity that feels like a heavy blanket is a given in the summer months, and the sky often opens up with rain only to return to sunshine a few minutes later. Hurricane season starts in June and lasts through November, and while the city took big hits from hurricanes Matthew and Irma, it usually stays out of the eye of the biggest storms. Winters can be surprisingly cold, always a shock to folks who show up in shorts and flip-flops.

## BRING BUG SPRAY

Tempering Savannah's many charms is the presence of myriad insects during warmer weather, including biting mosquitoes, flying roaches referred to as "palmetto bugs," and pairs of black-and-red "lovebugs" that are completely harmless. The worst kinds of bugs are the ones you can't see: tiny sand gnats—also known as "no-see-ums"—are particularly insidious, flying around in clouds and leaving nasty little welts. Also practically invisible are redbugs or "chiggers" that can live in the Spanish moss—it is highly advised not to touch it. Locals depend on "No Natz," a non-toxic spray found at the counter of many convenience stores.

## KNOW YOUR SOUTHERNISMS

While it sure seems like a nice thing, if a Savannahian says "bless your heart," it doesn't necessarily mean they're wishing you a good day. This expression has a multitude of meanings, from "I suppose you mean well, don't you?" to "Oh goodness, so you're wearing *that* dress?" It's usually good-natured, though. If a Savannahian really wants to land an insult, they'll say "It can't be helped, his mama didn't teach him right." Also, the term "y'all" can be singular or plural—though if there are more than four of you, you'll probably be referred to as "all y'all."

## DRIVERS BEWARE

Savannah's many squares and one-way streets can be a challenge. If you're driving downtown, mind the many street signs—Drayton, Lincoln, and Whitaker only go one direction.

Important: Cars already on the square have the right-of-way; you must yield before entering a square even if you're not going all the way around it. Pedestrians should always look both ways before stepping off the curb—not only are there cars to worry about, but there are also legions of trolleys, pedicabs, skateboarders, and horse-drawn carriages on the historic streets.

## CHECK YOUR ITINERARY

This city caters to tourists, but sleepy Southern habits die hard. Many locally owned businesses, museums, and institutions still close on Sundays and Mondays—and even Tuesdays! Double check hours before you make a plan.

## KEEP YOUR WITS ABOUT YOU

Crime in Savannah is an ongoing issue in the residential neighborhoods to the east and west of the historic district; if you're looking at the statistics, this is where the majority of violent crime

occurs. For tourists, however, the city is a relatively safe place as long as you stick to where the crowds gather. There are plenty of police patrolling downtown, though occasional pickpockets and purse snatchers find their way into the nightclubs or City Market. As with anywhere, it's always a good idea to be aware of your surroundings.

## THERE'S MORE THAN ONE CEMETERY

While iconic Bonaventure Cemetery receives tens of thousands of visitors a year, this isn't the only garden-like resting place worth visiting. Colonial Cemetery at Abercorn and Oglethorpe streets invites passersby to stroll among ancient oaks and brick mausoleums dating back to the Revolutionary War. On the west side of the city, Laurel Grove North and South contain acres of natural beauty and paved pathways that lead past the tombs of some of Savannah's most storied residents.

# Getting Here and Around

## ✈ Air

Savannah is serviced by Allegiant, Avelo, American, Breeze, Delta, Frontier, JetBlue, Silver Airways, Southwest, Sun Country, and United.

### AIRPORT

Savannah/Hilton Head International Airport (SAV) is 11 miles west of downtown. The airport is only 20 minutes by car from the Historic District and around 40 minutes from Hilton Head Island. Another option is the tiny Hilton Head Island Airport (HHH). Low-cost carriers like JetBlue and Frontier now offer flights to and from Savannah—but if you have to drive from Jacksonville, approaching Savannah from the south gives you an opportunity to stop at Jekyll Island and other treasures of southeastern Georgia. From the north, visit scenic Beaufort or Bluffton.

■TIP→ **If the flights into Savannah/Hilton Head International Airport aren't convenient, consider the international airport in Jacksonville. The drive time to Savannah is just shy of two hours.**

### AIRPORT TRANSFERS

For transportation into Savannah, taxis circle outside the baggage claim area and rideshare apps like Uber and Lyft pick up at the north entrance of baggage claim. Some of the larger hotels offer shuttles. There are no airport shuttles other than those operated by hotels, so visitors not renting a car must taxi to their lodging accommodations. The going rate for the approximately 11-mile trip to the Historic District is about $30. Several limousine and sedan services allow you to choose your vehicle with rates starting at less than $100 an hour. Another option for transporting groups into Savannah is Old Savannah Tours, which has larger vehicles that can be chartered.

## ⚓ Boat

Located on the Savannah River, the Port of Savannah is the busiest port between New Orleans and New York. A limited number of yacht slips are available on the river; contact City Hall for information. The Savannah Belles Ferry is part of the citywide transit system and provides regular service from the City Hall dock in the Historic District to the Westin Savannah Harbor Golf Resort & Spa at the International Convention Center on Hutchinson Island.

# 🚌 Bus

Savannah is a coastal stop for Greyhound. The newly renovated station is conveniently located on the western edge of the Historic District.

# 🚗 Car

Interstate 95 slices north–south along the Eastern Seaboard, intersecting 10 miles west of town with east–west Interstate 16, which dead-ends in downtown Savannah. U.S. 17, the Coastal Highway, also runs north–south through town. U.S. 80 is another east–west route through Savannah, starting from Tybee Island.

If you plan to stick to the Historic District, Savannah is one destination where smart city planning and abundant public transportation render a rental car unnecessary. If you'll be centrally located during your visit, choose from the plentiful buses, taxis, pedicabs (up to two persons can be pedaled in a cart attached to a bicyclist), horse carriages, trolley tours (some of which allow on-and-off privileges), free ferries, and rental bikes, scooters, and Segway rentals. This is a walking city, so bring a pair of comfortable shoes.

## CAR RENTALS

Major rental agencies can be found in town and at the airport, and many provide pickup and delivery service. Some rental offices are closed on Sunday, though most national chains operate seven days a week.

## GASOLINE

In general, gas prices in Savannah hover around the national average. Gas stations are not difficult to find; there are several on Martin Luther King Jr. Boulevard and 37th Street, the thoroughfares that access Interstate 16 to route back to Interstate 95 and the airport.

## PARKING

Downtown parking can be a challenge, though the city has taken steps to ameliorate the issue. Tourists should download the "Park Savannah" app for the most ease in paying for metered spaces, which are designated by a four-digit number in the corner of the parking space. Rates vary between 50¢ to $2 an hour. There are also kiosks located around the city where you can pay and receive a ticket to display on the dashboard as well as a few old-fashioned meters that take American coins. Meters are enforced from 8 am to 8 pm Monday through Saturday north of

# Getting Here and Around

Liberty Street. On weekdays, south of Liberty Street, meters are enforced from 8 am to 5 pm. You can add time as often as you wish. Rates vary at local parking garages, but in a City of Savannah–owned lot you should expect to pay at least $1 to $2 per hour during business hours on weekdays, a $2 flat rate in the evenings, and a flat rate of $3 on weekends. Special events parking can double the rates. Most downtown hotels have their own paid parking lots, and some B&Bs and inns have their own lots or advise guests on how to park on the street. Few restaurants have parking.

### ROAD CONDITIONS

Roads in Savannah are a mixed bag. Certain streets in the Historic District are brick or cobblestone, which makes for a bumpy ride. In other areas—particularly in the Midtown and Southside neighborhoods—roads are paved and in good condition. Traffic can be tricky in the Historic District, with one-way streets and large numbers of pedestrians, cyclists, and other vehicles; you may encounter slow-moving trolleys and horse-drawn carriages, but please don't honk at the horses. Remember to yield when entering a square by car! There's heavy truck traffic on

Interstate 95 due to the port, where the speed limit is 70 mph. Interstate 16 gets backed up around the 5pm rush hour.

## 🚢 Cruise

No ocean-going cruise lines depart from or dock in Savannah, but it's an occasional port of call for ships sailing up and down the east coast of the United States. More often, it's a popular stop for river cruise ships offering intracoastal canal cruises along the East Coast.

## Ⓜ Public Transport

Chatham Area Transit (CAT) operates buses in Savannah and Chatham County Monday through Saturday from just before 6 am to just shy of midnight, Sunday from 7 am to 9 pm; download the app to see the full schedule. Visitors can also take advantage of "the Dot," Savannah's fare-free downtown transportation system. This shuttle serves 24 stops through the Historic District and runs from 7 am to 7 pm weekdays, 10 am to 7 pm on Saturday, and 10 am to 6 pm on Sunday. Holiday hours are 10 am to 6:30 pm on Martin Luther King Jr. Day, Memorial Day, 4th of July,

Labor Day, Christmas Eve, and New Year's Eve. There is no service on Thanksgiving, Christmas, or New Year's Day.

## 🚗 Ride-Sharing

Ride-sharing apps Uber and Lyft are ubiquitous throughout the city. Both are available for pickup and drop-off at SAV/HHI and HHH airports. However, some drivers who are new to town may be unfamiliar with the city and its areas, even the most popular ones. Check driver ratings before finalizing your ride.

## 🚕 Taxi

You can hail cabs on the street if they don't have riders or assignments, although with the advent of Uber and Lyft these are few and far between. Most cab services offer flat rates to and from the airport, usually in the range of $28–$30, plus $5 for each additional person. Yellow Cab Company charges $2.94 per mile.

**Savannah Pedicab**, Savannah's first pedicab company, is a people-pedaled vehicle that costs $45 per hour and $25 per half hour; if your ride is less than a half hour, Savannah

Pedicab abides by a "trips for tips" policy in which the passenger pays whatever they see fit for rides (most riders pay $5 to $10 for a quick trip from a restaurant to a nightclub; another rule of thumb is that whatever you pay should be somewhere between the value of a sandwich and a pizza). Savannah Pedicab operates from 11 am to midnight (2 am on weekends). Another pedicab company, **Royal Bike Taxi**, charges a dollar per block per passenger for trips less than a half-hour, $25 for half-hour trips, and $45 for hour-long trips. Call to schedule a pick-up or just flag one down—they often congregate at the corner of Bull and Broughton streets.

## 🚆 Train

Amtrak runs its Silver Service/ Palmetto route down the East Coast from New York to Miami and stops in Savannah. However, the station is about 6 miles from downtown and not walkable.

# Essentials

## 🏃 Activities

Savannah is an excellent place to take advantage of life on the coast. The neighboring areas and barrier islands of the Lowcountry are conducive to nearly all types of water sports. Swimming, stand-up paddleboarding, sailing, kiteboarding, fishing, kayaking, parasailing, and surfing are popular pastimes. The Savannah River flows alongside the city on its way to the Atlantic Ocean and is easily accessible by boat. A multitude of tidal creeks and marshlands intertwine the river and the barrier islands, most notably Tybee Island, where you can enjoy sun-drenched beaches, casual bars and restaurants, friendly people, and a quirky vibe. The water here is cloudy due to the tides that churn in and out twice a day and is generally warm enough for swimming from May through October.

For those who would prefer keep their legs on land, bicycling, golf, and tennis dominate. During the hot and humid summer months, limit the duration of strenuous activity, remember to drink lots of water, and protect your skin from the sun.

### BASEBALL

A baseball game under a summer sky is an all-American pleasure, and Savannah's historic Grayson Stadium has been hosting games since 1926. The Savannah Bananas, formerly a Coastal Plain League team, has become a national sensation for its entertaining take on "Banana Ball," featuring its own rules, audience interaction, and fun hijinks for the whole crew. Games last no longer than two hours, making it a perfect evening outing for the family.

### BIKING

Navigating Savannah by bike is a wonderful way to explore the city—though be aware that the streets can be crowded. Forsyth and Daffin parks are favored destinations for locals, and there are designated bike routes on Lincoln, Price, and Washington streets. If you have a trailer or bike rack for your car, Tom Triplett Park, 8 miles east of town on U.S. 80 in Pooler, offers three bike loops—3.5 miles, 5 miles, and 6.3 miles. Bike rentals and helmets are available downtown at Perry Rubber Bike Shop (✉ *240 Bull St.*), Savannah Bike Tours (✉ *502 E. Broughton St.*), and Savannah on Wheels (✉ *405 W. Hall St.*) for $30 a day. On Tybee Island, gear up at Tim's Bikes, Beach & Disc Golf, and Fat Tire Bikes.

## GOLF

The weather here, particularly in the spring and fall, is custom-ordered for a round or two on the back nine. Though the courses aren't as famous as those on Hilton Head, players looking for a challenge can count on gems like the Westin's Club at Savannah Harbor and the Wilmington Island Club. The city-owned Bacon Park Golf Course on the southside of the city was renovated in 2014 and features 27 holes.

## WATER SPORTS

Water sports are the obvious choice for a city surrounded by rivers, creeks, marshes, and the Atlantic Ocean. Kayaking, sailing, stand-up paddleboarding, and kiteboarding are all popular, and there are plenty of options for guided tours, charter boats, and equipment rental. Savannah Canoe & Kayak in Thunderbolt offers an excellent selection of gear.

# 🍴 Dining

Southern cuisine is rich in tradition, but the dining scene in Savannah is more than just fried chicken and barbecue. Many of the city's restaurants have been exploring locally sourced ingredients as a way to tweak their usual homespun offerings, a change that is now attracting chefs and foodies alike.

Although the farm-to-table trend was first spotted at upscale spots like **Noble Fare** or **Local 11ten**, more neighborhood restaurants are now getting in on the action. In the Victorian District, Starland District, and Thomas Square District, places like **The Vault Kitchen + Market** and **Cotton & Rye** serve elegant dishes with local flavor and thoughtful wine pairings. Downtown, take in the star power of **The Grey**, home of James Beard Award-winner Chef Mashama Bailey, or Southern food titan Sean Brock's **Husk**.

The arrival of some new kids on the block doesn't mean the old standbys have ridden off into the sunset just yet. For traditional, exquisitely prepared menus, be sure to visit **Elizabeth on 37th** or **the Olde Pink House**, both of which have been pleasing local palates for decades. Or follow the crowds to either Paula Deen's famous **Lady & Sons** or the ever-popular **Mrs. Wilkes Dining Room**, where you'll find all the fried chicken, collard greens, and mac and cheese you can handle. Or beat the lines at locals-only places like **Sisters of the New South** on the city's Eastside.

If you're looking for barbecue, several spots throughout Savannah can satisfy your urge for slow-cooked meats of

# Essentials

all kind. For lunch, check out **Tricks BBQ** in the Starland District, a gas station-turned-take-out spot with pulled pork and slabs of ribs. Another popular spot with local meat lovers is **Wiley's Championship BBQ** on nearby Wilmington Island.

That's just a few ideas to get you started. While exploring Savannah, you're sure to find any number of other exciting options that reach beyond typical Southern fare, whether you're craving a noodle bowl or a Cuban sandwich.

## MEALS AND MEALTIMES

Some popular restaurants serve both lunch and dinner, though they may close in between meal service and reopen at 5 pm. Kitchens typically serve until 9 pm, though pubs serving food often keep the burners hot until midnight. Sunday brunch is a beloved institution, but be prepared to wait for a table at most of the popular spots.

## PAYING

Most restaurants take credit cards, but some smaller places do not. Others, like Starland Yard which houses multiple restaurants and food trucks, don't accept cash at all—another new trend. Servers garner a 20% tip at high-end restaurants; expect an automatic gratuity for groups of six or more.

⇨ *Restaurant prices are for a main course at dinner, not including taxes (7% on food, 8.25% tax on liquor).*

| What It Costs in U.S. Dollars | | | |
|---|---|---|---|
| $ | $$ | $$$ | $$$$ |
| **RESTAURANTS** | | | |
| under $15 | $15–$25 | $26–$35 | over $35 |

## RESERVATIONS AND DRESS

Always make a reservation at a restaurant when you can. Some are booked weeks in advance, but some popular restaurants don't accept reservations. While most places are fairly casual, the way you look can influence how you're treated—and where you're seated.

Some locals and restaurant owners have a laid-back attitude about dressing for a night out. And if you are hitting a River Street tourist restaurant, a small neighborhood eatery, or a barbecue joint, jeans and flip-flops are just fine. However, if you are going to one of the city's upscale restaurants, you'll look out of place among the sophisticated folks in suit jackets, ties, and cocktail dresses. If it's expensive, it's worth dressing up for, especially on weekend nights.

## SMOKING

Smoking and vaping is banned inside all restaurants and bars, but many have outdoor patios or balconies where smokers can light up.

# ⊕ Health & Safety

## CRIME

Savannah officials are serious about your safety, and you'll notice both police cars and security patrol cars through-out the downtown area. The streets are safe for pedestrians during the day, but at night you should exercise reasonable caution, especially in poorly lit areas along the perimeter of the Historic District. Always lock your car and remove val-uables that are visible through the windows. Utilize your hotel's safe for your cash and valuables.

# 🧭 Immunizations

There are no current immuni-zation requirements for visitors traveling to the United States for tourism.

# 📶 Internet

Many hotels and inns offer complimentary internet access, though rates may vary. The City of Savannah offers free Wi-Fi via "surfsavannah"—the signal can be picked up on River Street, Bay Street, Reynolds Square, Ellis Square, Franklin Square, and the south end of Forsyth Park. It can also be accessed along Martin Luther King Jr. Boulevard from Victory Drive to River Street. Users must register and usage is limited to two hours a day; if you're planning an extended stay, purchase a 30-day Wi-Fi pass via Seimitsu (☎ 912/525–0345). Live Oak Public Libraries also offer free Internet access at all of its branches.

# 🛏 Lodging

The Hostess City opens its doors every year to millions of visitors who are drawn to its historic and vibrant downtown. Because the majority of attrac-tions are within the Historic District, most of the city's best hotels are there, too. Many are within easy walking distance of the city's premier restaurants and historic sites. In terms of accommodations, Savannah is best known for its many inns and B&Bs, which have moved into the stately antebellum mansions, renovated cotton warehouses, and myriad other historic buildings stretching from the river out to the Victorian neighborhoods in the

# Essentials

vicinity of Forsyth Park. Most are beautifully restored with the requisite high ceilings, ornate carved millwork, claw-foot tubs, and other quaint touches. Some stay in close touch with the past and do not offer televisions or telephones; others have mixed in the modern luxuries that many travelers have grown accustomed to, including flat-screen TVs, Wi-Fi, and upscale bath amenities. Often, Southern hospitality is served up in the form of evening wine-and-cheese socials, decadent breakfasts, and pralines at turndown service.

The arrival of newer boutique hotels has shaken some of the dust out of Savannah's lodging scene and raised the bar for competing properties. Properties like JW Marriott's Plant Riverside, The Thompson, Perry Lane Hotel, the Brice, the Alida, and the Cotton Sail would be at home in a much larger city, but all have figured out how to introduce a sleek, cosmopolitan edge without bulldozing over Savannah's charm. Airbnb and VRBO have made massive inroads in recent years, and these short-term vacation rentals can be condos, rooms in someone's home, or an entire private house. If you take this route, be aware that you're sharing these historic neighborhoods with local residents; loud parties and bad behavior are not tolerated.

## FACILITIES

You can assume that all rooms have private baths, phones, TVs, and air-conditioning, unless otherwise indicated. Breakfast is noted when it is included in the rate. There are several Savannah hotels with pools and rooftop bars.

## PARKING

Most hotels have private or underground lots for guests, though many will charge a daily rate to park. Some will require valet parking due to the crowded facilities and tight entryways, especially on Bay Street. For all other parking, download the "Park Savannah" app and be sure to enter the correct space number. Many of the Airbnbs in the historic district provide only on-street parking, which can be tricky on busy weekends. While proprietors may pay for your parking fees, you will still have to move the car on days and nights when the street sweeper comes by—there are signs posted, and the city is merciless about giving out tickets. Parking is free downtown on Sundays.

## PRICES

The central location and relatively high standards of quality in Savannah's Historic District hotels do drive up room rates, especially during peak seasons, holidays, and special events like St. Patrick's Day. The number of hotel rooms has more than doubled in the past 15 years, and occupancy rates have grown accordingly, even in the former slow season from September through January. October is another relatively busy time thanks to the pleasant temperatures and packed events calendar. You can expect to pay anywhere from $79/night for a room outside of downtown up to $650/night downtown during peak season.

You will sometimes save by booking online or purchasing a package deal. Look for good last-minute deals online when bookings are light. These are often available in late summer, when the heat and humidity are at their highest. If you're on a tight budget, there are plenty of nice, new, mid-range options from trusted hotel chains in less-traveled but conveniently located areas a short drive from downtown, midtown, and the airport. Just keep in mind that what you are gaining in affordability you will often be losing in convenience and historic charm.

⇨ *Hotel prices are for two people in a standard double room in high season.*

### What It Costs in U.S. Dollars

| $ | $$ | $$$ | $$$$ |
|---|---|---|---|
| **HOTELS** | | | |
| under $150 | $150–$225 | $226–$300 | over $300 |

## RESERVATIONS

Researching lodging and making reservations is always a good idea in Savannah. However, given the sheer volume of downtown hotels and other options like Airbnbs, you will likely still find something in your price range. That said, do not leave the good weather seasons like April and October, the Christmas holidays, and the city's famous St. Patrick's Day celebration (when a million revelers descend upon the city) to chance.

## SAVANNAH LODGING TIPS

**Know what "historic" really means.** When booking in one of the city's historic homes-turned-hotels, among the negatives can be antique beds that are short, albeit beautifully canopied. If you are tall or are used to a California King, this could be an issue. Rooms can be small, especially if they were originally back-rooms meant for children or servants; rooms below street

# Essentials

level—often called garden or courtyard rooms—can be damp. Windows aren't usually soundproof, and some squares are noisy in the morning or late at night, depending on the proximity to bars. Some accommodations in old homes may require patrons to share bathrooms.

**Savannah has hotels, too.**
Full-service hotels such as Hyatt Regency, Marriott, and Westin—as well as newer boutique hotels—may be more appealing to visitors who prefer a larger property with an elevator or swimming pool, not to mention soundproof walls.

**Don't forget the chains.** Mid-range chain hotels and motels that normally would not excite or even interest you can be surprisingly appealing in Savannah. Some in the Historic District are creatively renovated historic structures. If you can't afford to stay downtown, you'll find many mid-range chains in midtown and the Southside (still less than 7 miles from downtown), as well as near the airport. The farther out you go, the less expensive your lodging will be.

## 🍸 Nightlife

There's no shortage of entertainment in the Hostess City, whether you're looking for a live band, a crowded dance floor, or any number of more laid-back options. Plus, you can carry alcoholic beverages with you on the street—the city's famous "to go" policy allows folks to travel with cocktails in plastic cups in the historic district up to Jones Street, adding a festive touch to life after dark. This can also mean folks often get sloppy; beware of drunk bridesmaids who can't hold their liquor and watch your step.

Congress Street and River Street have the highest concentrations of bars with live music, especially if you're looking for rock 'n' roll, jazz, or blues. Many of the most popular dance clubs are scattered across the same area. If you're in the mood for something more sedate, there are plenty of chic enclaves known for their creative cocktails and cozy nooks that encourage intimate conversation. But just because the city enjoys its liquor doesn't mean that there's nothing going on for those who'd rather not imbibe. There are coffee shops that serve up live music and film screenings, as well as arts venues offering theater, films, karaoke, and comedy.

# 🌐 Passport

Every visitor to the United States is required to have a passport that is valid for six months beyond the expected period of stay.

# 👜 Shopping

Anyone with even the slightest inclination toward shopping would be hard pressed to leave Savannah empty-handed. The downtown streets are alive with an array of boutiques and shops running the gamut from kitschy to glamorous, locally owned to nationally renowned.

Broughton Street has come full circle over the past 30 years: What was once a string of abandoned storefronts has been transformed into a world-class shopping district. As you stroll along Broughton, note the original tenant names etched into historic facades and the sidewalk mosaics.

Antiques malls and junk emporiums with eye-catching facades and eclectic offerings beckon you to take home treasures from the city's rich past. Meanwhile, contemporary design shops feature the latest lighting and sleek designer furnishings. Some of the newest additions to the shopping landscape are specialty food stores that offer tastings throughout the day. Don't miss trendy boutiques that offer modern fashions with a Southern twist, and be sure to visit the city's two wonderful independent bookstores, **The Book Lady** and **E. Shaver Booksellers.**

Since a great many of the city's attractions are centrally located, a day of shopping can go hand-in-hand with visits to nearby museums or long meals at one of the well-regarded restaurants. The tree-lined streets promise a vista at every turn, so be sure to bring along a comfortable pair of walking shoes as you snap selfies. Should you tire along the way, horse-drawn carriages, trolley tours, or pedicabs abound to help you get off your feet without sacrificing a full itinerary.

## BEST BETS FOR SAVANNAH SHOPPING

**Art galleries.** The Savannah College of Art and Design has indelibly imprinted the city with a love of fine arts, and the school's shopSCAD boutique showcases decorative and functional pieces from notable alums. City Market features dozens of local artists and artisans. On the western edge of town, Laney Contemporary presents Southern artists in a fabulous Brutalist edifice.

**Clothing and accessories.** Several areas offer designer clothing,

# Essentials

chic shoes, and one-of-a-kind jewelry and accessories to outfit the most discerning shoppers. Along Broughton Street, Globe Shoes has been keeping Savannah's feet gorgeous for generations, and J. Parker Ltd and Joseph's are where Savannah's Southern gentlemen pick up their seersucker suits. The Design District just north of Forsyth Park offers home decor from Madame Chrysanthemum and boutiques like Custard and StoneLords. For funky apparel and thrifted scores, head to the Starland District's Vintage Vortex and Starland Strange.

**Edible gifts.** The Savannah Bee Company's flagship store on Broughton is a haven of honey-based delights. Pair that with a box of pralines from River Street Sweets or homemade treats from Byrd Cookie Company for a take-home taste of Savannah.

**Home decor and antiques.** The charming Paris Market & Brocante occupies two floors with a feel reminiscent of a turn-of-the-20th-century French bazaar, and One Fish, Two Fish exemplifies coastal chic. Don't neglect the city's many antiques shops, including Jere's and Picker Joe's.

## 💲 Taxes

The sales tax is 7%. Hotel room tax is 8%.

## 💱 Tipping

Tip as you would in any other U.S. city; waiters in restaurants expect to receive 18% to 25% (the larger amount in more upscale establishments); 20% is the norm here for good service. Tip hotel maids about $2–$5 per day, depending on how expensive your lodgings and the mess you've left behind.

## 🏴 U.S. Embassy/ Consulate

All foreign governments have embassies in Washington, D.C., approximately 575 miles from Savannah. Most offer consular services in the embassy building.

## 🛂 Visa

Except for citizens of Canada and Bermuda, most visitors to the United States must have a visa. If you are from one of the designated members of the Visa Waiver Program, then you only require an ESTA

## Tipping Guide for Savannah

| | |
|---|---|
| Bartender | $1–$5 per round of drinks, depending on the number of drinks |
| Bellhop | $1–$5 per bag, depending on the level of the hotel |
| Coat check | $1–$2 per coat |
| Hotel concierge | $5 or more, depending on the service |
| Hotel door staff | $1–$5 for help with bags or hailing a cab |
| Hotel maid | $2–$5 a day (in cash, preferably daily since cleaning staff may be different each day you stay) |
| Hotel room service waiter | $1–$2 per delivery, even if a service charge has been added |
| Porter at airport or train station | $1 per bag |
| Restroom attendants | $1 or small change |
| Skycap at airport | $1–$3 per bag checked |
| Spa personnel | 15%–20% of the cost of your service |
| Taxi driver | 15%–20% |
| Tour guide | 10%–15% of the cost of the tour, per person |
| Valet parking attendant | $2–$5, each time your car is brought to you |
| Waiter | 15%–25%, with 20% being the norm; nothing additional if a service charge is added to the bill |

(Electronic System for Travel Authorization) as long as you are staying for 90 days or less. However, some changes were made in the Visa Waiver Program in 2015, and nationals of Visa-Waiver nations who have traveled to Iran, Iraq, Libya, Somalia, Sudan, Syria, or Yemen no longer qualify for ESTA. Also, if you have been denied a visa to visit the United States, your application for the ESTA program most likely will be denied.

# Essentials

## 📍 Visitor Information

The **Savannah Visitor Center** on MLK Jr. Blvd. is easily accessed from all major thoroughfares and is open daily 9 am to 4 pm. The center has a useful audiovisual overview of the city and a staff of knowledgeable trip counselors. Other downtown information centers include the **River Street Information Center**, open daily from 10 am to 6 pm with a staff member on site. At the Savannah/HHI airport, there is a visitor's desk open 8:30 am to 11 pm daily.

For detailed information about Tybee Island, drop by the island's visitor center, just off Highway 80. It's open daily 9 am to 4 pm.

## 📅 When to Go

**Low season:** Hotel rates drop with the temperatures in Savannah, though premium prices reign during the holiday season. Winter months can be surprisingly cold, often delving below freezing in the early mornings through February and early March.

**Shoulder season:** Though summer in Savannah can bring barely tolerable levels of heat and humidity, it's still travel season, after all. Still, many hotel deals can be scored during August, the hottest, slowest month of the calendar.

**High season:** Savannah's high season begins with a bang in March, when the city is flooded with visitors for its massive St. Patrick's Day festival. Hotel rooms—all lodgings, really—are at a premium then, with rates hardly dipping through April and May, when the spring weather is balmy and beautiful. After the terrific heat of summer, prices rise again in October and November, when the breezy weather returns.

### WEATHER

Savannah experiences a subtropical climate of hot, humid summers that can reach up to 99°F, lovely springs and autumns, and mild winters with occasional freezes. Its location places it in the path of hurricanes, and inclement weather including heavy thunderstorms is a given during the summer. The city's many camellia trees begin showing their stuff in December, petering out just in time for the azalea season, when the streets are awash in pinks, corals, and whites. Magnolias offer up flowers as big as dinner plates in May, and the summer's color is provided by the smooth-barked crepe myrtle trees. There can be a lot of pollen in the air during the spring, which may aggravate some people's allergies.

# Essentials

There are specialty forays into whatever your interests may be, whether it is food, cocktails, or of course, ghosts.

## BOAT TOURS

**Captain Mike's Dolphin Adventure.** Pushing off at Lazaretto Creek on the way to Tybee Island, the legendary Captain Mike has a knack for knowing where the dolphins gather, as well as sea turtles and shorebirds. He and his crew are also experts on local ecology and fishing spots and always have a great story to share. You can enjoy one-hour group excursions on a 35-person boat or inquire about private charters. ⊠ *1 Old U.S. Highway 80 E., Savannah* ☏ *855/436–5744* ⊕ *captainmikesdolphintours. com* ⊠ *From $16.*

**Savannah Riverboat Cruises.** Savannah Riverboat Cruises has daily departures from docks on River Street. The lovely white paddleboat shares the causeway with huge commercial ships and drifts past industrial sites. It has a full bar and kitchen and is a relaxing, fun activity, especially at sunset. Among the offers are 1½-hour afternoon cruises; luncheon or dinner cruises, which feature a truly fabulous Southern buffet spread with all the fixins'; and a Monday Gospel Dinner Cruise with entertainment by a choir.

Reservations are recommended. ⊠ *9 E. River St., Savannah* ☏ *912/232–6404* ⊕ *savannahriverboat.com* ⊠ *Scenic cruises from $36.95; dinner cruises from $82.95.*

**Sundial Charters.** Captain Rene Heidt and her team of skippers know the backwaters and secret sandbars of Tybee Island and Little Tybee like the natives they are. If dancing with dolphins, taking in glorious sunsets, and searching for giant sharks' teeth is on your agenda, booking an outing with Sundial is a sure bet. ⊠ *1615 Chatham Ave, Savannah* ☏ *912/786–9470* ⊕ *www.sundialcharters.com* ⊠ *Starting at $240 for a three-hour tour.*

## BUS, CARRIAGE, AND TROLLEY TOURS

**Carriage Tours of Savannah.** Operating 50-minute tours out of City Market, Carriage Tours of Savannah travels the Historic District at a 19th-century clip-clop pace, with coachmen spinning tales and telling ghost stories along the way. The tours are closed Mondays and the schedule can change during the winter months; check the website for the most up-to-date tours. ⊠ *19 Jefferson St., Savannah* ☏ *912/236–6756* ⊕ *carriagetoursofsavannah. com* ⊠ *From $35.*

# Best Tours

**Day Clean Journeys.** Historian, educator, and entertainer Amir Jamal Touré leads stimulating, informative tours around Savannah, offering in-depth details about African American life and its African origins in locations missed by other tours, especially the area's Gullah Geechee culture. Interesting fact: Touré served as the model for the bronze sculpture memorial on River Street. ⊠ Savannah ☎ 912/220–5966 ⊕ daycleansoul.com ⊠ From $35.

**Hearse Ghost Tours.** These tours may be like nothing you've ever experienced before. For years these hearses did the job they were intended for; when they were retired, their roofs were removed to make space for eight live bodies. You'll cruise past creepy cemeteries, haunted houses, and shady lanes, all while hearing the sordid stories of Savannah's darker past from the comfort of a real hearse. Count on macabre guides for irreverently funny narration. It's a great value. ⊠ 1410 E. Broad St., Savannah ☎ 912/695–1578 ⊕ hearseghosttours.com ⊠ From $30.

**Old Savannah Tours.** This is the city's award-winning company with years of experience, a wide variety of tours, and live historical re-enactors. Popular options include the historic hop-on, hop-off trolley tour, the 90-minute Historic Overview, and the ghost tour that includes dinner at the Pirates' House. Leashed pets under 25 pounds are welcome to ride along. ⊠ 255 Montgomery St., Savannah ☎ 912/234–8128 ⊕ oldsavannahtours.com ⊠ From $13.

**Old Town Trolley Tours.** Old Town Trolley Tours has personally narrated 90-minute tours traversing the Historic District. Trolleys stop at 15 designated stops every 30 minutes daily, from 9 am to 5 pm (August to March) or 9 am to 6 pm (April to July). You can hop on and off as you please, and free parking is available. In the evening, the company offers ghosts tours and visits to the American Prohibition Museum. ⊠ Savannah ☎ 855/245–8992 toll-free ⊕ www.trolleytours.com/savannah ⊠ From $33 (online purchases are discounted).

**Savannah Carriage Tours.** There's nothing like the sound of hooves on cobblestones to evoke Savannah's charm. Choose from a public history or ghost tour, or make it personal with a private history tour. You can hire their horse-drawn carriages for any special occasion, like a post-wedding stroll or a proposal. ⊠ 98 W. Bay St., Savannah ☎ 912/443–9333 ⊕ savannahcarriage.com

✉ From $32 for group tours, from $150 (2 people) for private tours.

## SEGWAY TOURS

**Segway of Savannah.** Mix it up by exploring the Historic District, Bonaventure Cemetery, and Tybee Island on a one-hour or 90-minute guided tour atop one of these unique two-wheeled vehicles. With two-way radios, it's easy to hear the guide and ask questions. Helmets are provided, and riders must be 16 years or older to participate. The company also offers tours by electric bicycles and van. ✉ 412 Whitaker St., Savannah ☎ 912/233–3554 ⊕ segwayofsavannah.com ✉ From $49.

## WALKING TOURS

**Bonaventure Don.** Take a deep dive into the storied history of Savannah's beloved Bonaventure Cemetery, the final resting place for notable Savannah greats like songwriter Johnny Mercer and author Conrad Aiken. Fifth-generation Savannahian Bonaventure Don offers a factual, history-based tour from a past chairman of the Bonaventure Historical Society. Tours last 2½ hours, and Don asks his customers to name their own price. ✉ 330 Bonaventure Road, Savannah ☎ 912/658–1748 ⊕ bonaventuredon.com ✉ Guests name their own price.

**Bonnie Blue Tours.** Local historian and witty raconteur Bonnie Rae Terrell guides visitors through her hometown like only a native could. Choose between two downtown tours, the Slo-Vannah Saunter and Lightly Sauced (the latter is for folks 21 and older); both run a leisurely three hours. ✉ Savannah ☎ 912/398–2640 ⊕ bonniebluetours.com ✉ From $45.

**Cobblestone Tours.** Cobblestone Tours provides a deep historical context for Savannah's spooky occurrences. This popular tour company offers two touring options: the Savannah Ghosts & Folklore tour, an all-ages 90-minute candlelit stroll through the Historic District, and the adults-only two-hour Savannah Haunted Pub Crawl that meets at Moon River Brewing Company on Bay Street. Guides travel in period costume for extra effect. ✉ Colonial Cemetery, 201 E. Oglethorpe Ave., Savannah ☎ 912/604–3007 ⊕ ghostsavannah.com ✉ From $20.

**Creepy Crawl Haunted Pub Tour.** Any good ghost story is better while imbibing adult beverages. Believers say there are so many ghosts in Savannah they're actually divided into subcategories, and these charismatic guides specialize in tavern ghosts. They'll regale you with tales

# Best Tours

of secret subbasements, possessed gumball machines, and animated water faucets. Tours traditionally depart from the Six Pence Pub at 8 pm and last for 2½ hours. Because this is a cocktail tour, children are not permitted. Routes can vary, so call for departure times and locations. ⊠ *245 Bull St., Savannah* ☎ *912/238–3843* ⊕ *savannahtours.com* ✉ *From $30.*

**Footprints of Savannah Tours.** You'll gain a comprehensive history of slavery in Savannah and the roles that African Americans have played in shaping the Hostess City's story with noted historian Vaughnette Goode-Walker, who leads tours through the landmarks you thought you knew and explains how they fit in with the cotton trade. Tours depart daily from Wright Square and last about 90 minutes. ⊠ *Savannah* ☎ *912/695–3872* ⊕ *footprintsofsavannah.com* ✉ *From $25.*

**Genteel & Bard.** A tour operator focused on storytelling, family-owned Genteel & Bard offers audio-enhanced tech for easy listening—guests are provided earbuds while a tour guide speaks into a wireless microphone. Choose from the Historic Savannah Daytime Walking Tour, Savannah Dark History & Ghost Encounter

Tour, or the Savannah Women's Walking Tour. ⊠ *24 E. Liberty, Savannah* ☎ *912/373–6651* ⊕ *genteelandbard.com* ✉ *From $30.*

**Ghost Talk Ghost Walk Tour.** Savannah's original, affordable ghost tour sends chills down your spine during an easygoing 1-mile jaunt through the downtown, the city's oldest area, but it's still appropriate for children. Tours last 1½ hours and leave from the middle of Reynolds Square at the John Wesley Memorial at 7:30 pm and 9:30 pm, weather permitting. Reservations are required. ⊠ *Savannah* ☎ *912/233–3896* ⊕ *www.ghosttalkghostwalk. com* ✉ *From $10.*

**Savannah Taste Experience.** Experience Savannah through your taste buds with forays into the city's food scene. All ages and fitness levels welcome. Come hungry! ⊠ *108 W. Broughton St., Savannah* ☎ *912/221–4439* ⊕ *savannahtasteexperience.com* ✉ *From $64.95.*

**Sixth Sense Savannah.** Hunt ghosts and explore cemeteries on one of Sixth Sense's chilling tours, including the Bonaventure Cemetery Tour, the America's Most Haunted City Tour, Sixth Sense Savannah Ghost Tour, The Midnight Tour, and the cozy Fireside Tales experience. Reservations are required. ✉ *415 Bonaventure Rd., Savannah* ☎ *912/292–0960* ⊕ *sixthsenseworld.com* ✉ *From $30.*

**Underground Tours of Savannah.**
Join Master Storyteller Sistah Patt Gunn for an exploration of Savannah from the Gullah Geechee perspective, told in its native tongue. Tours begin at the African American Monument on River Street and follow the cobblestones to the Cluskey Vaults and Cotton Exchange, where enslaved people marked the bricks with African Adinkra symbols. ✉ *25 Bull St., Savannah* ☎ *912/547–5937* ⊕ *undergroundtoursofsavannah.net* ✉ *From $25.*

# On the Calendar

## January

**New Year's Day Polar Plunge on Tybee Island.** Join the hundreds of brave (or some say crazy) folks who start the new year with a raucous dip in the Atlantic near the Pier. While it is not required, you can register to benefit the historic Tybee Post Theater to receive a commemorative T-shirt marking your courageous act. ⊕ *tybeeisland.com*.

## February

**Savannah Black Heritage Festival.** Celebrate local and national Black history with lectures, dance concerts, art shows, kids' activities, and more in a celebration sponsored by the City of Savannah and Savannah State University. Events take place throughout the month, culminating in an all-day festival that draws thousands. ⊕ *savannahblackheritagefestival.org*.

## March

**St. Patrick's Day Festival.** More than a million folks descend upon the city to carouse and take part in this annual parade and party dedicated to Irish heritage. Enjoy traditional Irish food, song, dance, and, if you're over 21, plenty of whiskey. Make sure to wear your green! ⊕ *savannahsaintpatricksday.com*.

## April

**Savannah Music Festival.** Beginning in late March and running through April, this world-class showcase features more than 80 performances in classical, blues, and global genres for music lovers who travel from far-flung destinations to attend. Concerts take place around the city, from formal theaters to exquisite, intimate private rooms. ⊕ *www.savannahmusicfestival.org*.

## May

**Savannah Doggie Carnival.** It's all about the puppers at this annual fundraiser in Forsyth Park that benefits the Humane Society for Greater Savannah and welcomes everyone with two and four legs to participate in fun games, healthy refreshments, and lots of lazing in the sun. ⊕ *www.humanesocietysav.org*.

## July

**Fourth of July Fireworks.** Watch the skies sparkle on River Street as the city celebrates American Independence all day long with kids' activities and entertainment, culminating with a spectacular fireworks show after dark. Tybee Island has its own pyrotechnic spectacle launched from the Pier as well. ⊕ *gosouthsavannah.com.*

## September

**Savannah Jazz Festival.** Sponsored by the City of Savannah, this weeklong extravaganza of hot licks, big band sounds, and classic standards brings together different generations and multiple genres in a series of free concerts in Forsyth Park. ⊕ *savannahjazz.org.*

## October

**Tybee Island Pirate Festival.** Say "arrrgh" for this annual homage to the coast's pirate past with live music, good-natured debauchery, and of course, plenty of eyepatches at the beach. ⊕ *www.tybeepiratefest. com.*

## November

**Picnic in the Park.** The weather is always perfect for this gorgeous gathering in Forsyth Park, where locals compete for the most glorious table setting, and where the talented musicians of the Savannah Philharmonic provide the serenade. Pack your own picnic and chairs, or just show up and let some of the city's finest food trucks make you dinner. ⊕ *savannahphilharmonic.org.*

## December

**Christmas Boat Parade.** The Savannah Harbor Foundation teams up with local hotels and ship captains to transform the Savannah River into a magical twinkling winter wonderland, best enjoyed with a hot cocoa from the riverfront. ⊕ *savannahboatparadeoflights.com.*

# Contacts

## ✈ Air

**AIRPORTS Hilton Head Island Airport. (HHH).** ✉ *120 Beach City Rd., North End* ☎ *843/255–2950* ⊕ *hiltonheadairport.com.* **Savannah/Hilton Head International Airport.** ✉ *400 Airways Ave., Northwest* ☎ *912/964–0514* ⊕ *savannahairport.com.*

**AIRPORT TRANSFERS Old Savannah Tours.** ☎ *912/234–8128* ⊕ *oldsavannahtours.com.*

## ⬤ Boat

**CONTACTS Savannah Belles Ferry.** ✉ *City Hall Dock, River St., Historic District* ☎ *912/233–5767* ⊕ *catchacat.org.*

## 🚗 Car

**PARKING Savannah Parking Mobility.** ✉ *100 E. Bryan St., Savannah* ☎ *912/651–6470* ⊕ *savannahga.gov/2519/ Mobility-Parking-Services.*

## Ⓜ Public Transport

**CONTACTS Chatham Area Transit.** ☎ *912/233–5767* ⊕ *catchacat.org.* **dot.** ✉ *1 International Dr., Savannah* ☎ *912/233–5767* ⊕ *connectonthedot.com.*

## 🚕 Taxi

**CONTACTS Savannah Pedicab.** ☎ *912/232–7900* ⊕ *savannahpedicab.com.* **Yellow Cab.** ☎ *912/236–1133, 912/236-1133* ⊕ *yellowcabsavannah.com.*

## 🚆 Train

**CONTACTS Savannah Amtrak Station.** ✉ *2611 Seaboard Coastline Dr., Savannah* ☎ *800/872–7245* ⊕ *www. amtrak.com.*

## 📍 Visitor Information

**CONTACTS The River Street Visitor Information Center.** ✉ *1 West River St., Historic District* ☎ *912/651–6662* ⊕ *visitsavannah.com.* **Savannah/Hilton Head International Airport Visitors Center.** ✉ *400 Airways Ave., Savannah* ☎ *912/966–3743* ⊕ *visitsavannah.com.* **Savannah Visitor Information Center.** ✉ *301 Martin Luther King Jr. Blvd., Historic District* ☎ *912/944–0455* ⊕ *visitsavannah.com.* **Tybee Island Visitor Information Center.** ✉ *802 1st St., Tybee Island* ☎ *877/786–5444* ⊕ *visittybee.com.*

# Chapter 3

# HISTORIC DISTRICT

Updated by
Summer Bozeman

| ◉ Sights | 🍴 Restaurants | 🛏 Hotels | 🛍 Shopping | 🍸 Nightlife |
|----------|---------------|----------|-------------|-------------|
| ★★★★☆ | ★★★★★ | ★★★★☆ | ★★★★★ | ★★★★★ |

# NEIGHBORHOOD SNAPSHOT

## TOP EXPERIENCES

■ **Forsyth Park:** This 30-plus acre park is perfect for walking and picnicking; it's one of Savannah's most beautiful and most-photographed spots.

■ **Telfair museums:** This family of three museums is comprised of the contemporary Jepson Center for the Arts, historic Telfair Academy, and the Owens-Thomas House and Slave Quarters.

■ **Savannah riverboat cruises:** Learn about Savannah's river-driven economy from its founding to the modern day with a cruise by the port.

■ **Haunted history:** Although Georgia is the youngest of the original 13 colonies, Savannah has a variety of ghostly tours and creepy house museums.

■ **The Olde Pink House:** A city staple dining experience since the 1990s, this iconic restaurant has always been near the top of travelers' Savannah bucket lists.

■ **St. Patrick's Day:** Savannah's signature annual festival celebrating Irish cultural heritage kicks off in mid-February.

## GETTING HERE

The Savannah/Hilton Head International Airport is about 10 miles from downtown Savannah. If you aren't staying in the Historic District, you'll probably need to rent a car. If you're planning on bringing your own car, Savannah is easily accessible via Interstates 95 and 16. Parking downtown is metered (mostly taking only credit and debit cards) but not plentiful. There's a free Dot shuttle to 24 major stops while you're in the Historic District (look for its green, gold, and purple signs). The Savannah Belles ferries are also free.

## QUICK BITES

■ **Dottie's Market.** This one-stop shop on Broughton Street offers a blend of a Southern-style sandwich-and-coffee café with an NYC-style grab-and-go bodega. ⊠ *207 W Broughton St., Historic District* ⊕ *dottiesmarketsav.com.*

■ **The Coffee Fox.** This award-winning local roaster and coffee crafter offers a full espresso menu plus pour-overs, craft beer, and freshly roasted beans in a historic spot where revolutionaries met to organize against British rule. ⊠ *102 W Broughton St., Historic District* ⊕ *thecoffeefox.com.*

■ **Zunzi's.** South African, Dutch, and Swiss-inspired fare with chicken, Boerewors sausage, and more are offered here. Sit under a rainbow umbrella and enjoy a flavorful South African iced tea. ⊠ *236 Drayton St., Historic District* ⊕ *zunzis.com.*

Georgia was established as a utopian experiment by General James Oglethorpe, with Savannah as its original and oldest city.

Georgia's sage founder guaranteed each male citizen a lot with a 24-by-16-foot frame house, a 5-acre garden lot outside of town, and a 45-acre farm lot past the garden lots. Each ward had home lots on the north and south sides and trust lots on the east and west sides for churches or other public buildings and an open green space in the center where each ward's militia could muster. Originally there were four squares—Johnson, Wright (then called Percival), Ellis, and Telfair (then called St. James)—and there have been as many as 24, but several were lost to development over the years. Some of those have been restored, and 22 squares exist today. The unique Oglethorpe Plan ensured that Savannah's Historic District is the earliest example of urban planning in America; it's also a National Historic Landmark.

Savannah's Historic District is neatly hemmed in by the Savannah River, Gaston Street, East Broad Street, and Martin Luther King Jr. Boulevard. Streets are arrow-straight, and public squares are tucked into the grid at precise intervals. Bull Street, anchored on the north by City Hall and the south by Forsyth Park, charges down the center of the grid and maneuvers around the five public squares that stand in its way. The squares provide shaded, quiet spots to enjoy public art or a picnic lunch, and also serve to slow traffic.

# Historic District North

Stretching from the edge of the sparkling Savannah River over a mile to the top of Forsyth Park at Gaston Street, Savannah's National Historic Landmark District is the area including Savannah's most well-known feature: its 22 city squares. The oldest parts of the district make up Historic District North, which ends at Oglethorpe Avenue.

## ◉ Sights

### American Prohibition Museum
HISTORY MUSEUM | FAMILY | In the heart of City Market, America's only museum dedicated to the Prohibition era shares history from 1907 to 1933. In the 6,000-square-foot space, guests wander 13

**KEY**

- ● Sights
- ● Restaurants
- ● Quick Bites
- ● Hotels

Williamson Street
West River Street
West Bay Street
West Bay Lane
West Bryan Street
Franklin Square
West Congress Street
Orange St.
Zubley St.
Martin Luther King Jr. Blvd
West Broughton Street
Montgomery Street
West York Street
Jefferson Street
West President St.
West State Street
Telfair Square
Barnard Street
West Oglethorpe Avenue
West Oglethorpe Ln.
West Hull Street
Orleans Square
Whitaker Street
Ellis Square
East Bay Street
East Bryan Street
Barnard Street
East Congress Street
West Congress Lane
West Broughton Lane
Johnson Square
Bull Street
East Broughton St.
East Broughton Lane
East State Street
Wright Square
E. President St.
East York Street
East Oglethorpe Avenue
Drayton Street
Cit Ha

0 — 1,000 ft
0 — 250 m

| Sights | Juliette Gordon Low Birthplace, **16** | Restaurants | Little Duck Diner, **7** |
|---|---|---|---|
| American Prohibition Museum, **4** | Owens-Thomas House & Slave Quarters, **17** | a.lure, **4** | The Olde Pink House, **15** |
| Christ Church Episcopal, **7** | Reynolds Square, **8** | B&D Burgers, **6** | The Ordinary Pub, **5** |
| City Market, **3** | Rousakis Riverfront Plaza, **9** | Cha Bella, **21** | Pacci Italian Kitchen, **19** |
| Davenport House Museum, **18** | Ships of the Sea Maritime Museum, **1** | The Collins Quarter, **11** | The Pirates' House, **20** |
| Ellis Square, **5** | Telfair Academy, **13** | The Flying Monk Noodle Bar, **9** | Treylor Park, **16** |
| Emmet Park, **10** | Waving Girl Statue, **12** | 45 Bistro, **14** | Vic's on the River, **1** |
| Factors Walk, **11** | Wright Square, **15** | Franklin's, **12** | Vinnie Van Go-Go's, **2** |
| First African Baptist Church, **2** | | Garibaldi, **3** | Zunzi's, **13** |
| Jepson Center for the Arts, **14** | | The Grey, **1** | |
| Johnson Square, **6** | | Huey's on the River, **18** | **Quick Bites** |
| | | Husk Savannah, **10** | The Coffee Fox, **2** |
| | | The Lady & Sons, **8** | Cup to Cup Cafe, **4** |

# Historic District North

*Savannah River*

Hutchinson Island

Morrell Park

East River Street

Factors Walk

Emmet Park

East Bay Street

Reynolds Square

E. St. Julian St.

East Congress Lane

Warren Square

E. St. Julian St.

East Bryan Street

East Bay Lane

Washington Square

East Congress Street

East Broughton Street

E. Broughton Ln.

Oglethorpe Square

E. President St.

East York Street

Columbia Square

East York Lane

East State Street

Greene Square

E. President St.

Burney Drive

East Oglethorpe Avenue

Wilder Drive

Avery Street

Abercorn Street

Lincoln Street

Habersham Street

Price Street

Houston Street

East Broad Street

W. Boundary St.

Leopold's Ice Cream, **3**

The Little Crown by Pie Society, **1**

**Hotels**

The Alida, Savannah, a Tribute Portfolio Hotel, **2**

Andaz Savannah, **3**

Bohemian Hotel Savannah Riverfront, Autograph Collection, **4**

The Drayton Hotel Savannah, Curio Collection by Hilton, **6**

The Grant, **17**

Green Palm Inn, **21**

Hampton Inn & Suites Savannah-Historic District, **10**

Holiday Inn Express Savannah-Historic District, **9**

Hyatt Regency Savannah, **5**

JW Marriott Savannah Plant Riverside District, **1**

Kehoe House, **20**

The Kimpton Brice Hotel, **14**

The Marshall House, **18**

Olde Harbour Inn, **12**

Planters Inn, **15**

The President's Quarters Inn, **19**

River Street Inn, **7**

Savannah Marriott Riverfront, **13**

SpringHill Suites by Marriott Savannah Downtown/Historic District, **16**

Staybridge Suites Savannah Historic District, **11**

Westin Savannah Harbor Golf Resort & Spa, **8**

City Market is a busy area filled with shops, galleries, and attractions.

galleries, a theater, and a real speakeasy. From stories of Southern rumrunners to the history of moonshine, the museum offers a fun and informative look at the past—there are even four antique cars on the premises. Make sure to enjoy a specially crafted cocktail at the museum speakeasy bar, Congress Street Up, which stays open long after the museum closes and uses period-authentic recipes and ingredients. ⊠ *209 W. Julian St.* ✛ *In City Market* ☎ *912/220–1249* ⊕ *www.americanprohibitionmuseum.com* 🖾 *From $17.*

### Christ Church Episcopal

**CHURCH** | This was the first church—then Anglican—established in the Georgia colony in 1733. It is often called the "Mother Church of Georgia." George Washington attended services here when he visited the city in 1791 (although in the building prior to the current 1838 structure), as did Juliette Gordon Low, founder of the Girl Scouts. From its location on Johnson Square, an 1819 Revere & Son bell still chimes today in the imposing white-columned steeple. ⊠ *28 Bull St., Historic District* ☎ *912/236–2500* ⊕ *www. christchurchsavannah.org.*

### City Market

**BUSINESS DISTRICT** | Although the 1870s City Market was razed years ago, its atmosphere and character are still evident. Adjacent to Ellis Square, the area is a lively destination because of its galleries, boutiques, street performers, and open-air cafés. Local favorites include Byrd Cookie Company, a popular Savannah-based bakery with great edible souvenirs, and Pie Society, offering

specialty British meat pies. City Market is also a good spot to purchase trolley tickets, take a ride in a horse-drawn carriage, or dive
into history at the American Prohibition Museum. ⊠ *W. St. Julian
St., between Barnard and Montgomery Sts., Historic District*
☎ *912/232–4903* ⊕ *www.savannahcitymarket.com.*

## ★ Davenport House Museum

**HISTORIC HOME | FAMILY |** Semicircular stairs with wrought-iron rail-
ings lead to the recessed doorway of the redbrick Federal home
constructed by master builder Isaiah Davenport for his family
between 1815 and 1820. Three dormered windows poke through
the sloping roof of the stately house, and the interior has polished
hardwood floors and fine woodwork and plasterwork, showcasing
Davenport's talents to potential clients. The proposed demolition
of this historic Savannah structure galvanized the city's residents
into action to save their treasured buildings. The home endured
a history of dilapidation that had lingered since the 1920s, when
it was divided into tenements. When someone proposed razing
it to build a parking lot in 1955, a small group of neighbors raised
$22,000 in 24 hours to buy and restore the property. This action
was the inception of the Historic Savannah Foundation and the
first of many successful efforts to preserve the architectural
treasure that is the city today. ⊠ *324 E. State St., Historic District*
☎ *912/236–8097* ⊕ *www.davenporthousemuseum.org* 🎫 *$10*
⊘ *Closed mid-Jan. and on Sun.*

## Ellis Square

**PLAZA/SQUARE | FAMILY |** Converted from a public square to a park-
ing garage in the 1970s, Ellis Square has been restored in recent
years and is once again one of Savannah's most popular spots.
Near the western end stands a statue of legendary songwriter
Johnny Mercer, a Savannah native. Nearby is a visitor center
with a touch-screen city guide, maps and brochures, and public
restrooms. To the east is a life-size chess board; the pieces can
be requested at the visitor center. A treat for youngsters (and
the young at heart) is the square's interactive fountain, which is
entertaining and refreshing in the warmer months. ⊠ *Barnard St.,
between W. Congress and W. Bryan Sts., Historic District.*

## Emmet Park

**CITY PARK |** Once a Native American burial ground, the lovely
tree-shaded park is named for Robert Emmet, a late-18th-century
Irish patriot and orator. The park contains monuments to Georgia
Hussars, fallen soldiers from the Vietnam War, and the Celtic
Cross Irish memorial, among others. Various small festivals are
held in the park each year. ⊠ *E. Bay St. from E. Broad St. to Lincoln St., Historic District.*

## Did You Know?

Emmet Park was once known as Irish Green because of its proximity to the Irish residents of Savannah's Old Fort neighborhood.

## Factors Walk

**PLAZA/SQUARE** | A network of iron crosswalks and steep stone stairways connects Bay Street to Factors Walk below. The congested area of multistory buildings was originally the center of commerce for cotton brokers (also called factors), who walked between and above the lower cotton warehouses. Ramps lead down to River Street. ■**TIP→ This area is paved in cobblestones and features steep, historic stone staircases, so wear comfortable shoes and step carefully.** ✉ *Bay St. to Factors Walk, Historic District.*

## First African Baptist Church

**CHURCH** | **FAMILY** | Enslaved people constructed this church at night by lamplight after having worked the plantations during the day, finishing it in 1859. It is one of the first organized black Baptist churches on the continent, constituted in 1777. The basement floor still shows signs of its time as a stop on the Underground Railroad. Holes drilled in the floor are designed in a prayer symbol known as an "African cosmogram," and are rumored to actually have been air holes for slaves hiding underneath, waiting to be transported to the Savannah River for their trip to freedom. It was also an important meeting place during the civil rights era. ✉ *23 Montgomery St., Historic District* ☎ *912/233–6597* ⊕ *www.firstafricanbc.com* ⊠ *$15* ⊙ *No tours on Sun., closed Mon.* ⚄ *Group tours must be reserved in advance.*

## ★ Jepson Center for the Arts

**ART MUSEUM** | **FAMILY** | This contemporary building is one of a kind among the characteristic 18th- and 19th-century architecture of historic Savannah. The modern art extension of the adjacent Telfair Academy museum, the Jepson was designed by renowned architect Moshe Safdie. Within the marble-and-glass edifice are rotating exhibits, on loan and from the permanent collection, ranging from European masters to contemporary locals. There's also an outdoor sculpture terrace and an interactive, kid-friendly area on the third level. ✉ *207 W. York St., Historic District* ☎ *912/790–8800* ⊕ *www.telfair.org/visit/jepson-center* ⊠ *$30, includes admission to the Owens-Thomas House & Slave Quarters and the Telfair Academy.*

## Johnson Square

**PLAZA/SQUARE** | The oldest of James Oglethorpe's original squares was laid out in 1733 and named for South Carolina governor Robert Johnson. A monument marks the grave of Nathanael Greene, a hero of the Revolutionary War and close friend of George Washington. The square has always been a popular gathering place: Savannahians came here to welcome President Monroe in 1819, to greet the Marquis de Lafayette in 1825, and to cheer for Georgia's secession in 1861. ■**TIP→ Locals call this Bank Square**

**because of the plethora of nearby banks—perfect if you need an ATM.**
⊠ *Bull St., between Bryan and Congress Sts., Historic District.*

### Juliette Gordon Low Birthplace

**HISTORIC HOME | FAMILY |** This early-19th-century town house, attributed to William Jay, was designated in 1965 as Savannah's first National Historic Landmark. "Daisy" Low, founder of the Girl Scouts, was born here in 1860, and the house is now owned and operated by the Girl Scouts of America. Mrs. Low's paintings and other artwork are on display in the house, restored to the style of 1886, the year of Mrs. Low's marriage. Droves of Girl Scout troops make the regular pilgrimage to Savannah to see their founder's birthplace and earn merit badges. In addition to its value as a pilgrimage site for Girl Scouts, the home is a beautiful look into the lives of Savannahians during the Victorian era. ■ TIP→ **Tickets sell fast, so book in advance if you want to tour the house on a specific day.** ⊠ *10 E. Oglethorpe St., Historic District* 🕾 *912/233–4501* ⊕ *www.juliettegordonlowbirthplace.org* 🖭 *$15 adult; $10 Girl Scout* ⊙ *Closed Sun. and early Jan.*

### ★ Owens-Thomas House & Slave Quarters

**HISTORIC HOME | FAMILY |** Designed by William Jay, the Owens-Thomas House is widely considered to be one of the finest examples of English Regency architecture in America. Built in 1816–19, the house was constructed with local materials. Of particular note are the curving walls, Greek-inspired ornamental molding, half-moon arches, stained-glass panels, original Duncan Phyfe furniture, the hardwood "bridge" on the second floor, and the indoor toilets, which it had before the White House or Versailles. In 2018, the site renamed itself the Owens-Thomas House & Slave Quarters and revealed a new interpretive exhibition that includes the restored dwellings of those enslaved here and stories of their lives and work. Owned and administered by Telfair Museums, this home gives an inside perspective on Savannah's history. ⊠ *124 Abercorn St., Historic District* 🕾 *912/790–8889* ⊕ *www.telfair.org/visit/owens-thomas* 🖭 *$30, includes admission to the Jepson Center and the Telfair Academy.*

### Reynolds Square

**PLAZA/SQUARE |** Anglican cleric and theologian John Wesley is remembered here. He arrived in Savannah in 1736 at the behest of General James Oglethorpe to minister to the newly established colony. During his short stay, the future founder of the Methodist Church preached and wrote the first English hymnal in the city. His monument in Reynolds Square is shaded by greenery and surrounded by park benches. The landmark Planters Inn, formerly the John Wesley Hotel, is also located on the square. Ironically,

Savannah's many squares, like Reynolds Square, offer a peaceful environment to relax, read a book, or have a takeout meal.

though it was named after a man of the cloth, it was considered the best brothel in town at the turn of the 20th century. ✉ *Abercorn St., between E. Congress and E. Bryan Sts., Historic District.*

### Rousakis Riverfront Plaza

**PLAZA/SQUARE** | From River Street's main pavilion you can watch a parade of freighters and pug-nosed tugs glide by along the river. River Street is the main venue for several of the city's grandest celebrations, including the First Friday Fireworks. The plaza is named for former Savannah mayor John Rousakis and fills with locals for Savannah's signature St. Patrick's Day festivities and Fourth of July celebration. Rousakis, like greater River Street, is flanked by an abundance of shops and restaurants and draws colorful street entertainers. ✉ *River St., near Abercorn St., Historic District* ⊕ *www.savannahswaterfront.com.*

### ★ Ships of the Sea Maritime Museum

**HISTORIC HOME** | **FAMILY** | This exuberant Greek Revival mansion was the home of William Scarborough, a wealthy early-19th-century merchant and one of the principal owners of the *Savannah*, the first steamship to cross the Atlantic. The structure, with its portico capped by half-moon windows, is another of architect William Jay's notable contributions to the Historic District and Regency-style architecture. These days, it houses the Ships of the Sea Maritime Museum, with displays of model ships and exhibits detailing maritime history. The ambitious North Garden nearly doubled the original walled courtyard's size and provides ample space for naturalist-led walks and outdoor concerts. ✉ *41 Martin*

## Full Steam Ahead

The first steam-powered ship to cross the Atlantic was the SS *Savannah*, which sailed from Savannah north to Newark and then finally to Scotland, England, and Russia during its maiden voyage in 1819. The ship was funded by local shipping magnate William Scarborough, whose home still stands on Martin Luther King Jr. Boulevard (formerly West Broad Street). While the SS *Savannah*'s first trip was a success as a major landmark in the evolution of maritime travel and commerce, the endeavor didn't work out so well for Scarborough as a businessman. He ended up bankrupt and eventually was forced to sell his newly constructed home, which is now the Ships of the Sea Maritime Museum—an appropriate homage to its original tenant. Before the building underwent substantial restorations prior to becoming the museum, it spent nearly a century as a public school. Opened in the 1870s, the West Broad Street School was the first officially sanctioned school for African American children in the city.

*Luther King Jr. Blvd., Historic District* ☎ *912/232–1511* ⊕ *www. shipsofthesea.org* ✉ *$15* ⊘ *Closed Mon.*

### ★ Telfair Academy

**ART MUSEUM | FAMILY |** The oldest public art museum in the South was designed by William Jay in 1819 as a residence for Alexander Telfair. Within its marble rooms are a variety of paintings from American and European masters, plaster casts of the Elgin Marbles and other classical sculptures, and some of the Telfair family furnishings, including a Duncan Phyfe sideboard and Savannah-made silver. ✉ *121 Barnard St., Historic District* ☎ *912/790–8800* ⊕ *www.telfair.org/visit/telfair-academy* ✉ *$30, includes admission to the Jepson Center and the Owens-Thomas House & Slave Quarters.*

### Waving Girl Statue

**PUBLIC ART | FAMILY |** This statue at River Street and East Broad Ramp is a beloved symbol of Savannah's Southern hospitality. It commemorates Florence Martus, a sister to the lighthouse keeper, who waved to ships as they came into Savannah's port for more than 44 years. She would wave a white towel and, when young, always had her dog by her side. Late in her life, locals threw her a huge birthday party at Fort Pulaski with more than 5,000 guests. Despite having welcomed so many sailors to port, she died without ever having been wed. ✉ *River St. near E. Broad Ramp, Historic District.*

Telfair Academy, the oldest art museum in the South, houses the Bird Girl statue made famous in the novel and film *Midnight in the Garden of Good and Evil*.

### Wright Square

**PLAZA/SQUARE** | Named for James Wright, Georgia's last colonial governor, this square has an elaborate monument in its center that honors William Washington Gordon, founder of the Central of Georgia Railroad. A granite boulder from Stone Mountain adorns the grave of Tomochichi, the Yamacraw chief who befriended General Oglethorpe and the colonists, giving his permission for the English settlers to establish their colony on Yamacraw Bluff. ⊠ *Bull St., between W. State and W. York Sts., Historic District.*

## 🍴 Restaurants

The Plant Riverside district anchors the west end of River Street and extends Savannah's famous riverwalk with an acre-and-a-half public park, outdoor concert venue, and many new restaurants, including those serving wood-fired pizza, Mexican food, smokehouse barbecue, and more.

### a.lure

**$$$** | **AMERICAN** | This simple, sophisticated dining room is smartly designed so there isn't a bad seat in the house. Don't be afraid to fill up on light bites—like the lamb carpaccio with house-made blue-cheese ice cream or the fried green tomatoes paired with American speck ham, pimento cheese, and green goddess dressing—and then skip right to dessert: the frozen goat-cheese soufflé is delightful in both flavor and architectural presentation. **Known for:** shrimp and grits; intimate ambience; reimagined Southern fare.

$ *Average main: $31* ⊠ *309 W. Congress St., City Market* ☎ *912/233–2111* ⊕ *aluresavannah.com* ⊘ *No lunch.*

## B&D Burgers

$ | **BURGER** | **FAMILY** | Locally owned and operated B&D Burgers is a great bet for a quick, low-key bite to eat with offerings like tempura-battered chicken fingers and a grand assortment of locally themed burgers. The large, two-story

### Money-Saving Tips

Download the Savannah ePASS (⊕ *epass.app*) for culinary savings during your stay in the Hostess City. You might get a free appetizer or dessert or a discount on your final check.

dining room is decorated in Lowcountry flair, including faux trophy alligators and nets and buoys, but be encouraged to venture outside; this place has some of the best outdoor dining in the city and the expansive patio is equipped with a video screen for sports events and large umbrellas that protect against the rain and sun. **Known for:** big-screen sports viewing; kid-friendly menu; locations on Broughton Street, Southside, and Pooler. $ *Average main: $11* ⊠ *209 W. Congress St., Historic District* ☎ *912/238–8315* ⊕ *bdburgers.net.*

## ★ Cha Bella

$$$ | **AMERICAN** | The first farm-to-table restaurant in Savannah, Cha Bella continues to serve only dishes made with the finest local ingredients, so even if you've been here recently, there may be some surprises. With no walk-in freezer, all ingredients must be used within three days of delivery, so the menu is guaranteed to be fresh. **Known for:** Savannah's first farm-to-table restaurant; a delightful array of cocktails; menu changes regularly based on what's fresh and available. $ *Average main: $27* ⊠ *102 E. Broad St., Historic District* ☎ *912/790–7888* ⊕ *www.cha-bella.com* ⊘ *No lunch.*

## ★ The Collins Quarter

$$ | **CAFÉ** | Modeled after the cozy coffee cafés of Melbourne, Australia, this bustling locale serves espresso, cold brew, and its famous spiced lavender mochas, as well as a curated menu that features favorites like smashed avocado toast at brunch and duck confit, served alongside fingerling potatoes and oyster mushrooms, at dinner. The beer selection includes favorites from craft breweries around the country, and the wines are carefully selected from some of the world's most unique regions to complement the food. **Known for:** chic café setting; walk-up window service; spiced lavender mochas. $ *Average main: $17* ⊠ *151 Bull St.,*

*Historic District* ☎ *912/777–4147* ⊕ *thecollinsquarter.com* ⊗ *No dinner Mon. and Tues.*

## The Flying Monk Noodle Bar

$ | ASIAN | Noodle, rice, and soup dishes from across Asia come together on the eclectic, flavorful menu at the Flying Monk. The well-appointed space and laid-back atmosphere complement the savory dishes. **Known for:** authentic Asian fare; quick service; vegetarian-friendly menu. ⑤ *Average main: $12* ⊠ *5 W. Broughton St., Historic District* ☎ *912/232–8888* ⊕ *www.flywiththemonk.com.*

## 45 Bistro

$$$ | AMERICAN | On the ground floor of the Marshall House, 45 Bistro has some of the best views of Broughton Street from the floor-to-ceiling windows that run the length of the room. Most of the menu abounds with regional flavors—local crab, wild shrimp, spiced pecans—but standards like the wet-aged rib eye are equally as satisfying, as are the updated old favorites like shrimp and grits with fried Vidalia onion rings, or the grilled romaine hearts in the exceptional Caesar salad. **Known for:** elevated comfort foods; historic charm; a great steak. ⑤ *Average main: $34* ⊠ *Marshall House, 123 E. Broughton St., Historic District* ☎ *912/234–3111* ⊕ *45bistro.com* ⊗ *Closed Sun. No lunch.*

## ★ Franklin's

$$ | AMERICAN | This elegant garden-level spot is moody but bright and cozy, and the menu is chock-full of delicious treats for any time of day. The quiche is some of the richest in town, the homemade tomato soup will knock your socks off, and the Butcher's B.L.T. features thick-cut bacon and soft sourdough. **Known for:** coffee cocktails; steamed eggs with amazing cheese; croque madame with delicate béchamel. ⑤ *Average main: $15* ⊠ *5 W. Liberty St., Historic District* ☎ *912/200–4045* ⊕ *www.ilovefranklins.com.*

## Garibaldi

$$$ | ITALIAN | This well-appointed restaurant is known to locals and travelers alike for its contemporary cuisine and Italian classics at reasonable prices. Dark wood and burnished tin ceilings evoke a romantic brasserie. **Known for:** elegant and intimate setting; crispy flounder with apricot and shallot sauce; Italian classics. ⑤ *Average main: $27* ⊠ *315 W. Congress, Historic District* ☎ *912/232–7118* ⊕ *www.garibaldisavannah.com* ⊗ *No lunch; closed Sun.*

## ★ The Grey

$$$ | AMERICAN | In a restored Greyhound bus depot, James Beard Award–winner Chef Mashama Bailey and her talented team create gorgeous dishes that fuse Southern cuisine with

Housed in a former bus station, The Grey has been serving the food of Chef Mashama Bailey, a transplant from New York City, since 2014.

European inspiration. Whether you're tucked in the more casual diner bar or perched in the luster of the Art Deco–inspired dining room, service is impeccable, and the ever-changing menu offers sumptuously made mains from water, earth, and sky. **Known for:** impressive collection of accolades; port city Southern cuisine; reservations recommended. ⑤ *Average main: $31 ⊠ 109 Martin Luther King Jr. Blvd., Downtown ☎ 912/662–5999 ⊕ www. thegreyrestaurant.com ⊘ Closed Mon.*

### Huey's on the River

$$ | **CREOLE** | **FAMILY** | As Southern food goes, Huey's is decidedly more New Orleans than Coastal Georgia, as you'll discover with one bite of the sinfully rich beignets served with praline sauce— they are a taste of perfection. Although lunch and dinner items like po'boys and muffaletta accompanied by red beans and rice are delicious, the breakfast and brunch menu is the highlight. **Known for:** kid-friendly menu; people-watching and great views of passing ships; Bloody Marys. ⑤ *Average main: $18 ⊠ 115 E. River St., Savannah ☎ 912/234–7385 ⊕ www.hueysontheriver.net.*

### Husk Savannah

$$$ | **SOUTHERN** | After transforming the Charleston restaurant scene with internationally recognized, elevated Southern cuisine crafted from heirloom ingredients, James Beard Award–winning chef Sean Brock has brought his unique flavor to Savannah. Housed in a restored (and rumored to be haunted) Historic District home, Husk Savannah features an ever-changing menu of coastal Georgia and Deep South delights. **Known for:** award-winning chef

Sean Brock as its creator; Sunday brunch; classic Southern building with modern decor. $ *Average main: $22* ⊠ *12 W. Oglethorpe Ave., Historic District* ☎ *912/349–2600* ⊕ *www.husksavannah.com* ☉ *No lunch weekdays.*

### The Lady & Sons

$$$ | AMERICAN | FAMILY | Y'all, this is the place that made Paula Deen famous. There are plenty of crowds these days, but everyone patiently waits to attack the family-style service which is stocked for both lunch and dinner with crispy fried chicken, mashed potatoes, collard greens, lima beans, and other favorites. **Known for:** celebrity chef Paula Deen; gut-busting Southern eats; homemade dessert classics like banana pudding. $ *Average main: $24* ⊠ *102 W. Congress St., Historic District* ☎ *912/233–2600* ⊕ *www.ladyandsons.com.*

### Little Duck Diner

$ | DINER | FAMILY | This enchanting family-friendly diner perched on the corner of bustling Ellis Square offers an array of comfy bites all day long. With a full menu of milkshakes and diner favorites like apple pie à la mode and crispy chicken and waffles, a trip to Little Duck's white marble and brass-accented space is a special occasion for all. **Known for:** vintage diner-inspired space with modern touches; comfy eats; lavender "bubble bath" bellinis topped with a rubber ducky. $ *Average main: $12* ⊠ *150 W. Julian St., Historic District* ☎ *912/235–6773* ⊕ *www.littleduckdiner.com.*

### ★ The Olde Pink House

$$$ | AMERICAN | This Georgian mansion was built in 1771 for James Habersham, one of the wealthiest Americans of his time, and the historic atmosphere comes through in the original Georgia pine floors of the tavern, the Venetian chandeliers, and the 18th-century English antiques. The menu is just as classic and Southern, with chicken pot pie, shrimp and grits, and sweet potato biscuits gracing the menu. **Known for:** exceptional Southern dining; historical ambience; remarkable wine menu. $ *Average main: $27* ⊠ *23 Abercorn St., Historic District* ☎ *912/232–4286* ⊕ *www.plantersinnsavannah.com/the-olde-pink-house-menu* ☉ *No lunch Sun. and Mon.*

### ★ The Ordinary Pub

$$ | AMERICAN | Savannah's most-beloved brunch is tucked away in the basement level of bustling Broughton Street's shopping and dining corridor. The neighborhood eatery serves bottomless Baron D'Arignac mimosas, Bloody Marys made with Savannah-based Ghost Coast Distillery vodkas, cold brew coffee-based cocktails with ingredients from local roaster Perc, and a full menu of brunch favorites—don't miss the gouda grits and the pork belly doughnut

The Olde Pink House is one of Savannah's oldest structures, dating to 1771; it now houses a beloved piano bar and restaurant.

sliders—and gastropub dinner dishes. **Known for:** bottomless mimosas ("togosas" when poured in a portable plastic cup); lively brunch served seven days a week; eclectic pub fare. $ *Average main: $16* ⊠ *217 ½ W. Broughton St., Historic District* ☎ *912/238–5130* ⊕ *www.theordinarypub.com.*

### Pacci Italian Kitchen

**$$ | ITALIAN |** Pacci has the look and taste of a high-end Italian eatery, but with a laid-back and welcoming atmosphere. Guests gather in the beautifully designed dining room or the open-air patio for signature cocktails like the Biarritz or the Negroni before moving on to some of the best charcuterie and crudites platters in the city. **Known for:** farm-fresh ingredients; homemade pastas; thoughtful interior. $ *Average main: $22* ⊠ *The Kimpton Brice Hotel, 601 E. Bay St., Historic District* ☎ *912/233–6002* ⊕ *www. paccisavannah.com.*

### ★ The Pirates' House

**$$ | AMERICAN | FAMILY |** A Savannah landmark that gets its name from its time in the 1750s as a tavern for seafarers, the oldest parts of this bucket list destination date to 1734, only a year after the colony's founding, making this the oldest standing structure in Georgia. The lunch buffet has all the Southern standards, including a particularly delicious squash casserole, but the food is better on the à la carte menu; there's no buffet for dinner, but the dessert menu is worth sticking around for. **Known for:** fanciful history; Chatham Artillery Punch; busy atmosphere. $ *Average main:*

*$22* ✉ *20 E. Broad St., Historic District* ☎ *912/233–5757* ⊕ *www. thepirateshouse.com.*

### Treylor Park

**$** | **AMERICAN** | Expect whimsical takes on lowbrow eats at this bustling favorite, where the taco menu alone is a playground of flavor with options like the peppery fried chicken and pancake tacos or the savory shrimp and grits tacos. With all-day breakfast options, an interior that honors the restaurant's camp influences while keeping it hip and modern, and a robust beer and cocktail menu, it's no wonder this is one of Savannah's hot spots. **Known for:** creative takes on comfort food like PB&J chicken wings; late-night bites; patio seating. $ *Average main: $14* ✉ *225 E. Bay St., Downtown* ☎ *912/495–5557* ⊕ *www.treylorpark.com.*

### Vic's on the River

**$$$** | **AMERICAN** | This upscale Southern charmer is one of the finest spots in town for well-executed Southern delicacies like andouille hash and seafood po'boys. The five-story brick building was originally designed by the famous New York architect John Norris as a warehouse in the 19th century and was painstakingly renovated into the elegant space you'll find these days; reserve a window table for great views of the Savannah River. **Known for:** spectacular views; Sunday brunch; award-winning crawfish beignets. $ *Average main: $26* ✉ *26 E. Bay St., Historic District* ☎ *912/721–1000* ⊕ *www.vicsontheriver.com.*

### Vinnie Van Go-Go's

**$** | **PIZZA** | **FAMILY** | With a secret dough recipe and a homemade sauce, Vinnie's is critically acclaimed by pizza and calzone enthusiasts from around the Southeast. Lots of visitors get a kick out of watching the cooks throw the dough in the air in the big open kitchen, but there are only a few tables inside, along with a long stretch of stools at the bar; the heart of the restaurant is its plentiful outdoor seating, great for people-watching. **Known for:** outdoor seating; bustling, casual dining; long waits. $ *Average main: $14* ✉ *317 W. Bryan St., City Market* ☎ *912/233–6394* ⊕ *www.vinnievangogo.com* ☾ *No lunch Mon.–Thurs.*

### ★ Zunzi's

**$** | **SOUTH AFRICAN** | The beloved sandwich shop has a fantastic lineup of saucy sandwiches, peri-peri marinated wings, and crispy chips made in-house—wash any of them down with Zunzi's South African sweet tea, and you won't be sorry. Don't skip the sauces! **Known for:** Conquistador sandwich (French bread piled high with grilled chicken and the signature sauce); marinated wings; housemade chips. $ *Average main: $14* ✉ *236 Drayton St., Historic District* ☎ *912/443–9555* ⊕ *zunzis.com.*

# ☕ Coffee and Quick Bites

### ★ The Coffee Fox

$ | CAFÉ | Specializing in locally roasted PERC coffee, house-made baked goods, and craft beers, the Coffee Fox is a great stop whether you're on the run or looking to perch. The cold brew will win the hearts of coffee aficionados in the hot summer months. **Known for:** Cubano-style coffee and Latin American–inspired drinks with horchata; vegan baked goods made by Auspicious Bakery; beer to go. ⑤ *Average main: $4* ✉ *102 W. Broughton St., Historic District* ☎ *912/401–0399* ⊕ *thecoffeefox.com.*

### ★ Cup to Cup Cafe

$ | CAFÉ | Tucked away just off of Oglethorpe Square, Cup to Cup roasts its beans in small batches right outside of downtown and serves the coffee creations in a tiny shop that is easy to miss if you don't know it's there. Not just a great place to grab an espresso or a bag of whole beans to take home, Cup to Cup even offers education, training, and consultation as a free service to customers looking to increase the quality of their coffee presentation. **Known for:** expertly made lattes; restful environment; wide tea selection and local honey. ⑤ *Average main: $3* ✉ *140 Abercorn St., Historic District* ☎ *912/376–9173* ⊕ *www.cuptocupcoffee.com* ☾ *Closed Sun.*

### ★ Leopold's Ice Cream

$ | CAFÉ | FAMILY | One of the best ice-cream parlors in the area is Leopold's, a Savannah institution since 1919. It's owned by Stratton Leopold, grandson of the original owner and the producer of films like *Mission: Impossible III*. Posters and paraphernalia from his films make for an entertaining sideline to the selection of ice cream made with the old family recipe, methods, and ingredients. **Known for:** lemon custard or honey almond and cream flavors; seasonal flavors like rose petal cream, Guinness, or mint-lime sorbet; floats and shakes. ⑤ *Average main: $5* ✉ *212 E. Broughton St., Historic District* ☎ *912/234–4442* ⊕ *www.leopoldsicecream.com.*

### The Little Crown by Pie Society

$$ | BRITISH | This British-style bakery sells everything from traditional meat pies to savory quiches to crusty bread and dessert pies, all of it baked fresh daily. The owners hail from Staffordshire and make remarkable and authentic meat pies in such varieties as steak and ale, chicken and thyme, and steak and kidney. **Known for:** full-size savory and sweet pies for take-away (perfect for a family meal at a short term rental); warm hand-held savory pastries that can be carried on the go; pecan pie is considered some of the best in town. ⑤ *Average main: $15* ✉ *19 Jefferson St.,*

*City Market* ☎ 912/856–4785
⊕ *www.thebritishpiecompany.*
*com* ☞ *No table service.*

## 🛏 Hotels

### The Alida, Savannah, a Tribute Portfolio Hotel

$$$ | HOTEL | A newer addition
to Savannah's Riverfront, the
Alida collaborated with the
Savannah College of Art and
Design to create the industri-
al-meets-mid-century-modern
vibe that's peppered with
vibrant original, local artwork.
**Pros:** local/artisanal details feel
special; large, bright windows; can be booked through Marriott
with points. **Cons:** views from several floors are blocked by the JW
Marriott at Plant Riverside District; Williamson Street gets very
busy and rowdy with partiers at night; no in-room coffee (though
available on request). ⑤ *Rooms from: $288* ⊠ *412 Williamson
St., Historic District* ☎ *912/715–7000* ⊕ *www.thealidahotel.com*
⇴ *194 rooms* ⦿ *No Meals.*

### Andaz Savannah

$$$ | HOTEL | The interiors at the Andaz make quite a statement:
the exposed-brick walls in the spacious lobby are offset by cozy,
nested seating areas. **Pros:** concierge with extensive insider
knowledge; excellent location overlooking Ellis Square, two blocks
from the river; cosmopolitan rooftop pool. **Cons:** sounds of revelers on Congress Street can sometimes be heard in rooms; no
free parking; conference spaces don't match the designer appeal
of the rest of the hotel. ⑤ *Rooms from: $279* ⊠ *Ellis Sq., 14
Barnard St., Historic District* ⊹ *At Barnard and Bryan Sts. on Ellis
Sq.* ☎ *912/233–2116* ⊕ *savannah.andaz.hyatt.com* ⇴ *151 rooms*
⦿ *No Meals.*

### Bohemian Hotel Savannah Riverfront, Autograph Collection

$$$ | HOTEL | Giving you easy access to the hustle and bustle of
River Street, this boutique hotel is a much-needed addition to the
hotel landscape—instead of the Victorian decor that's so prev-
alent in Savannah; a stay at the Bohemian is like settling into a
gentleman's study in a regal English manse. **Pros:** can be booked
through Marriott with points; pets are allowed for a nonrefund-
able fee of $100; location on the river offers beautiful views and
convenience. **Cons:** decor is a little over-the-top; the Rocks on the

**Breakfast Included** 🛏

When you are trying to
decide on what kind of
accommodation to reserve
in Savannah, consider that
B&Bs include breakfast
(sometimes a lavish one),
complimentary wine and
cheese nightly, and even
free bottled water. Hotels,
particularly the major ones,
usually do not even give
you a bottle of water.

**3** Historic District HISTORIC DISTRICT NORTH

Roof lounge stays open late and the noise can sometimes be heard in guest rooms; not very kid-friendly. $ *Rooms from: $250* ✉ *102 W. Bay St., Historic District* ☎ *912/721–3800, 888/213–4024* ⊕ *www.kesslercollection.com/bohemian-savannah* ⊅ *75 rooms* ❄ *No Meals.*

### The Drayton Hotel Savannah, Curio Collection by Hilton

$$$$ | **HOTEL** | Boasting an ideal location directly across from Savannah's Cotton Exchange on Bay Street, The Drayton Hotel takes advantage of a gorgeous 19th-century building to accommodate guests in cozy, modern luxury. **Pros:** upscale without feeling stodgy; plenty of dining and drinking amenities; super-convenient location. **Cons:** bustling location means there can be some noise; the bars are frequented by visitors and locals and can be crowded; rooms are comfortable but can feel a little sterile. $ *Rooms from: $391* ✉ *7 Drayton St., Historic District* ☎ *912/662–8900* ⊕ *www.thedraytonhotel.com* ⊅ *50 luxury rooms and suites* ❄ *No Meals.*

### ★ The Grant

$$ | **APARTMENT** | Offering the best of both worlds, the Grant provides a boutique-hotel environment with the freedom of vacation-rental accommodations, the first establishment in Savannah to embrace the so-called urban suite trend. **Pros:** quality plus affordability; multiple-room suites great for large parties; overlooks Broughton Street. **Cons:** Broughton Street can be noisy at night; no hotel amenities; parking can be a challenge. $ *Rooms from: $174* ✉ *5 W. Broughton St., Downtown* ☎ *912/257–4050* ⊕ *www.stayblackswan.com/book-the-grant* ⊅ *17 suites* ❄ *No Meals.*

### Green Palm Inn

$$ | **B&B/INN** | This gingerbread inn built in 1897 is a pleasing little discovery with its spacious, high-ceilinged and elegantly furnished cottage-style rooms inspired by Savannah's British Colonial heritage. **Pros:** innkeeper is knowledgeable about Savannah's history; quiet location with a garden patio; affordable rates. **Cons:** with only four guest rooms, it might be too intimate for some; location on the eastern edge of the Historic District isn't as convenient as other hotels; designated guest parking is limited. $ *Rooms from: $191* ✉ *548 E. President St., Historic District* ☎ *912/447–8901* ⊕ *www.greenpalminn.com* ⊅ *4 suites* ❄ *Free Breakfast.*

### Hampton Inn & Suites Savannah-Historic District

$$ | **HOTEL** | **FAMILY** | The rooms and suites at this well-known chain hotel are a remarkably good value for Savannah's Historic District. **Pros:** spacious accommodations; Continental breakfast with plenty of hot options; suites start at only $10 more than a standard room. **Cons:** avoid the suite next to the noisy boiler; charge for parking; noise from nearby traffic. $ *Rooms from: $204* ✉ *603 W.*

*Oglethorpe Ave., Historic District* 🕾 *912/721–1600, 800/426–7866* ⊕ *www.hamptoninn.com* 🖙 *154 rooms* ❍❙ *Free Breakfast.*

### Holiday Inn Express Savannah-Historic District

**$** | **HOTEL** | **FAMILY** | Since all buildings in the Historic District must conform to the local charm, Holiday Inn went all-out, creating a handsome interior design in the public spaces, with tasteful animal-print settees, leather club chairs, fireplaces, and classy chandeliers. **Pros:** impressive Wi-Fi throughout; soundproof rooms; on-site fitness center. **Cons:** rates are higher than at most similar properties; taupe palette could be considered bland rather than neutral; could use some updates. ⑤ *Rooms from: $121* ✉ *199 E. Bay St., Historic District* 🕾 *912/231–9000, 877/834–3613* ⊕ *www. savannahlodging.com* 🖙 *146 rooms* ❍❙ *Free Breakfast.*

### Hyatt Regency Savannah

**$$** | **HOTEL** | A study in modernity amid the history of River and Bay streets, the seven-story Hyatt Regency Savannah has marble floors, glass elevators, and a towering atrium. **Pros:** modern decor; comfortable bedding; views from everywhere including the heated pool and lounge. **Cons:** valet parking is very expensive; many large groups; views don't come cheap. ⑤ *Rooms from: $169* ✉ *2 W. Bay St., Historic District* 🕾 *912/238–1234, 866/899–8039* ⊕ *www.hyatt.com* 🖙 *351 rooms* ❍❙ *No Meals.*

### JW Marriott Savannah Plant Riverside District

**$$$$** | **RESORT** | The name is a mouthful, and that's appropriate for this massive, entertainment-packed property with an enviable location on the Savannah riverfront. **Pros:** activity-packed area of town; plenty of dining options; Electric Moon Skytop Lounge is one of the city's best. **Cons:** this trendy area of River Street is noisy in the evenings; as Savannah's newest lodging property, prices are high; the decor can be gauche and overstimulating. ⑤ *Rooms from: $429* ✉ *400 W. River St., Historic District* 🕾 *912/373–9100* ⊕ *www.plantriverside.com* 🖙 *419 rooms* ❍❙ *No Meals.*

### ★ Kehoe House

**$$$** | **B&B/INN** | Known for its remarkably friendly and attentive staff, this 1890s-era house, handsomely appointed in Victorian splendor, was originally the family manse of William Kehoe, a prominent Savannah businessman whose Kehoe Iron Works are now an event venue near the Eastern Wharf. **Pros:** romantic, photo-worthy setting; the two elevators are a rarity in a B&B; great, filling Southern breakfasts. **Cons:** a few rooms have the sink and shower in the room; soundproofing in guest rooms could be better; in-room fireplaces don't work. ⑤ *Rooms from: $251* ✉ *123 Habersham St., on Columbia Square, Historic District*

In a city of charming hotels, the Marshall House stands out with its wrought-iron balconies overlooking busy Broughton Street and its popular restaurant.

☎ *912/232–1020, 800/820–1020* ⊕ *www.kehoehouse.com* ⇆ *13 rooms* ❍ *Free Breakfast.*

### ★ The Kimpton Brice Hotel

**$$** | **HOTEL** | No detail was spared when they made a boutique hotel out of this 1860s warehouse, which later served as a Coca-Cola bottling plant and then a livery stable. **Pros:** staff is genuinely warm and helpful; artistic design mixed with old Southern touches; great view of the secret garden from many of the second-floor rooms. **Cons:** neighboring Bay Street can be loud; no free parking; given it's in a historic building, the rooms are smaller than one might expect for the price. ⑤ *Rooms from: $224* ⊠ *601 E. Bay St., Historic District* ☎ *912/238–1200* ⊕ *www.bricehotel.com* ⇆ *145 rooms* ❍ *No Meals.*

### ★ The Marshall House

**$$$** | **B&B/INN** | **FAMILY** | With original pine floors, handsome woodwork, and exposed brick, this hotel provides the charm and intimacy of a B&B. **Pros:** great location near stores and restaurants; exceptional restaurant; balconies offer great bird's-eye views of Broughton Street. **Cons:** no free parking; floors show their age in places; the sounds of bustling Broughton Street can be noisy. ⑤ *Rooms from: $259* ⊠ *123 E. Broughton St., Historic District* ☎ *912/644–7896* ⊕ *www.marshallhouse.com* ⇆ *68 rooms* ❍ *No Meals.*

### Olde Harbour Inn

**$$ | B&B/INN** | Dating from 1892, this pet-friendly riverfront lodging tries hard to please even if it doesn't always hit the heights; nevertheless, it's a good option for those who want to be near the action of River Street. **Pros:** hearty breakfast menu; welcomes families and pets; all suites have views of river. **Cons:** not luxurious; location has some negatives, including hard-partying crowds and late-night noise; decor feels a little old-fashioned. $ *Rooms from: $215 ⊠ 508 E. Factors Walk, Historic District ☎ 912/234–4100, 800/553–6533 ⊕ www.oldeharbourinn.com ⇨ 24 rooms* ⦿ *Free Breakfast.*

### Planters Inn

**$$ | HOTEL** | A Savannah landmark, the Planters Inn makes sure its guests mix and mingle—the evening wine-and-cheese reception is a house party where the concierge introduces fellow guests, a good cross-section of leisure and business travelers, many of whom are repeats. **Pros:** management and staff truly make you feel at home; great architectural details in the lobby; convenient location near the Olde Pink House, where the kitchen provides for room service. **Cons:** decor and bathrooms could benefit from an update; breakfast could be improved; smaller rooms due to historic nature. $ *Rooms from: $159 ⊠ 29 Abercorn St., Historic District ☎ 912/232–5678, 800/554–1187 ⊕ www.plantersinnsavannah.com ⇨ 60 rooms* ⦿ *Free Breakfast.*

### The Presidents' Quarters Inn

**$$ | B&B/INN** | You'll be impressed even before you enter this lovely historic inn, which has an exterior courtyard so beautiful and inviting that it's popular for wedding receptions. **Pros:** central-but-quiet location; private parking and some private entrances; romantic atmosphere. **Cons:** inn books up fast in spite of ghost rumors; some might not like the contemporary carpeted floors in guest rooms; ground floor rooms are at street level, which can be noisy. $ *Rooms from: $189 ⊠ 225 E. President St., Historic District ☎ 912/233–1600, 800/233–1776 ⊕ www.presidentsquarters.com ⇨ 16 rooms* ⦿ *Free Breakfast.*

### River Street Inn

**$$$ | HOTEL** | Housed in a five-story converted warehouse, this 1817 lodging has a harbor-from-yesteryear theme, with nautical murals and model schooners. **Pros:** fitness center; fifth-floor library; complimentary wine and hors d'oeuvres are laid out almost every evening. **Cons:** could use a renovation; no private parking (city garage across the street); beware of the wildly uneven floors. $ *Rooms from: $235* ✉ *124 E. Bay St., Historic District* ☎ *912/234–6400* ⊕ *www.riverstreetinn.com* ⬢ *87 rooms* ⦿ *No Meals.*

### Savannah Marriott Riverfront

**$$ | HOTEL |** One of the city's few high-rise hotels—and the major anchor of the east end of the River Street area—the Savannah Marriott Riverfront delivers the professional management demanded by business travelers while offering some of the resort amenities that vacationers crave. **Pros:** views from the balconies of the riverfront rooms are truly magical at night; indoor and outdoor pools; great spa. **Cons:** conventions often dominate the main floor, limiting access to the indoor pool; a fair walk to the hot spots up on River Street; pedicabs can't come here on the cobblestones. $ *Rooms from: $179* ✉ *100 General McIntosh Blvd., Historic District* ☎ *912/233–7722, 800/285–0398* ⊕ *www.marriott. com* ⬢ *387 rooms* ⦿ *No Meals.*

### SpringHill Suites by Marriott Savannah Downtown/Historic District

**$ | HOTEL | FAMILY |** Holding its own beside any of the city's boutique hotels, the SpringHill Suites has a lobby that's a study in sleek, contemporary design, with earthy wood elements contrasting with pops of color and ultramodern light fixtures. **Pros:** suites include refrigerators and microwaves; on-site gym; free Wi-Fi and hot buffet breakfast. **Cons:** some bathrooms are small and stark; parking is pricey; it's nice but doesn't have much Savannah character. $ *Rooms from: $139* ✉ *150 Montgomery St., Historic District* ☎ *912/629–5300* ⊕ *www.marriott.com* ⬢ *160 rooms* ⦿ *Free Breakfast.*

### Staybridge Suites Savannah Historic District

**$ | HOTEL | FAMILY |** Located in a historic building, the Staybridge Suites has a perfect downtown location, with rates that include free Wi-Fi, same-day dry cleaning, a well-equipped gym, continental breakfast, and a social evening receptions on Monday, Tuesday, and Wednesday with free wine, beer, and appetizers. **Pros:** breakfast and social hour treats included in stay; parking included in hotel fee; in the heart of everything. **Cons:** $100 pet fee may seem excessive to some; due to historic building, suites are smaller than newer builds; Bay Street is a thoroughfare and can be noisy with revelers and traffic. $ *Rooms from: $128* ✉ *301 E. Bay St., Historic District* ☎ *912/721–9000* ⊕ *www.staybridgesuites.com* ⬢ *104 rooms* ⦿ *Free Breakfast.*

### ★ Westin Savannah Harbor Golf Resort & Spa

**$$$ | RESORT | FAMILY |** Within its own fiefdom, this high-rise property with more resort amenities than any other property in the area—including tennis courts, a full-service spa, and a golf course—presides over Hutchinson Island, five minutes by water taxi from River Street and just a short drive over the Talmadge Bridge. **Pros:** heated outdoor pool boasts a great view of River Street; dreamy bedding; great children's program. **Cons:** you are close, but still removed, from downtown; lacks atmosphere; an expensive and annoying resort fee. ⑤ *Rooms from: $249* ⊠ *1 Resort Dr., Hutchinson Island* ☎ *912/201–2000* ⊕ *www.westinsavannah.com* ⇴ *403 rooms* ⦵*l No Meals.*

 ## Nightlife

### BARS AND CLUBS

#### ★ Alley Cat Lounge

**COCKTAIL BARS** | A trendy spot in downtown Savannah, the Alley Cat Lounge is a backdoor bar with a refined cocktailer attitude. The well-designed subterranean space can only be accessed via the lane south of Broughton Street. The menu is a triumph of content marketing, resembling a newsprint, with entertaining articles, sketches, and quotes, and features impressive craft liquors and conceptual beverages. Space is limited, so come early to guarantee your spot. ⊠ *207 W. Broughton St., Historic District* ☎ *912/677–0548* ⊕ *www.alleycatsavannah.com.*

#### Barrelhouse South

**LIVE MUSIC** | In the center of Congress Street's bustling nightlife scene, Barrelhouse South offers live music most nights of the week. Packed on the weekends with an enthused mix of bohemian and professional twenty- to thirtysomethings, the crowds dance the night away to bands playing covers and originals that range from funk and R&B to rock. Shoot a round of pool at the second bar in the basement. ⊠ *125 W. Congress St., Historic District* ✛ *Off Ellis Square on Congress St.* ☎ *912/228–5116* ⊕ *www.barrelhousesouth.com.*

#### ★ Circa 1875

**COCKTAIL BARS** | In a beautifully renovated space with pressed-tin ceilings and a gorgeous antique bar, this is the place to come for a bottle of wine or champagne by the glass. Recordings of jazz legends like Billie Holiday or Django Reinhardt are usually the soundtrack, and the bar area is filled with tucked-away nooks for couples on a date. The gastropub next door offers a full menu of French fare that can also be ordered late into the night. The gourmet burgers and the mussels are highly recommended. ⊠ *48 Whitaker St., Historic District* ☎ *912/443–1875* ⊕ *www.circa1875.com.*

### Congress Street Social Club

**BARS** | Part sports bar, part music venue, the Congress Street Social Club is always jam-packed on weekend nights. Enjoy drinks and street eats right off the grill on the patio, dance to live music or a DJ inside, or play a round of pool in Social's basement. For a more laid-back experience, stop by on a weekend afternoon for nibbles, beer, and dogspotting on the patio. ⊠ *411 W. Congress St., Historic District* ☎ *912/238–1985* ⊕ *congressstreetsocialclub. com.*

### Electric Moon Skytop Lounge

**COCKTAIL BARS** | In the JW Marriott's Power Plant building, this rooftop lounge is one of the city's best and busiest, offering views of the river, great bar food, and signature cocktails like the Fly Me to the Moon infused with vodka. ⊠ *JW Marriott Savannah Plant Riverside District, 400 W. River St., Historic District* ☎ *912/373–9100* ⊕ *www.plantriverside.com.*

### ★ Lulu's Chocolate Bar

**COCKTAIL BARS** | This laid-back spot invites you to indulge your sweet tooth. Walking through the door, you're immediately greeted by a dessert case full of freshly baked specialties—try some of the homemade truffles. The menu also includes a spectacular list of specialty drinks, including champagne cocktails, chocolate martinis, and a modest selection of beer and wines. Warm up with an Irish coffee or the truly divine "drinkable chocolate," an especially fulfilling twist on hot chocolate. ⊠ *42 Martin Luther King Jr. Blvd., Historic District* ☎ *912/480–4564* ⊕ *www.luluschocolatebar.com.*

### ★ Planters Tavern

**PUB** | Lighted by flickering candles, this tavern in the basement of The Olde Pink House is one of Savannah's most romantic late-night spots. There's a talented piano player setting the mood, two stone fireplaces, and an array of fox-hunt memorabilia. The upstairs menu is available, with the same quality of service but a slightly less formal approach. Keep your eyes peeled for the House's ghosts, said to be most commonly seen here in the tavern. ■TIP→ **The handful of tables fill up fast, but the staff will serve you wherever you find a spot.** ⊠ *The Olde Pink House, 23 Abercorn St., garden level, Historic District* ☎ *912/232–4286.*

### Savannah Smiles Dueling Piano Bar

**PIANO BAR** | Reminiscent of an old roadside honky tonk, Savannah Smiles features dueling piano players that take requests via napkins, and a tip will get your song bumped up in the playlist. Patrons are encouraged to participate in the onstage antics. The kitchen is open late. ⊠ *314 Williamson St., Historic District* ☎ *912/527–6453* ⊕ *www.savannahsmilesduelingpianos.com.*

**Top Deck Rooftop Bar**

BARS | Enjoy the best views of the Savannah River and the cargo ships coming to port from this bar on the rooftop of the Cotton Sail Hotel. During the daytime Top Deck is quite low-key, but it gets lively and packed during the evening hours. Enjoy tasty, eclectic light bites with classic mixed drinks or more inspired signature cocktails. ■ TIP→ **It's the best place in town to catch the sunset while enjoying a drink.** ⊠ *Cotton Sail Hotel, 125 W. River St., Downtown* ☎ *912/436–6828* ⊕ *www.topdeckbar.com.*

## BREWERIES AND DISTILLERIES

**Moon River Brewing Company & Beer Garden**

BREWPUBS | FAMILY | Savannah's first microbrewery, Moon River occupies a historic building that once served as a hotel, as well as a lumber and coal warehouse. The adjacent outdoor beer garden is known for great people-watching, live music, and breezes off the nearby river. Check out the amazing variety of handcrafted lagers, ales, and wheat beers, including the White Lady, named for this famously haunted building's most well-known apparition. A sweet potato harvest ale is available in autumn months, and all brews are nicely complimented by an array of pub-style dishes and snacks. ⊠ *21 W. Bay St., Historic District* ☎ *912/447–0943* ⊕ *www.moonriverbrewing.com.*

**Service Brewing Co.**

BREWPUBS | Opened by veteran Kevin Ryan and his partner Meredith Sutton, this local institution has been brewing since 2014. Stop by the taproom for beer (some varieties are brewed year-round, some are seasonal) and camaraderie. Wednesday is Trivia Night. ⊠ *574 Indian St., Historic District* ☎ *912/358–1002* ⊕ *servicebrewing.com.*

## LGBTQ+

**Club One**

DANCE CLUB | Savannah's mainstay gay bar offers three levels of fun: drag shows and occasional burlesque and theater productions upstairs; dance parties on the main floor; and a relaxing spot for conversation or karaoke in the basement bar. Although the decor is a little tacky, the scene is wildly fun when the lights go down and the music starts. ⊠ *1 Jefferson St., Historic District* ☎ *912/232–0200* ⊕ *www.clubone-online.com.*

## LIVE MUSIC CLUBS

**El-Rocko Lounge**

LIVE MUSIC | This trendy, 1970s-inspired nightclub, adorned in vintage decor, golden lighting, and authentic pachinko machines, serves a variety of audiences. At happy hour, you'll find young professionals enjoying a barrel-aged cocktail, conversation, and punching requests into the analog jukebox. After the sun sets, catch local and touring rock, hip-hop, and indie acts onstage. Late night, students flood the space to dance beneath the golden disco ball until last call. ⊠ *117 Whitaker St., Historic District* ✛ *At corner of Whitaker and State St.* ☎ *912/495–5808* ⊕ *www.elrockolounge. com.*

## 🎫 Performing Arts

### ARTS FESTIVALS

#### ★ Savannah Music Festival

**MUSIC FESTIVALS** | Georgia's largest and most acclaimed music festival brings together musicians from around the world for more than two weeks of unforgettable performances in late March and early April. The multigenre entertainment ranges from foot-stomping gospel to moody blues to mainstream rock to new takes on classical music. Performances take place in Savannah's premier theaters, as well as nontraditional venues like historic churches. ⊠ *Historic District* ☎ *912/525–5050* ⊕ *www.savannahmusicfestival.org.*

#### ★ Savannah Stopover Music Festival

**MUSIC FESTIVALS** | This intimate indie music festival held every March is a yearly "stopover" for bands headed to the massive South by Southwest event in Austin. The event features almost 100 acts in about a dozen different venues, providing indie music fans with an unmatched opportunity to experience their favorite up-and-coming acts in intimate spaces. ⊠ *Historic District* ⊕ *www. savannahstopover.com.*

### VENUES

#### ★ Lucas Theatre for the Arts

**PERFORMANCE VENUES** | Slated for demolition in 1976, the Lucas Theatre is now one of Savannah's most celebrated spaces. The beautifully renovated 1921 Beaux-Arts space hosts a variety of performances throughout the year, from ballet to bluegrass bands. It's a go-to venue for events hosted by the Savannah College of Art and Design, the Savannah Film Festival, and the Savannah Music Festival, and even occasionally screens classic and family films. ⊠ *32 Abercorn St., Historic District* ☎ *912/525–5040* ⊕ *www.lucastheatre.com.*

#### Trustees Theater

**THEATER** | When it opened in 1946, the Trustees Theater was one of the largest movie screens in the South. Now run by the Savannah College of Art and Design, it hosts a variety of events, including the Savannah Film Festival. It's also a popular venue for concerts

Book a ticket in advance to watch the Savannah Philharmonic at the Lucas Theatre to mark a memorable evening.

and lectures. ⊠ *216 E. Broughton St., Historic District* ☎ *912/525–5050* ⊕ *www.trusteestheater.com.*

# 👜 Shopping

## ART GALLERIES

### Kobo Gallery

**ART GALLERY** | Between the bustling hubs of Broughton Street and City Market sits the city's foremost cooperative art gallery. Near Ellis Square, the tasteful space is teeming with fine art across countless mediums. Noteworthy are industrial-style jewelry by Danielle Hughes Rose, the colorful landscapes of Dana Richardson, and Dicky Stone's intricate woodworking. ⊠ *33 Barnard St., Historic District* ☎ *912/201–0304* ⊕ *kobogallery.com.*

### Ray Ellis Gallery/Compass Prints

**ART GALLERY** | Ray Ellis Gallery/Compass Prints sells original artwork, prints, and books by acclaimed landscape artist Ray Ellis, whose scenic landscapes are included in permanent collections of the White House. ⊠ *205 W. Congress St., Historic District* ☎ *912/234–3537, 800/752–4865* ⊕ *www.rayellis.com.*

## CLOTHING

### Copper Penny

**CLOTHING** | Venture to this Broughton Street mainstay for women's clothing and footwear that is, as they say, "curated with the Southern eye." You'll find seasonal looks by Michael Stars, BB Dakota, and Citizens of Humanity, as well as shoes and accessories by Rebecca Minkoff, Vince Camuto, and Sam Edelman. ✉ *22 W. Broughton St., Historic District* 🕾 *912/629–6800* ⊕ *copperpennysavannah.com.*

### Harper Boutique

CLOTHING | Harper Boutique is a bright storefront overlooking Wright Square, offering a well-curated selection of ladies' fashion and accessories. Its elegant window displays will draw any shopper to peruse the shop's casual but sophisticated collection of dresses, tops, bottoms, jewelry, and bags by such brands as FRNCH and Hutch. ✉ *118 Bull St., Historic District* 🕾 *912/235–5172* ⊕ *harpersavannah.com.*

### J. Parker Ltd.

CLOTHING | This is where savvy Savannah gentlemen have been suiting up since 1972. Look for outerwear, sportswear, and dresswear by top men's designers like Filson, Southern Tide, High Cotton, and Mountain Khakis. If you need a seersucker suit on short notice, this is your best bet. ✉ *20 W. Broughton St., Historic District* 🕾 *912/234–0004* ⊕ *www.jparkerltd.com.*

## FOOD AND WINE

### Chocolat by Adam Turoni: The Chocolate Dining Room

CHOCOLATE | Local chocolatier Adam Turoni has two shops, but the biggest has a wide range of his delightful chocolates and many other treats for sale in the world's most delicious-looking living room, "where Marie Antoinette meets Alice in Wonderland." You'll find his creations at other coffee shops and upscale boutiques, but the widest selection can be found here. ✉ *323 W. Broughton St., Historic District* 🕾 *912/335–2068* ⊕ *www.chocolatat.com.*

### Paula Deen Store

SOUVENIRS | The "First Lady of Southern Cooking" sells her wares at this shop on Congress Street. You can find some very Southern spices and sauces, such as a smokin' barbecue sauce, and salad dressings—like peach pecan and blueberry walnut—that are so sweet they could double as dessert toppings. Two full floors of Paula's own label of cooking goodies and gadgets are cleverly displayed against bare brick walls. The shop is adjacent to Deen's famous Southern-style restaurant, The Lady and Sons. ✉ *108 W. Congress St., Historic District* 🕾 *912/232–1579* ⊕ *www.ladyand-sons.com/retail-store.*

### The Salt Table

FOOD | More than 200 flavors of salts are on offer here, as well as specialty sugars, peppers, and teas. Noteworthy are the popular black truffle, smoked bacon, and ghost pepper sea salts. Gourmands should not miss the Himalayan pink salt plates. These solid salt bricks or slabs come in various sizes and can be used as cutting boards for preparing meats, vegetables, seafood, or even cheeses. They can also be placed directly on the stovetop, adding flavor to every dish. ⊠ *190 W. Bryan St., Historic District* ☎ *912/447–0200* ⊕ *www.salttable.com.*

### ★ Savannah Bee Company

**FOOD | FAMILY** | Ted Dennard's Savannah Bee Company has been featured in such national magazines as *O, Vogue, InStyle,* and *Newsweek,* and with good reason—the whimsical shop features locally cultivated honey and bath products that are simply wonderful. You can sample and buy multiple varieties of honey and even raw honeycombs, and there's an entire bar dedicated to mead, a delicate honey wine; enjoy a tasting for a sweet experience. Children enjoy the life-size beehive. ⊠ *104 W. Broughton St., Historic District* ☎ *912/233–7873, 800/955–5080* ⊕ *www.savannahbee. com.*

### Savannah's Candy Kitchen

**CANDY | FAMILY** | One of the largest candy stores in the South, Savannah's Candy Kitchen has made its home on historic River Street for more than 30 years. Owner and head confectioner Stan Strickland grew up in Woodbine, Georgia, watching his mother bake pecan log rolls, pralines, and peanut brittle. You'll find every scrumptious delight imaginable here, but don't miss the world-famous praline layer cake. There's a second location in City Market. ⊠ *225 E. River St., Historic District* ☎ *912/233–8411* ⊕ *www. savannahcandy.com.*

## HOME DECOR

### ★ The Paris Market and Brocante

**SOUVENIRS** | A Francophile's dream from the time you open the antique front door and take in the intoxicating aroma of lavender, this two-story emporium is a classy reproduction of a Paris flea market. It sells furniture, vintage art, garden planters and accessories, and home fashions like boudoir items and bedding. Although the store will ship to your hometown, there are numerous treasures that can be easily packed away, like soaps, candles, vintage jewelry, kitchen and barware, and dried lavender. ⊠ *36 W. Broughton St., Historic District* ☎ *912/232–1500* ⊕ *www. theparismarket.com.*

## JEWELRY AND ACCESSORIES

### ★ 13 Secrets Jewelry Gallery

**JEWELRY & WATCHES** | Created to provide an elegant and approachable atmosphere for fine and custom jewelry, this store is both beautiful and welcoming. Jeweler Chad Crawford, who himself has created a collection for The Met, showcases his own designs from his Andrew Hamilton Crawford line as well as pieces from the studios of jewelry artists from around the world. The store recently opened a second location at Plant Riverside District on West River Street, so you can take a peek inside regardless of which side of town you're on. ⊠ *426 E. Oglethorpe Ave., Historic District* ☎ *912/484–0985* ⊕ *www.13secret.com.*

## SHOES, HANDBAGS, AND LEATHER GOODS
### Globe Shoe Co.
**SHOES** | Hands down Savannah's best shoe store, Globe has served both well-heeled women and well-soled men since 1892. There's an expansive storefront display, so it's easy to window shop for the perfect pair. It features footwear and accessories by Stuart Weitzman, Donald Pliner, Cole Haan, Sam Edelman, VanElli, Thierry Rabotin, Gentle Souls, and Jeffrey Campbell, to name a few. ⊠ *17 E. Broughton St., Historic District* ☎ *912/232–8161* ⊕ *instagram.com/globeshoecompany.*

## SHOPPING DISTRICTS
### Broughton Street
**NEIGHBORHOOD** | **FAMILY** | Savannah's "main street" has long served as an indicator of the city's changing economic and demographic trends. The first of Savannah's department stores, Adler's and Levy's, emerged on Broughton, followed by the post-WWII intro- duction of national chains Sears & Roebuck, JCPenney, and Kress. During the 1950s, ladies donning white gloves and heels did their shopping, while kids gathered at the soda counter or caught the matinee. Downtown's decline began in the late 1950s and continued through the '70s, when boarded-up storefronts were the norm rather than the exception. Today, Broughton is again thriving, not only with local boutiques and world-class shops, but with theaters, restaurants, and coffeehouses. ⊠ *Broughton St., between Congress and State Sts., Historic District* ⊕ *www. broughtonstreetcollection.com.*

### Riverfront/Factors Walk
**NEIGHBORHOOD** | **FAMILY** | Though it's often crowded and a little rowdy after dark, no visit to Savannah would be complete without a stroll through Riverfront/Factors Walk. These nine blocks of renovated waterfront warehouses were once the city's Cotton Exchange. Today, you'll discover more than 75 boutiques, galler- ies, restaurants, and pubs, as well as a spectacular view of the Savannah River. Glimpse impressive cargo ships as they head to port while you shop for souvenirs, specialty treats, and local art. Tired of shopping? Catch a dolphin tour or dinner boat and see the waterfront from a different perspective. ■ TIP→ **River Street's cobblestones and Factors Walk's steep stairwells can be rough, so**

Cross the Love Lock Bridge while strolling through Factors Walk.

**be sure to wear comfortable footwear.** ⊠ *River St., Historic District* ⊕ *savannahswaterfront.com*.

 ## Activities

### BIKING

Savannah is table-flat, to the enjoyment of many bicyclists. Like many towns and cities across the country, Savannah has introduced a bike-share program, allowing daily or weekly access to bikes at several solar-powered stations downtown. The city has also added a number of bike racks around the Historic District to make it easier for cyclists to find adequate parking without blocking foot traffic.

Sunday is the best day for riding in the Historic District, but be aware that throughout much of the area there are restrictions for bikers. Riding through the middle of squares and on the sidewalks of Broughton Street is illegal and carries a stiff fine if you're busted.

Bikers should always ride with traffic, not against it, and obey the lights. Riding after dark requires bicycles to display a white light visible from 300 feet on the front and a red reflector on the back. Helmets are legally required for those under the age of 16 (and a good idea for everyone). Be sure to lock up your bike securely if you're leaving it unattended, even for a few minutes.

### Sekka Bike

**BIKING** | Stop by this popular storefront shop for hourly or daily bike rentals. Take an afternoon spin at $10 for three hours, or opt for a weekly rental for only $60. ⊠ *206 E. Broughton St., Historic District* ☎ *912/233–3888* ⊕ *www.sekkabicycles.com/bike.html.*

## GOLF

### ★ The Club at Savannah Harbor

**GOLF** | The area's only PGA course, this resort property on Hutchinson Island is a free ferry ride from Savannah's riverfront. The lush championship course winds through pristine wetlands and has unparalleled views of the river and downtown. It is also home to the annual Liberty Mutual Legends of Golf tournament, which attracts golfing's finest each spring. A bit pricier than most local clubs, prices vary according to the season, but the course is packed with beauty and amenities. ⊠ *Westin Savannah Harbor, 2 Resort Dr., Hutchinson Island* ☎ *912/201–2240* ⊕ *www. theclubatsavannahharbor.com* ⊠ *Dynamic pricing $85–$145* 🏌 *18 holes, 7,300 yds, par 72.*

## SPAS

### Savannah Day Spa

**SPA** | In addition to traditional spa services, Savannah Day Spa offers a complete line of skincare products, accessories for home, and a line of vegan body products. This historic office building is a delightful place to take your treatments, be it one of the creative massages or a therapeutic facial for your particular skin type. It's also one of the more romantic settings for couples massages. ⊠ *15 E. York St., Downtown* ☎ *912/234–9100* ⊕ *www.savannah-dayspa.com.*

### ★ Spa Bleu

**SPA** | Consistently ranked as one of Savannah's top ways to pamper yourself, Spa Bleu offers a contemporary feel of true Southern comfort in a modern space. The signature Organic Thermal Body Treatments are not to be missed, and neither are spa nights where you can stay late and indulge in hors d'oeuvres and Champagne. ⊠ *101 Bull St., Historic District* ☎ *912/236–1490* ⊕ *www. spableu-sav.com.*

### Westin Heavenly Spa

**SPA** | Across the Savannah River from downtown, the Westin Heavenly Spa feels a world away with its standard menu of services and then some. The "quiet room," with its solarium-like setting, is a highlight. It's a little on the pricey side, but it's worth it for the relaxing, luxurious environment. It's also a great destination for bridal parties. ■**TIP→ If you're coming from downtown, consider traveling by water taxi.** ⊠ *Westin Savannah Harbor Golf Resort &*

The Girl Scouts were founded in the Andrew Low House in 1912 by Juliette Gordon Low, a Savannah native. Her birthplace on Oglethorpe Street is also a museum.

*Spa, 2 Resort Dr., Hutchinson Island* ☎ *912/201–2250* ⊕ *www. westinsavannahspa.com.*

# Historic District South

The lower boundary of the Historic District South at Gaston marks the end of the Oglethorpe Plan's squares and the beginning of the Victorian District, where large, decorative mansions line the streets and surround Forsyth Park like pastel-colored petit fours.

## ◉ Sights

### Andrew Low House

**HISTORIC HOME** | Built on the site of the former city jail, this residence was constructed in 1848 for Andrew Low, a native of Scotland and one of Savannah's merchant princes. Designed by architect John S. Norris, the residence later belonged to Low's son, William, who inherited his father's wealth and married his longtime sweetheart, Juliette Gordon. The couple moved to England and several years after her husband's death, Juliette returned to this house and founded the Girl Scouts here on March 12, 1912. The house has 19th-century antiques, stunning silver, and some of the finest ornamental ironwork in Savannah, but it is the story and history of the family—even a bedroom named after family friend and visitor General Robert E. Lee—that is fascinating and well told by the tour guides. ⊠ *329 Abercorn St., at Lafayette*

## Famous Faces of Savannah

Here's a sampling of the figures who have etched themselves into Savannah's collective memory.

**Antwan "Big Boi" Patton** (born 1975), best known as half of the legendary hip-hop duo OutKast, was born on the west side of the city.

Fiction writer **Flannery O'Connor** (1925–64) spent the first 13 years of her life in Savannah. Known for her Southern-Gothic style, her greatest achievement is found in her short stories, published in the collections *A Good Man Is Hard to Find* and *Everything That Rises Must Converge*.

**James L. Pierpont** (1822–93), a native of Medford, Massachusetts, became music director of Savannah's Unitarian church in the 1850s. In 1857 he obtained a copyright for "The One Horse Open Sleigh" (more popularly known as "Jingle Bells"). Tempers flared in the 1980s, when Medford claimed that Pierpont had written the song there instead. The dispute over where he wrote the timeless tune remains unresolved.

**Johnny Mercer** (1909–76), who penned such classic songs as "Moon River" and "Accentuate the Positive," was a fourth-generation Savannah native and helped found Capitol Records. He is buried in Bonaventure Cemetery next to his wife, Ginger.

**John Wesley** (1703–91), the founder of Methodism, arrived in 1735 and is commemorated by a statue in Reynolds Square. After returning to England, he became one of the towering figures in the history of Protestantism.

---

*Sq., Historic District* ☎ *912/233–1828* ⊕ *www.andrewlowhouse. com* 🎫 *$12.*

### Beach Institute
**HISTORY MUSEUM | FAMILY |** Works by African American artists from the Savannah area and around the country are on display in this building, which once housed the first school for African American children in Savannah. On permanent exhibit are more than 230 wood carvings by renowned folk artist Ulysses Davis. ✉ *502 E. Harris St., Historic District* ☎ *912/335–8868* ⊕ *www.beachinstitute.org* 🎫 *$10* ⊗ *Closed Sun. and Mon.*

### Cathedral Basilica of St. John the Baptist
**CHURCH |** Soaring over the city, this French Gothic–style cathedral, with pointed arches and free-flowing traceries, is the seat of the Catholic diocese of Savannah. It was founded in 1799 by the first French colonists to arrive in Savannah. Fire destroyed the early

By night, Colonial Park Cemetery is a popular stop for ghost tours; by day, it's an idyllic place to stroll.

structures; the present cathedral dates from 1876. Its architecture, gold-leaf adornments, and the entire edifice give testimony to the importance of the Catholic parishioners of the day. The interior spaces are grand and dramatic, including incredible stained glass and an intricately designed altar. ⊠ *222 E. Harris St., at Lafayette Sq., Historic District* ☎ *912/233–4709* ⊕ *www.savannah-cathedral.org* ⊗ *No tours Sun.*

### Chippewa Square

**PLAZA/SQUARE** | Anchoring this square is Daniel Chester French's imposing bronze statue of General James Edward Oglethorpe, founder of both the city of Savannah and the state of Georgia. The bus-stop scenes of *Forrest Gump* were filmed on the northern end of the square. The historic Savannah Theatre, on the corner of Bull and McDonough Streets, claims to be the oldest continuously operated theater site in North America and offers a variety of family-friendly shows. ⊠ *Bull St., between Hull and Perry Sts., Historic District.*

### Colonial Park Cemetery

**CEMETERY** | Stroll the shaded pathways and read some of the old tombstone inscriptions in this park, the final resting place for Savannahians who died between 1750 and 1853. Many of those interred here succumbed during the yellow fever epidemic in 1820. Notice the dramatic entrance gate on the corner of Abercorn and Oglethorpe Streets. Local legend tells that when Sherman's troops set up camp here, they moved some headstones around and altered inscriptions for their own amusement, which partially explains the headstones mounted against the far wall. This spooky spot is a regular stop for ghost tours—though this burial ground only covers a block, there are more than 9,000 people buried here, some beneath the sidewalk and the street. ⊠ *200 Abercorn St., Oglethorpe and Abercorn Sts., Historic District* ⊕ *www.savannahga.gov/879/Colonial-Park-Cemetery.*

### Georgia State Railroad Museum

**HISTORY MUSEUM | FAMILY** | This museum preserves the legacy of the Central of Georgia Railway, an integral part of the industrial heritage of Savannah and of the South. A step into a different era, the museum is home to numerous railcars and boxcars, working diesel and steam locomotives, and a rare functioning railroad turntable. Around the corner is an iconic 125-foot-tall smokestack and the original quarters for workers and managers. Children of all ages will appreciate the expansive model-train exhibit, a fully operable rendition of a train traveling through the region. Ride on a historic diesel or steam locomotive. ⊠ *Tricentennial Park, 303 Martin Luther King Jr. Blvd., Historic District* ☎ *912/651–6823* ⊕ *www.chsgeorgia.org/GSRM* 🎫 *$15.*

### Lafayette Square

**PLAZA/SQUARE** | Named for the Marquis de Lafayette, who aided the Americans during the Revolutionary War, the square contains a graceful three-tier fountain donated by the Georgia chapter of the Colonial Dames of America. The Cathedral Basilica of St. John the Baptist is located on this square, as are the Andrew Low House and the impressive and elegant Hamilton-Turner Inn. The childhood home of celebrated Southern author Flannery O'Connor also sits on this square. ⊠ *Abercorn St., between E. Harris and E. Charlton Sts., Historic District.*

### Madison Square

**PLAZA/SQUARE** | Laid out in 1839 and named for President James Madison, this square is home to a statue depicting Sergeant William Jasper hoisting a flag, a tribute to his bravery during the Siege of Savannah. Though mortally wounded, Jasper rescued the colors of his regiment in the assault on the British lines, and his valor is celebrated each year with an annual memorial ceremony. A granite marker denotes the southern line of the British defense during the 1779 battle. The Green-Meldrim House, General Sherman's headquarters after capturing the city in 1864, is here. ⊠ *Bull St., between W. Harris and W. Charlton Sts., Historic District.*

### ★ Mercer Williams House

**HISTORIC HOME** | A staple on the tourist circuit, this house museum has been the stuff of legend since the release of the longtime best-selling novel *Midnight in the Garden of Good and Evil,* which was based on the murder trial of local architectural restorer and antiques dealer Jim Williams.' Williams, who purportedly killed his lover in the front den while sitting at the desk where he later died, purchased the house in 1969. Scandal aside, Williams was an aficionado of historic preservation, and the Mercer House was one of some 50 Savannah properties that he purchased and restored. Designed by New York architect John S. Norris for General Hugh Mercer, great-grandfather of Johnny Mercer, the home was constructed in 1860 and completed after the end of the Civil War in 1868. Inside are fine examples of 18th- and 19th-century furniture and art from Jim Williams's private collection. ■TIP→ **Don't miss a look around the charming gift shop.** ⊠ *429 Bull St., Historic District* ☎ *912/236–6352* ⊕ *www.mercerhouse.com* ☎ *$13.50* ⌁ *Tours are first-come, first-served; Call 912/238–0208 for parties of 6 or more.*

### Monterey Square

**PLAZA/SQUARE** | Commemorating the victory of General Zachary Taylor's forces in Monterrey, Mexico, in 1846, this is the southernmost of Bull Street's squares. A monument honors General Casimir Pulaski, the Polish nobleman who lost his life in the Siege of Savannah during the Revolutionary War. On the square sits Temple Mickve Israel (one of the country's oldest Jewish congregations) and some of the city's most beautiful mansions, including the iconic Mercer Williams House. ⊠ *Bull St., between Taylor and Gordon Sts., Historic District.*

### Ralph Mark Gilbert Civil Rights Museum

**HISTORY MUSEUM | FAMILY** | This history museum, named after the late Dr. Ralph Mark Gilbert, the father of Savannah's modern-day civil rights movement and leader of the NAACP, has a series of engaging exhibits on segregation, from emancipation through the civil rights movement. The role of Black and white Savannahians in ending segregation in their city is well detailed and includes archival photographs and videos housed in this former Black-owned bank in what was once the heart of Savannah's Black business community. There's also a replica of a lunch counter where Black patrons were denied service. ⊠ *460 Martin Luther King Jr. Blvd., Historic District* ☎ *912/777–6099* ⊕ *facebook.com/ rmgcivilrightsmuseum* ☎ *$10* ☉ *Closed Sun.–Wed.*

### St. John's Episcopal Church

**CHURCH | FAMILY** | Built in 1852, this church is famous for its whimsical chimes and stained-glass windows. The extraordinary parish house is the revered Green-Meldrim House, the only remaining Gothic-style private home in the Historic District. An interesting bit of trivia: on Christmas 1864, after General Sherman moved

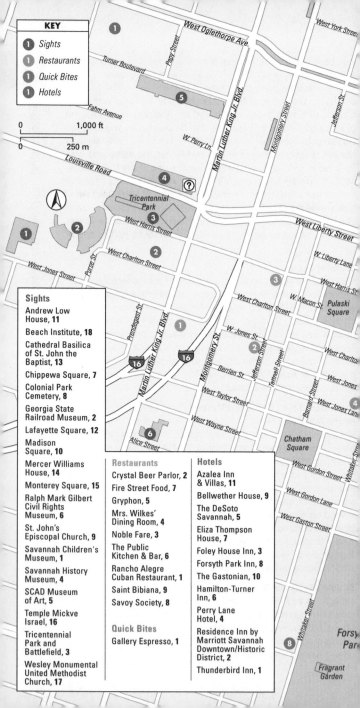

## KEY

- **1** Sights
- **1** Restaurants
- **1** Quick Bites
- **1** Hotels

West Oglethorpe Ave.
West York Street
Turner Boulevard
Fahm Avenue
W. Perry Ln.
Louisville Road
Tricentennial Park
West Harris Street
West Charlton Street
West Jones Street
Purse St.
West Liberty Street
W. Liberty Lane
West Harris St.
W. Macon St.
Pulaski Square
West Charlton Street
West Charlton
West Jones
Prembegart St.
W. Jones St.
Berrien St.
West Taylor Street
West Jones Lane
West Wayne Street
Alice Street
Chatham Square
West Gordon Street
West Gordon Lane
West Gaston Street
Forsyth Park
Fragrant Garden
Whitaker Street
Martin Luther King Jr. Blvd.
Montgomery Street
Jefferson St.
Jefferson Street
Tatnell Street
Barnard Street

0  1,000 ft
0  250 m

### Sights

Andrew Low House, **11**

Beach Institute, **18**

Cathedral Basilica of St. John the Baptist, **13**

Chippewa Square, **7**

Colonial Park Cemetery, **8**

Georgia State Railroad Museum, **2**

Lafayette Square, **12**

Madison Square, **10**

Mercer Williams House, **14**

Monterey Square, **15**

Ralph Mark Gilbert Civil Rights Museum, **6**

St. John's Episcopal Church, **9**

Savannah Children's Museum, **1**

Savannah History Museum, **4**

SCAD Museum of Art, **5**

Temple Mickve Israel, **16**

Tricentennial Park and Battlefield, **3**

Wesley Monumental United Methodist Church, **17**

### Restaurants

Crystal Beer Parlor, **2**

Fire Street Food, **7**

Gryphon, **5**

Mrs. Wilkes' Dining Room, **4**

Noble Fare, **3**

The Public Kitchen & Bar, **6**

Rancho Alegre Cuban Restaurant, **1**

Saint Bibiana, **9**

Savoy Society, **8**

### Quick Bites

Gallery Espresso, **1**

### Hotels

Azalea Inn & Villas, **11**

Bellwether House, **9**

The DeSoto Savannah, **5**

Eliza Thompson House, **7**

Foley House Inn, **3**

Forsyth Park Inn, **8**

The Gastonian, **10**

Hamilton-Turner Inn, **6**

Perry Lane Hotel, **4**

Residence Inn by Marriott Savannah Downtown/Historic District, **2**

Thunderbird Inn, **1**

# Historic District South

West State Street
East Broughton Lane
East Broughton St.
East Congress Lane
Telfair Square
East State Street
Whitaker Street
Barnard St.
Wright Square
East York Street
East York Lane
West Oglethorpe Avenue
Oglethorpe Square
West Oglethorpe Lane
Lincoln Street
West Hull Street
Orleans Square
W. Mc Donough St.
West Perry Street
❸
Bull Street
East Oglethorpe Avenue
Chippewa Square
❼
Drayton Street
Colonial Park Cemetery
East Mc Donough Street
❽
East Perry Street
❶
❼
❹
Whitaker Street
East Liberty Street
East Liberty Street
❻
❺
Floyd Street
Abercorn Street
❽
East Perry Lane
Habersham Street
Madison Square
❾
East Harris Street
East Liberty Street
❿
Drayton Street
East Macon Street
❺
East Charlton Street
⓫
Lafayette Square
⓬
⓭
East Liberty Ln.
❻
Troup Square
E Harris St.
East Macon St.
Bull Street
East Jones St.
❼
Abercorn Street
East Charlton St.
Price Street
E. Charlton Ln.
East Jones Lane
Lincoln Street
Habersham Street
E. Charlton Ln.
Monterey Square
East Taylor Street
⓯
Drayton Street
E. Jones St.
East Wayne Street
⓰
East Gordon Street
⓱
Calhoun Square
East Jones Lane
Bull Street
Whitefield Square
East Taylor Street
East Gaston Street
❿
East Gordon Street
❾
East Gordon Lane
East Gaston Lane
East Gaston St.
⓲
East Huntingdon Street
Abercorn Street
Lincoln Street
Habersham Street
Price Street
❾
Goodwin Street
⓫
Hartridge Street
Drayton Street

into the Green-Meldrim House, his army chaplain conducted the church's Christmas service. Though the house is still an active parish house, tours are available on a limited basis. Contact the church to learn whether a house tour is available for your selected date. ⊠ *325 Bull St., at Madison Sq., Historic District* ☎ *912/232–1251* ⊕ *www.stjohnssav.org* ⊠ *Church tours free ($10 donation suggested); Green-Meldrim House tours $15* ⚠ *Call to find out about last-minute closings for church events.*

## Savannah Children's Museum

**CHILDREN'S MUSEUM | FAMILY |** Adhering to the principle of learning through doing, the Savannah Children's Museum has open green spaces with several stations geared toward sensory play, including a water–sand play excavation station, sound station of percussion instruments, and an organic garden. The storybook nook is a partnership with the public library and encourages visiting youngsters to balance physical and mental recreation. One station includes costumes for stage performances. ⊠ *Tricentennial Park, 655 Louisville Rd., Historic District* ☎ *912/651–4292* ⊕ *www.chsgeorgia.org/scm* ⊠ *$10* ⊙ *Closed Sun. in June–Aug., and Mon. and Tues. in Sept.–May.*

## Savannah History Museum

**HISTORY MUSEUM | FAMILY |** This history museum houses exhibits on Savannah's cultural and military history. Inside you'll find much about the lives of early Native American settlers, including the development of tabby (crushed oyster shells with lime, sand, and water) for use in early construction. Subsequent historical periods are portrayed, including the Revolutionary and Civil War eras and the Industrial Revolution. More modern highlights include the city's countless Hollywood film appearances over the years, the most memorable of which might be *Forrest Gump*. The very bench that Tom Hanks sat on can be seen here. ⊠ *Tricentennial Park, 303 Martin Luther King Jr. Blvd., Historic District* ☎ *912/651–6840* ⊕ *www.chsgeorgia.org/SHM* ⊠ *$10.*

## ★ SCAD Museum of Art

**ART MUSEUM | FAMILY |** This architectural marvel rose from the ruins of the oldest surviving railroad building in the United States. Appropriately, the architect chosen for the lofty design and remodel project was Christian Sottile, the valedictorian of Savannah College of Art and Design's 1997 graduating class and the former dean of the School of Building Arts. Sottile rose to the hearty challenge of merging the past with the present, preserving key architectural details of the original structure while introducing contemporary design elements. SCAD Museum of Art houses two main galleries with rotating exhibits by some of the most acclaimed figures in contemporary art: the Evans Gallery features works of African American arts and culture, while the André Leon Talley Gallery is devoted to fashion and high style. ⊠ *601 Turner Blvd., Historic District* ☎ *912/525–7191* ⊕ *www.scadmoa.org* ⊠ *$10* ☺ *Closed Tues.*

### Temple Mickve Israel

**SYNAGOGUE | FAMILY** | This unique Gothic-revival synagogue on Monterey Square houses the third-oldest Jewish congregation in the United States; its founding members settled in town only five months after the establishment of Savannah in 1733. The synagogue's permanent collection includes documents and letters (some from such notables as George Washington, James Madison, and Thomas Jefferson) pertaining to early Jewish life in Savannah and Georgia, as well as a 15th-century Torah, the oldest Torah in North America. ⊠ *20 E. Gordon St., Historic District* ☎ *912/233–1547* ⊕ *www.mickveisrael.org* ⊠ *Tour $10* ☺ *Closed weekends except for Super Museum Sunday* ♿ *Call to reserve a tour time.*

### Tricentennial Park and Battlefield

**HISTORY MUSEUM | FAMILY** | This 25-acre complex is home to the Savannah History Museum, the Georgia State Railroad Museum, and the Savannah Children's Museum, as well as Battlefield Memorial Park. This site offers an unbeatable introduction to the city and a full day of fun for the whole family. The battlefield was the site of the second-bloodiest battle of the Revolutionary War, where on October 9, 1779, 800 of the 8,000 troops who fought lost their lives. ⊠ *303 Martin Luther King Jr. Blvd., Historic District* ☎ *912/651–6840* ⊕ *chsgeorgia.org/CHS/Tri-Centennial-Park* ⊠ *$10.*

### Wesley Monumental United Methodist Church

**CHURCH | FAMILY** | This Gothic revival–style church memorializes the founders of Methodism, brothers John and Charles Wesley, who both lived in Savannah for a brief time in the 1730s. The sanctuary is patterned after Queen's Kerk in Amsterdam. It dates from 1868 and is particularly noted for its magnificent stained-glass windows. ⊠ *429 Abercorn St., Historic District* ☎ *912/232–0191* ⊕ *www.wesleymonumental.org.*

## 🍴 Restaurants

### Crystal Beer Parlor

**$$ | AMERICAN | FAMILY** | This former speakeasy has been serving hungry locals since 1933, and the back dining rooms are covered in historic newspaper clippings and local ephemera, while those around the bar maintain several of the original high-back booths.

As you can tell from the decor, this place is a landmark—and that goes for the menu, which includes basics like delicious burgers, wings, sandwiches, and some of the best shrimp salad you'll ever have. **Known for:** historic tavern setting; bustling environment and long lines; the creamy Crystal crab stew. ⑤ *Average main: $15* ✉ *301 W. Jones St., Historic District* ☎ *912/349–1000* ⊕ *www. crystalbeerparlor.com* ⊘ *Closed Mon.*

### Fire Street Food

$ | ASIAN | FAMILY | Restauranteurs Ele and Sean Tran brought Asian-style street food to Savannah with their menu that boasts everything from sushi rolls to noodle soups, and some of the best sweet-and-spicy chicken wings in town. Occupying a bright, hypermodern space, this eatery offers an offbeat alternative to the slow-paced Southern Savannah feel. **Known for:** bright and modern space; late-night bites; street food staples. ⑤ *Average main: $14* ✉ *13 E. Perry St., Historic District* ☎ *912/234–7776* ⊕ *firestreet-food.com.*

### Gryphon

$$ | AMERICAN | Shimmering stained glass, stunning woodwork, and magnificent decor make this old-time pharmacy one of the most handsome settings in town. Delectable sandwiches and salads are the main bill of fare, but for more ambitious selections, opt for the ratatouille and shrimp orzo, served with locally caught wild Georgia shrimp. **Known for:** sandwiches and salads; traditional afternoon high tea, with wide selection of teas; menu as groomed as the atmosphere. ⑤ *Average main: $15* ✉ *337 Bull St., Historic District* ☎ *912/525–5880* ⊕ *www.scad.edu/experience/gryphon* ⊘ *No dinner.*

### ★ Mrs. Wilkes' Dining Room

$$$ | AMERICAN | FAMILY | The gold standard for authentic Southern fare in Savannah has kept folks lined up to enjoy family-style offerings at big tables for decades. Mrs. Wilkes's granddaughter and great-grandson are keeping it a family affair in more ways than one (kids under 10 eat for half-price). **Known for:** Southern cooking served family-style; former president Barack Obama and his entourage had lunch here when he visited Savannah; cash-only policy. ⑤ *Average main: $30* ✉ *107 W. Jones St., Historic District* ☎ *912/232–5997* ⊕ *www.mrswilkes.com* ▭ *No credit cards* ⊘ *Closed weekends and Jan. No dinner* ☞ *Cash or check only. ATM on site.*

### Noble Fare

$$$ | ECLECTIC | This eatery's clientele ranges from thirtysomethings celebrating a special occasion to well-heeled older residents who love the elegant atmosphere. The bread service includes honey

## Sunday Brunch

On Sunday, Savannah's churches are packed to the choir loft, so follow the hungry, postservice crowds for some great cuisine. Given the local fishing traditions and the city's proximity to the ocean, it should be no surprise that seafood appears as brunch items more often in these parts than in other parts of the country. Keep an eye out for seafood omelets with hollandaise sauce, or eggs Benedict, served with a crab cake rather than Canadian bacon. Another local staple is shrimp and grits, which you'd be remiss not to try at least once while in town. If you're not a fan of seafood, don't fret: the ever-popular Southern tradition of sausage-gra-vy-smothered biscuits is a fine way to start the day, and there's always bacon and eggs, if you're not feeling adventurous.

butter, pistachio pesto, olive oil, and balsamic vinegar for your biscuits, flatbreads, rolls, and focaccia, all of which are artistically presented on contemporary dishes. **Known for:** perfectly fresh fish; melt-in-your-mouth honey-cured pork chop; prix-fixe tasting menu. $ *Average main: $33* ⊠ *321 Jefferson St., Historic District* ☎ *912/443–3210* ⊕ *www.noblefare.com* ☉ *No lunch. Closed Sun. and Mon.*

### The Public Kitchen & Bar

$$ | **AMERICAN** | A prime location at the corner of Liberty and Bull streets, café-style outdoor dining, and a chic bar adorned with an industrial-style chandelier—Public Kitchen & Bar has it all. Despite the upscale atmosphere, the food is approachable and affordable with contemporary classics like shrimp and grits, and mussels steamed with chorizo and leeks. **Known for:** elevated Southern cuisine; outdoor dining; handsome interior. $ *Average main: $16* ⊠ *1 W. Liberty St., Historic District* ☎ *912/200–4045* ⊕ *www. thepublickitchen.com.*

### ★ Rancho Alegre Cuban Restaurant

$$ | **CUBAN** | **FAMILY** | Offering Cuban-, Caribbean-, and Spanish-style food since 1999, Rancho Alegre is a standout that has often flown under the radar. Authentic Cuban dishes like croquetas de jamón, boliche, and ropa vieja are served with traditional-style rice and black beans alongside your choice of tostones or sweet maduros. **Known for:** authentic Carribbean cuisine; jazz performances on the weekends; private parking lot. $ *Average main: $15* ⊠ *402 Martin Luther King Jr. Blvd., Historic District* ☎ *912/292–1656* ⊕ *rancho-alegrecuban.com.*

### ★ Saint Bibiana

**$$$$ | ITALIAN |** Named after the patron saint of hangovers, this new dining concept brings authentic flavors from coastal Italy to Savannah. Executive Chef Derek Simcik draws upon his worldly experience to deliver elevated dishes that are as innovative as they are inviting—try the impeccable Florentine steak served with Calabrian green salsa. **Known for:** the signature Saint Bibiana Sorella made by local Two Tides Brewing and only available here; fresh pastas handmade in house; low-intervention wine program. ⑤ *Average main: $42* ⊠ *Hotel Bardo, 700 Drayton St., Victorian District* ☎ *912/721–5002* ⊕ *saint-bibiana.com* ⊙ *No lunch weekdays.*

### ★ Savoy Society

**$ | AMERICAN |** Filling a sparse concrete and glass space on the ground floor of the mid-century Drayton Tower, this restaurant has a distinctly 1970s Palm Beach vibe with shiny brass fixtures, bamboo settees, and lots of lush greenery. The menu is light, featuring shareable tapas like pickled deviled eggs, tuna tartare, and a caprese mega toast (with vegan mozzarella available as a substitute option), alongside classic salads, sandwiches, and sourdough flatbreads (the Moroccan spiced beef flatbread with a cucumber crema is of particular note). **Known for:** avant-garde cocktails; shareable tapas and starters; vegan substitutions. ⑤ *Average main: $12* ⊠ *Drayton Tower, 102 E Liberty St., Suite 109, Historic District* ☎ *912/662–6665* ⊕ *www.savoysociety.com* ⊙ *Closed Tues.*

## ☕ Coffee and Quick Bites

### Gallery Espresso

**$ | CAFÉ |** This long-established coffee haunt and art enclave features a steady rotation of local artists, with house-made pastries, cheesecakes, muffins, scones, and luscious desserts. Gallery Espresso is a real neighborhood joint and a popular destination for art students, and the comfortable vintage couches and chairs are a great place to curl up with a book. **Known for:** interesting and inviting art-filled space; Tex-Mex–style taco selection; "Fire & Wine Saturdays" with live music in the courtyard. ⑤ *Average main: $4* ⊠ *234 Bull St., Historic District* ☎ *912/233–5348* ⊕ *www.galleryespresso.com.*

##  Hotels

### Azalea Inn & Villas

**$$ | B&B/INN |** Expect a hospitable ambience, a wonderful breakfast, and afternoon wine service at this 1889 mansion built for a

Cotton Exchange tycoon. **Pros:** rooms exude romance and luxury; baked goods are put out during the day; this is one of the few local B&Bs with a pool. **Cons:** just outside the heart of the Historic District, and it's a bit of a walk to many attractions; less expensive rooms are small; the carriage house is not as distinctive. $ *Rooms from: $179* ✉ *217 E. Huntingdon St., Historic District* ☎ *912/236–6080, 800/582–3823* ⊕ *www.azaleainn.com* ⇌ *10 rooms, 3 villas* ❍| *Free Breakfast.*

### Bellwether House

$$$ | **B&B/INN** | This rambling Italianate town house from the late 19th century is a standout for its ornate exterior, relaxing front porch, and comfortable ambience as a luxury accommodation in a B&B configuration. **Pros:** rooms are well-appointed and un-fussy; included afternoon tea and evening "sabering" of a bottle of wine; free parking in a private lot plus option for valet service. **Cons:** lacks the privacy of a large property; just off the beaten path allows for quiet at night but longer walks to central areas; only one ADA room. $ *Rooms from: $262* ✉ *211 E. Gaston St., Historic District* ☎ *646/397–9720* ⊕ *bellwether.house* ⇌ *16 rooms* ❍| *Free Breakfast.*

### The DeSoto Savannah

$$ | **HOTEL** | Expect tasteful contemporary furnishings at this 15-story property with a rooftop pool, multiple dining options, and a downtown location in the heart of a thriving shopping and dining neighborhood. **Pros:** overlooking Madison Square; nice skyline views from the upper floors; complimentary Wi-Fi. **Cons:** on-street parking or pricey valet; walking distance to the riverfront can be a little far for some; no refrigerator in room. $ *Rooms from: $185* ✉ *15 E. Liberty St., Historic District* ☎ *912/232–9000* ⊕ *www. thedesotosavannah.com* ⇌ *251 rooms* ❍| *No Meals.*

### Eliza Thompson House

$$ | **B&B/INN** | Afternoon wine, cheese, and appetizers and luscious evening desserts and sherry are served in the atmospheric main parlor of this fine town house built by Eliza Thompson's loving husband, Joseph, for their family in 1847. **Pros:** on one of Savannah's most beautiful streets; in a lively residential neighborhood; multi-night specials are available. **Cons:** must purchase parking passes; breakfast can be hit or miss; some of the back rooms are small. $ *Rooms from: $159* ✉ *5 W. Jones St., Historic District* ☎ *912/236–3620, 800/348–9378* ⊕ *www.elizathompsonhouse. com* ⇌ *25 rooms* ❍| *Free Breakfast.*

### Foley House Inn

$$$ | **B&B/INN** | In the center of the Historic District, this elegant inn is made up of two town houses built 50 years apart. **Pros:**

gorgeous architecture and decor; luxury bath products; complimentary wine and hors d'oeuvres served in the evening. **Cons:** old pipes can make for slow drainage; fee for parking pass; no elevator. Ⓢ *Rooms from: $259* ✉ *14 W. Hull St., Historic District* ☎ *912/232–6622, 800/647–3708* ⊕ *www.foleyinn.com* 🛏 *19 rooms* ⦿ *Free Breakfast.*

### Forsyth Park Inn

$ | **B&B/INN** | Done up in a sunny shade of yellow, this wood-frame Queen Anne home dating from 1893 is surrounded by an appealing courtyard and gardens. **Pros:** excellent Southern breakfast; complimentary homemade desserts; on-street parking is free. **Cons:** some rooms are just adequate; bathrooms need an upgrade; children and pets only allowed in the cottage. Ⓢ *Rooms from: $139* ✉ *102 W. Hall St., Historic District* ☎ *912/233–6800, 866/670–6800* ⊕ *www.forsythparkinn.com* 🛏 *11 rooms, 1 cottage* ⦿ *Free Breakfast.*

### ★ The Gastonian

$$$ | **B&B/INN** | Guest rooms—many of which are exceptionally spacious—in this atmospheric Italianate inn dating from 1868 all have fireplaces and are decorated with a mix of funky finds and antiques from the Georgian and Regency periods. **Pros:** cordial and caring staff; hot breakfast is hard to beat; afternoon tea and wine and cheese at night. **Cons:** accommodations on the third floor are a climb; some of the furnishings are less than regal; plumbing is old and sometimes problematic. Ⓢ *Rooms from: $279* ✉ *220 E. Gaston St., Historic District* ☎ *912/232–2869, 800/322–6603* ⊕ *www.gastonian.com* 🛏 *17 rooms* ⦿ *Free Breakfast.*

### ★ Hamilton-Turner Inn

$$$ | **B&B/INN** | With bathrooms the size of New York City apartments, this French Empire mansion is celebrated, if not in song, certainly in story, and definitely has a "wow" effect, especially the rooms that front Lafayette Square. **Pros:** wonderfully furnished rooms; breakfast is a treat, with baked items such as scones and hot entrées like perfect eggs Benedict; long and interesting history. **Cons:** sedate atmosphere won't appeal to everyone; no guest elevator (except for accessible Room 201); street parking only. Ⓢ *Rooms from: $259* ✉ *330 Abercorn St., Historic District* ☎ *912/233–1833, 888/448–8849* ⊕ *www.hamilton-turnerinn.com* 🛏 *18 rooms* ⦿ *Free Breakfast.*

### Perry Lane Hotel

$$$ | **HOTEL** | Luxurious and artful with an edge, Perry Lane Hotel raises the bar for upscale accommodations in Savannah. **Pros:** beautiful and chic; staff goes above and beyond; a favorite spot for locals and tourists alike. **Cons:** in a high-traffic area that can

If you stay at the ornate Hamilton-Turner Inn, try to get one of the rooms facing Lafayette Square, but whichever room you get will be beautifully furnished and have a large bathroom.

be noisy; no coffee makers in rooms; expensive daily amenity fee. $ *Rooms from: $226* ✉ *256 E. Perry St., Historic District* ☎ *912/415–9000* ⊕ *www.perrylanehotel.com* ⇘ *179 rooms* ⊙❘ *No Meals.*

### Residence Inn by Marriott Savannah Downtown/Historic District

**$$** | **HOTEL** | **FAMILY** | Some of the architecture at this reasonably priced lodging re-creates the 19th-century cottages that were used to house executives of the Central of Georgia Railroad. **Pros:** outdoor pool; complimentary hot breakfast; Wi-Fi throughout the hotel. **Cons:** location on the western edge of Historic District isn't the best; looks and feels like a chain hotel; parking for a fee. $ *Rooms from: $177* ✉ *500 W. Charlton St., Historic District* ☎ *912/233–9996* ⊕ *www.marriott.com* ⇘ *109 rooms* ⊙❘ *Free Breakfast.*

### Thunderbird Inn

**$** | **HOTEL** | **FAMILY** | A stay in this funky motor lodge will transport you back to the 1960s with hot popcorn awaiting your arrival, white leather chairs in the rooms, and Moon Pies on your pillow with the complimentary turndown, but it offers all the modern amenities of standard brand hotels—flat-screen TVs, fridges, coffeepots—at a highly competitive rate for this part of town. **Pros:** free parking; hip furnishings; great location. **Cons:** as far as the towels go, you get what you pay for; traffic noise can be a little loud; it was a motel, so the rooms open directly onto outdoor walkways. $ *Rooms from: $98* ✉ *611 W. Oglethorpe Ave., Historic*

District ☎ 912/232–2661, 866/324–2661 ⊕ www.thethunderbird-inn.com ⇌ 42 rooms ⦿⦿ No Meals.

# ⓨ Nightlife

## BARS AND CLUBS

### ★ Artillery

**COCKTAIL BARS** | The award-winning Daniel Reed group renovated this unique, intimate space that was once home to the Georgia Hussars pre-Revolutionary cavalry regiment, and later a showroom for the Model T Ford. The end result is one of Savannah's classiest cocktail bars and a resplendent example of contemporary design mixed with historical accuracy. Intricate cocktails feature inspired ingredients like muddled corn, shishito peppers, and smoked pipe tobacco. The wine list is as formidable as the cocktail menu. ■**TIP→ There is an enforced code of conduct in a classy joint like this; usage of cell phones is highly frowned upon and the dress code is on the border of business-casual and semiformal.** ⊠ 307 Bull St. ☎ 912/335–5200 ⊕ www.artillerybar.com.

### ★ The Original Pinkie Masters

**BARS** | This dive bar's biggest claim to fame was that Georgia's own Jimmy Carter stood up on the bar to announce his bid for the presidency. The people are friendly, the drinks are cheap, the analog jukebox is loaded with an unexpected mix of soul, R&B, and punk, and the vibe is laid-back with zero frills. ⊠ 318 Drayton St., Historic District ☎ 912/999–7106 ⊕ theoriginalpinkies.com ☞ Cash only.

### Peregrin

**BARS** | Perched on top of the Perry Lane Hotel, Peregrin offers the best view of the city's church steeples and architectural details on a lush, colorful patio. Revelers can play cornhole while sipping frosé (frozen rosé) or the planter's punch. Wine lovers will revel in the curated menu, and there's a small array of bites, like dill pickle dip and crab-and-shrimp lettuce wraps, if you're feeling peckish. ⊠ Perry Lane Hotel, 256 E. Perry St., Historic District ☎ 912/559–8365 ⊕ www.peregrinsavannah.com.

### The Wayward

**BARS** | The Perry Lane Hotel's take on an elevated dive bar, the Wayward combines grimy punk aesthetics with sleek, modern design touches like a salon-style gallery wall with paintings of Bill Murray and a vintage motorcycle hanging over the bar. Order a boilermaker, enjoy some free popcorn, and play a round of pinball in the small arcade. ⊠ Perry Lane Hotel, 257 E. Perry St., Historic District ☎ 912/559–8362 ⊕ www.waywardsavannah.com.

# 🎭 Performing Arts

## ARTS FESTIVALS

### Savannah Jazz Festival

**MUSIC FESTIVALS | FAMILY |** A local favorite since 1982, this free outdoor musical event is held annually in late September. Thousands of concertgoers pack Forsyth Park's expansive lawn with chairs, blankets, and picnic spreads for several nights of live jazz performances. Given the ideal weather this time of year, this festival puts Savannah's foremost green space to great use. After the evening headliner, head to local clubs to check out the nightly jam sessions, where unexpected collaborations are the norm. ✉ *Forsyth Park, Gaston St., between Drayton and Whitaker Sts., Historic District* ☎ *912/228–3158* ⊕ *www.savannahjazzfestival.org.*

### ★ SCAD Savannah Film Festival

**FILM FESTIVALS |** This star-studded affair, hosted by the Savannah College of Art and Design in late October and early November, offers multiple daily screenings of award-winning films in various venues on or near Broughton Street. Sir Patrick Stewart, Salma Hayek, William H. Macy, John Krasinski, Emily Blunt, Hugh Jackman, Ava DuVernay, and Kevin Bacon are among the celebrities who've attended in recent years. Q&A sessions with visiting celebrities and industry professionals are always popular. ■ TIP→ **Be ready to purchase your screening and panel tickets as soon as sales open, as the most popular often sell out in half an hour or less.** ✉ *Broughton St., Historic District* ⊕ *filmfest.scad.edu.*

### ★ SCAD Sidewalk Arts Festival

**ARTS FESTIVALS | FAMILY |** Savannah College of Art and Design's Sidewalk Arts Festival, held the last Saturday in April, is an opportunity to experience Forsyth Park in abundant glory. At no other time in the year is the park so packed with people of all ages, coming out in droves to see students past and present take to the park's winding sidewalks with rainbow colors of chalk. By the day's end, the park is lined with out-of-this-world drawings as far as the eye can see, plus fun stains of chalk throughout the grass and on scraggling artists. ✉ *Forsyth Park, Gaston St., between Drayton and Whitaker Sts., Historic District.*

## VENUES

### ★ The Historic Savannah Theatre

**THEATER | FAMILY |** Said to be the country's oldest continuously operating theater, the beautifully maintained Savannah Theatre presents family-friendly comedies and musical revues. The 600-seat theater is a throwback to the glory days of the stage. Don't miss the *Savannah Live* variety show and the popular holiday

## Savannah on Film

In the 1970s, some scenes from the legendary television miniseries *Roots* were shot at various spots around Savannah. In 1989, the Academy Award–winning film *Glory* was filmed near Fort Pulaski. One of Savannah's most famous film appearances came in 1994, when scenes for *Forrest Gump* were set on the north end of Chippewa Square. *Midnight in the Garden of Good and Evil* was filmed in the Historic District in 1997, and two years later *The General's Daughter* was shot at Wormsloe Plantation State Historic Site. *The Legend of Bagger Vance,* starring Will Smith, brought film crews to Savannah and Jekyll Island in 2000. Robert Redford's historical drama about Mary Surratt, *The Conspirator,* used Savannah for its backdrop in 2009.

Broughton Street was transformed into Salty Shoals for box office smash *The SpongeBob Movie: Sponge Out of Water,* starring Antonio Banderas, in 2015. Funnymen Adam Sandler and David Spade filmed *The Do-Over* in 2016—Spade even surprised locals with an impromptu comedy set at The Wormhole, a local dive. In 2019, Disney shot its live-action version of *Lady and the Tramp* throughout the Historic and Victorian Districts, so you may see some homes, buildings, and alleyways you recognize when you watch the film.

Tybee Island has welcomed heartthrob visitors like Channing Tatum for *Magic Mike XXL* and Zac Efron and Dwayne "The Rock" Johnson for 2017's *Baywatch.*

---

production *A Christmas Tradition.* ✉ *222 Bull St., at Chippewa Sq., Historic District* ☎ *912/233–7764* ⊕ *www.savannahtheatre.com* 🎟 *From $46.*

## 🛍 Shopping

### ANTIQUES

#### V&J Duncan Maps, Prints and Books
**ANTIQUES & COLLECTIBLES** | Originally opened by Virginia and John Duncan in 1983, V&J Duncan was purchased by new owners and relocated to picturesque Madison Square in 2022. The shop specializes in antique maps and prints and carries a vast collection of engravings, photographs, and lithographs. There are also rare books on Southern culture and signed editions of John Berendt's famous *Midnight in the Garden of Good and Evil.* The shop's hours aren't strictly observed, so call ahead to make sure they're open.

■ **TIP→ With so much to see, plan to spend some time here.** ⊠ *13 W. Charlton St., Historic District* ☏ *912/232–0338* ⊕ *vjduncan.com.*

## ART GALLERIES

### Gallery Espresso

**ART GALLERY** | Gallery Espresso is Savannah's oldest coffee shop and has a new show every couple of weeks focusing on work by local artists. The house-made desserts complement the heavy dose of caffeine and art. The location at the foot of lush Chippewa Square is ideal for enjoying your beverage on the brick sidewalk and watching the world go by under the live oak canopy. ⊠ *234 Bull St., Historic District* ☏ *912/233–5348* ⊕ *www.galleryespresso. com.*

## BOOKS

### ★ Books on Bay

**BOOKS** | **FAMILY** | Specializing in vintage and antiquarian children's books, this tucked-away bookshop has titles going all the way back to the 1600s. It's not a musty, dusty, look-but-don't-touch kind of place, though: the walls of the colorful store are lined with stacks of Nancy Drew, Dick and Jane, and The Hardy Boys titles. Owner Betsy Hoit-Thetford is knowledgeable and pleasant, and the shop is open daily from 10 to 5, including most holidays, so even if you're not looking for something specific, it's an excellent way to keep the kids entertained before your riverboat cruise or trolley tour. ⊠ *411 Abercorn St., Historic District* ☏ *912/398–6222* ⊕ *booksonbay.com.*

### The Book Lady

**BOOKS** | Located on the garden level of a Liberty Street row house, the Book Lady stocks around 50,000 new, used, and vintage books spanning 40 genres. The friendly staff is always available for a lively literary discussion, and the shop hosts the occasional book signing by noted authors. ⊠ *6 E. Liberty St., Historic District* ☏ *912/233–3628* ⊕ *www.thebookladybookstore.com.*

### ★ E. Shaver, Bookseller

**BOOKS** | Among the city's most beloved bookshops, E. Shaver, Bookseller is the go-to spot for bibliophiles and book-clubbers, considering they have groups meeting monthly for fans of Jane Austen, social justice and culture reads, graphic novels, and much more. Among other services, staff can curate a book collection to fit the customer's taste, ranging in size from a few feet of shelves to an entire library. ⊠ *326 Bull St., Historic District* ☏ *912/234–7257* ⊕ *www.eshaverbooks.com.*

## CLOTHING

### Custard Boutique

**CLOTHING** | This quaint corner shop has stylish statement pieces that are locally and sustainably sourced and sure to turn heads. Clothing, shoes, jewelry and charming gifts and housewares can be found at the boutique, which has an eclectic, bohemian vibe. ✉ *422 Whitaker St., Historic District* 🕾 *912/232–4733* ⊕ *www.custardboutique.com.*

### James Hogan

**CLOTHING** | Tucked in a storefront in the Historic District, this shop has brought a touch of glamour to the city. Featured here is apparel designed by James Hogan himself, as well as upscale women's fashions from well-regarded American and European designers. ✉ *124 W. Gwinnett St., Historic District* 🕾 *912/234–0374* ⊕ *www.jameshogan.com.*

### Red Clover

**CLOTHING** | This is the place to be if you want fashionable and affordable apparel, shoes, and handbags. It features sharp looks from up-and-coming designers, all at under $100. It's also a great place to search for unique jewelry. ✉ *244 Bull St., Historic District* 🕾 *912/236–4053* ⊕ *shopredclover.com.*

## FOOD AND WINE

### Le Chai Galerie du Vin

**WINE/SPIRITS** | This is a long-cherished establishment for Savannah's wine aficionados. With a devoted following, proprietor Christian Depken has a trained palate for old-world wines—trust him to recommend the perfect accompaniment to any dish. Plus, its temperature- and humidity-controlled environment is the only one of its kind in Georgia. ✉ *15 E. Park Ave.* 🕾 *912/713–2229* ⊕ *www.lechai.com.*

## GIFTS AND SOUVENIRS

### Saints & Shamrocks

**SOUVENIRS** | In a neo-Gothic storefront rich with architectural detail, Saints & Shamrocks features hand-smocked children's clothing, Irish imports, and religious gifts. The gift selection embraces Irish and Southern heritage in the form of jewelry, bath products, and seasonal items. ✉ *309 Bull St., Historic District* 🕾 *912/233–8858* ⊕ *www.saintsandshamrocks.com.*

### ★ ShopSCAD

**ART GALLERY** | Inside historic Poetter Hall, the Savannah College of Art and Design's shop is filled with handcrafted items guaranteed to be one of a kind. Handmade and hand-dyed silk accessories are cutting-edge, as are original fashion pieces and experimental purses by design students. Just remember that these originals are often truly unique and may not come cheap. ⊠ *340 Bull St., Historic District* ☎ *912/525–5180* ⊕ *www.shopscad.com.*

## HOME DECOR
### One Fish Two Fish
**HOUSEWARES** | Whimsically named for the classic Dr. Seuss book, One Fish Two Fish is a high-end home decor shop located in the Downtown Design District. Look for contemporary furnishings, fine linens, and bedroom and bathroom accessories. Every corner of the store has something charming to offer, including elegant handbags and jewelry and colorful modern lighting fixtures. For fine wearables, cross over Whitaker Street to visit the Annex, its sister store. ⊠ *401 Whitaker St., Historic District* ☎ *912/447–4600* ⊕ *onefishstore.com.*

## JEWELRY AND ACCESSORIES
### Ordinary Magic Shop
**JEWELRY & WATCHES** | Have fun browsing the unique jewelry, crystals, organic beauty care, tarot cards, yoga accessories, and other mystical items at this cute corner shop owned by longtime local yogi Kelley Boyd. You'll find lots of interesting gifts and souvenirs for the New Age–minded. ⊠ *509 Barnard St., Historic District* ☎ *912/244–3755* ⊕ *shopordinarymagic.com.*

## SHOES, HANDBAGS, AND LEATHER GOODS
### ★ Satchel.
**JEWELRY & WATCHES** | This artisanal-leather studio and shop is owned by Elizabeth Seeger, a New Orleans native and graduate of SCAD. The store specializes in custom leather clutches, handbags, travel bags, and accessories and offers a wide selection of leathers to choose from, including python and alligator. At lower price points are the sharp and handy beverage cozies, cuff bracelets, and wallets. ⊠ *4 E. Liberty St., Historic District* ☎ *912/233–1008* ⊕ *shopsatchel.com.*

## SHOPPING DISTRICTS
### Downtown Design District
**NEIGHBORHOOD** | Known for its array of fine antiques shops, galleries, lighting showrooms, and interior design boutiques, the Downtown Design District is worth a visit. Stop in some of Savannah's trendier fashion stores, many of them housed in charming historic storefronts. Nearby are the famed Mercer Williams House and the landmark Mrs. Wilkes' Dining Room, known for some of the area's best family-style Southern food. The picturesque surrounding neighborhoods are also enjoyable for a nice afternoon stroll. ⊠ *Whitaker St., between Charlton and Gaston Sts., Historic District.*

### ★ Liberty Street Corridor

**NEIGHBORHOOD** | With the redevelopment of Broughton Street came an influx of national and high-end retailers that left local shops in search of lower rent. Many set up shop a half-mile south along the oak-lined Liberty Street Corridor. The crossroads of Liberty and Bull is a particularly thriving shopping neighborhood, with outdoor cafés, pubs, clothing boutiques, art galleries, bookshops, and more. ⊠ *Liberty St. at Bull St., Historic District.*

### Madison Square

**NEIGHBORHOOD** | You'll discover an array of unique local shops nestled around historic Madison Square. Grab lunch on the rooftop of The Public Kitchen and Bar before stopping in longtime favorites like Saints & Shamrocks and E. Shaver, Bookseller. ShopSCAD offers some of the finest gifts, clothing, and home decor items designed and produced by students of the highly regarded Savannah College of Art and Design. Take afternoon tea at the college's Gryphon Tea Room, located inside a remodeled old-time pharmacy. For something a little stronger, head to Artillery, a speakeasy-inspired bar housed in a restored cavalry artillery; the bartenders make some of the city's best handcrafted cocktails. ⊠ *Bull St., bordered by Liberty and Charlton Sts., Historic District.*

# 🏃 Activities

## BIKING

### Perry Rubber Bike Shop

**BIKING** | At the pulsing corner of Bull and Liberty Streets, Perry Rubber is the go-to shop for repairs and your best bet for rentals. It offers trendy hybrid or city bikes at $25 for a half-day or $40 for the full day—helmet, lock, and city map included. ⊠ *240 Bull St., Historic District* ☎ *912/236–9929* ⊕ *www.perryrubberbikeshop. com.*

## TENNIS

### Forsyth Park Tennis Courts

**TENNIS** | Tucked away in the southern side of the city's central park, these four lighted courts are available for free, though securing a spot can be competitive. ⊠ *Drayton St. at Park Ave., Historic District.*

# Chapter 4

# VICTORIAN DISTRICT AND EASTSIDE

Updated by
Chantel Britton

| ◉ Sights | 🍴 Restaurants | 🛏 Hotels | 🛍 Shopping | 🍸 Nightlife |
|---|---|---|---|---|
| ★★☆☆☆ | ★★★★☆ | ★★★☆☆ | ★★★★☆ | ★★★★☆ |

# NEIGHBORHOOD SNAPSHOT

## TOP EXPERIENCES

■ **Ogle the architecture:** Ornate ironwork, pineapple finials, and other fine flourishes decorate blocks of historic Victorian homes.

■ **Frolic in Forsyth Park:** Bask in grassy green fields and shady nooks, all centered around the city's iconic white fountain.

■ **Sway to the music:** The park's bandshell hosts concerts, local cafes spotlight local bands, and talented musicians busk on the streets.

■ **Chill like a local:** The tables in front of the Sentient Bean and Brighter Day Natural Foods at the south end of the park provide a people-watching haven.

■ **Behold the bounty:** Come to Forsyth Farmers' Market every Saturday for the local produce and baked goods, stay for the dog-petting.

■ **Find African American history:** Explore a deeper narrative at The King-Tisdell Cottage and folk artist James Kimble's Black Holocaust Memorial on the eastside.

## GETTING HERE

Forsyth Park and the surrounding neighborhoods are an easy walk from downtown; just head south down Bull Street. All major tour trolleys stop at the south end of the park, as does the city's free DOT shuttle. Parking is ample at the south end as well, with a mixture of free and paid spots (download the "Park Savannah" app.) Public transportation runs through the eastside neighborhoods; check for updated schedules.

## QUICK BITES

■ **PERC Coffee.** Roasted aromas, fresh-baked pastries, and industrial vibes abound for hard-core coffee folk who can watch beans bagged and sent out to international destinations. ⊠ *1802 E. Broad St., Eastside* ☎ *912/209–0025.*

■ **The Mate Factor.** This charming hideaway can only be described as a woodland fantasy made real, featuring yerba mate beverages, made-to-order sandwiches, and baked treats. ⊠ *401 E. Hall St., Victorian District* ☎ *912/235–2906.*

Built after the Civil War, the Victorian District and Eastside neighborhoods evolved from General Oglethorpe's antebellum layout of centralized squares at what was then the edge of the city. Allot a half-day's walk from the middle of Forsyth Park to take in its unique architectural touches, sidewalk cafés, and lesser-known historic sights.

Bordered by Gwinnett, Abercorn, 31st Street, and MLK Jr. Blvd., the Victorian District and the Eastside neighborhoods were Savannah's first suburbs built to accommodate streetcars with the picturesque Forsyth Park at their heart. This is where you'll find blocks of gorgeous, restored homes in a rainbow of colors and the Saturday morning Farmers Market. Farther east toward East Broad Street, the King-Tisdell Cottage and the Black Holocaust Memorial continue the story of Savannah's African American heritage.

## ◉ Sights

### Black Holocaust Memorial
**PUBLIC ART** | Folk artist and Savannah resident James "Double Dutch" Kimble created this outdoor sculpture in 2002 as a testament to the city's African American and slave history. He continually adds to the amalgam of found objects and painted items, creating an ever-evolving statement and legacy. ⊠ *537 E. Anderson La., Eastside* ⇻ *Outdoors in the alley on the corner of East Broad St. and Anderson La.*

### ★ Forsyth Park
**CITY PARK** | **FAMILY** | The heart of the city's outdoor life, Forsyth Park hosts a number of popular cultural events, including film screenings, sports matches, and the annual Savannah Jazz Festival. Built in 1840 and expanded in 1851, the park was part of General Oglethorpe's original city plan and made possible by the donation of land from Georgia governor John Forsyth. A glorious white fountain dating to 1858, Confederate and Spanish-American War

# Victorian District and Eastside

## KEY

- **1** *Sights*
- **1** *Restaurants*
- **1** *Quick Bites*
- **1** *Hotels*

## Sights

Black Holocaust
Memorial, **3**

Forsyth Park, **1**

King-Tisdell
Cottage, **2**

## Restaurants

Betty Bombers, **4**

The Black
Rabbit, **2**

Collins Quarter
at Forsyth Park, **1**

Local 11ten, **5**

Sisters of
the New South, **6**

Strangebird, **3**

## Quick Bites

Brighter Day
Natural Foods, **1**

## Hotels

Catherine Ward
House Inn, **1**

The King-Tisdell Cottage was home to Sara King and Robert Tisdell, two African American entrepreneurs in turn-of-the-20th-century Savannah.

memorials, a fragrant garden, multiple playgrounds, tennis and basketball courts, and an old fort (which houses the gorgeous Collins Quarter Forsyth Café, with indoor/outdoor seating) are spread across this grand, green space. Be sure to stop by the south end on Saturday mornings for the bustling farmers' market. The park's 1-mile perimeter is among the prettiest walks in the city and takes you past many beautifully restored historic homes. ✉ *Gaston St., between Drayton and Whitaker Sts., Historic District* ✛ *If you're walking up Bull Street from downtown, you'll walk right into the park.*

### King-Tisdell Cottage

**HISTORIC HOME** | Built in 1897, this restored Victorian cottage with gingerbread flourishes pays homage to Savannah's thriving African American entrepreneurial community of the 20th century. Artifacts, maps, and educational installations present a multidimensional, nuanced narrative of local Black history. ✉ *514 E. Huntingdon St., Eastside* ☎ *912/335–8868* ⊕ *beachinstitute.org* ⊘ *Closed Sun.–Mon.*

## 🍴 Restaurants

### Betty Bombers

**$ | AMERICAN | FAMILY** | Located inside the American Legion Post 135 on Forsyth Park, this throwback mess hall is a hit with the locals. World War II–theme decor lines the walls, and "Bettys" in period-inspired dress smile and serve classics like chili dogs, cheesesteaks, juicy burgers, and baskets of French fries. **Known for:** cheap eats; specialty burgers; milkshakes. $\boxed{\$}$ *Average main: $11 ⊠ American Legion Post 135, 1108 Bull St., Victorian District* ⟊ *opposite Forsyth Park* ☎ *912/272–9326* ⊕ *www.bettybombers. com* ⊗ *Closed Sun.*

### The Black Rabbit

$ | **AMERICAN** | On bustling Barnard Street in the Victorian District, this neighborhood café and bar serves up affordable, scrumptious sandwiches and creatively crafted cocktails in a small, intimate space. With a name inspired by the black rabbit painted on its roll-down door, the property stands today as a compelling concept from seasoned Savannah restaurateurs who know how to make unforgettable food at unbeatable prices. **Known for:** cozy space; late-night bites like the Three Piggies sandwich (Spam, pit ham, and sliced pork shoulder); modern luncheonette vibes. $\boxed{\$}$ *Average main: $12 ⊠ 1215 Barnard St., Victorian District* ☎ *912/200–4940* ⊕ *www.blackrabbitsav.com.*

### Collins Quarter at Forsyth Park

$ | **ECLECTIC** | The white fort in the middle of Forsyth Park opened in 2020 with a full-service restaurant, bar, and café that bustles from early mornings to late afternoons. Sophisticated Southern brunch and lunch fare like shrimp 'n' grits, pork belly Benedict and avocado toast (of course) pair with a drink bar that offers signature coffees, beautifully garnished craft cocktails, and fun treats for the kids. **Known for:** outdoor brunch and mimosas; music on the patio; avocado toast. $\boxed{\$}$ *Average main: $14 ⊠ Forsyth Park, 621 Drayton St., Victorian District* ☎ *912/298–6674* ⊕ *thecollinsquarter.com.*

### ★ Local 11ten

$$$ | **AMERICAN** | This farm-to-table staple features an upbeat and contemporary menu that draws young chefs on their nights off. Seasonally driven, the menu is continually changing depending on the local harvest and the chef's vision, but dishes tend to be perfectly prepared and presented. **Known for:** seasonal menu with farm-sourced ingredients; sea scallops over black rice; open-air rooftop bar. $\boxed{\$}$ *Average main: $33 ⊠ 1110 Bull St., Victorian District* ☎ *912/790–9000* ⊕ *local11ten.com* ⊗ *Closed Mon. and Tues. No lunch.*

### Sisters of the New South

$ | **SOUTHERN** | Traditional Southern home cookin' comes with a smile at Sisters of the New South, where you'll be greeted as "honey" or "baby" (or both) as you place your order. Try the

## Moss Mystique

Spanish moss—the silky gray garlands that drape over the branches of live oaks—has come to symbolize the languorous sensibilities of the Deep South. A relative of the pineapple, this moisture-loving plant requires an average year-round humidity of 70%, and thus thrives in subtropical climates—including Georgia's coastal regions.

Contrary to popular belief, Spanish moss is not a parasite—it's not even moss.

Or Spanish. It's an epiphyte, or "air plant," taking water and nutrients from the air and photosynthesizing in the same manner as soil-bound plants and reproduces using tiny flowers. When water is scarce, it turns gray, and when the rains come it takes on a greenish hue. Although it is tempting to grab handfuls of Spanish moss as a souvenir, be careful! It harbors biting menaces commonly known as chiggers.

smothered pork chops or the fried whiting, though you can't go wrong with the generous "Meat & Three"—a choose-your-own foodie adventure. **Known for:** smothered pork chops; traditional Southern cooking; collard greens. $ *Average main: $12* ✉ *2605 Skidaway Rd., Eastside* ☎ *912/335–2761* ⊕ *thesistersofthenewsouth.com.*

### Strangebird

$$ | **MODERN MEXICAN** | Operating inside of a well-preserved 1938 Worcester Streamliner, Strangebird serves up casual, approachable eats with a Mexican flair. The appetizing aromas of smoked meats and Yucatan marinades fill the cozy diner car, which has already amassed a flock of devoted patrons since its opening in July 2023. **Known for:** birria burger; smokehouse tacos; retro streamliner. $ *Average main: $15* ✉ *1220 Barnard St., Victorian District* ☎ *912/250–9500* ⊕ *www.strangebirdsavannah.com* ⊗ *Closed Tues.*

## ☕ Coffee and Quick Bites

### Brighter Day Natural Foods

$ | **SANDWICHES** | This natural foods haven has been serving Savannah's organically minded since the 1970s. In the back of this full-fledged grocery and supplement store is a busy deli counter busting out custom sandwiches with meat, vegetarian, and vegan options as well as house-made side dishes, salads, and cakes.

The Catherine Ward House Inn is one of many Savannah B&Bs in what were once grand private homes.

**Known for:** baked cheese and avocado sandwich; walk-up window 9–2 for fresh juices and smoothies; large assortment of vegan and vegetarian options. ⑤ *Average main: $8* ✉ *1102 Bull St., Victorian District* ☎ *912/236–4703* ⊕ *brighterdayfoods.com.*

## 🛏 Hotels

### Catherine Ward House Inn

**$$ | B&B/INN |** Elegance meets comfort at this bed-and-breakfast, applauded for warm and inviting touches like soft music, cozy lighting, and crackling fires in period fireplaces. **Pros:** rooms have antique mantels and fireplaces, some of which work; some rooms have two-person whirlpool tubs; tasty breakfasts. **Cons:** less expensive rooms are small; carriage-house rooms are not as atmospheric as the main house; two-night minimum usually required for weekends. ⑤ *Rooms from: $219* ✉ *118 E. Waldburg St., Victorian District* ☎ *912/234–8564* ⊕ *www.catherineward-houseinn.com* ⇝ *9 rooms* ⦿ *Free Breakfast.*

## 🍸 Nightlife

### American Legion Post 135

**COCKTAIL BARS |** This old-school watering hole is where the locals go for easy camaraderie and cheap drinks. Built in 1913, the handsome, fortress-like brick building is the birthplace of the

The Victorian District is known for having block after block of large, lovingly restored homes in a rainbow of colors.

"Mighty Eighth" Air Force, and the decor pays homage to those who've served. Pick up a friendly game of pool, or listen to wild stories on the smokers' balcony. ✉ *1108 Bull St., Victorian District* ☎ *912/233–9277* ⊕ *alpost135.com.*

### Perch

**BARS** | Above restaurant Local 11ten, this secret lair nestled in the oak trees is the perfect place to enjoy specialty drinks on a weekend evening. Try a Honeydew It with its melon-infused gin or the satisfyingly spicy Jalapeño Lime Spritzer, or choose wine by the glass from the thoughtful selection. They also have a few mocktails for patrons who wish to avoid the intoxication factor. ✉ *1110 Bull St., Victorian District* ⊕ *Use stairs on side of building* ☎ *912/790–9000* ⊕ *perchsavannah.com.*

## 💼 Shopping

### ART GALLERIES

#### Cleo the Gallery

**ART GALLERY** | This gallery gives under-exhibited artists well-deserved honorariums along with a platform to showcase their artworks, which range from painting and sculpture to video and installation. With five major exhibitions each year, there's always something fresh on view here, and visitors can enjoy artist talks with local makers nearly every Saturday. ✉ *915 B Montgomery St., Victorian District* ☎ *912/328–4776* ⊕ *cleothegallery.com.*

## CLOTHING
### Future on Forsyth
**SECOND-HAND** | Your fashion future is always bright at this super cool vintage shop on the western edge of Forsyth Park. From whimsical window dressings to reasonable prices, this unique spot delivers delightful surprises. ⊠ *106 W. Gwinnett St, #1A, Victorian District* ☎ *912/235–2476* ⊕ *thefutureonforsyth.com.*

#  Activities

## BIKING
### Bike Walk Savannah
**BIKING** | Savannah's foremost bicycle advocate, this nonprofit membership organization helps to educate cyclists, motorists, and elected officials about cyclist and pedestrian safety and promotes improved bicycle facilities in Chatham County. They also host rides and events, such as the Moonlight Garden Ride, that are family-oriented and open to the public. Visit the website for information on upcoming activities. ⊠ *1301 Lincoln St., Suite A, Savannah* ☎ *912/228–3096* ⊕ *bikewalksavannah.org.*

## SPAS AND GYMS
### Savannah Yoga Center
**YOGA** | Established in 2003, SYC is Savannah's longest-running yoga studio, with a variety of styles and classes seven days a week. The space is clean and sunny, and there are mats, blocks and towels available for use. Drop-ins are welcome, and beginners are encouraged—all you have to do is show up. ⊠ *509 Barnard St., Victorian District* ☎ *912/232–2994* ⊕ *savannahyoga.com.*

### Strong Gym
**HEALTH CLUB** | Offering personal training, group fitness, post-rehabilitation and massage therapy, Strong Gym regular wins local "Best of" awards for its trainers' expertise and professional knowledge. One-on-one sessions start at $75; massages start at $90. ⊠ *1321 Bull St., Victorian District* ☎ *912/443–4006* ⊕ *strong-savannah.com.*

### Temple Day Spa
**SPA** | Presenting a compelling invitation to worship yourself, this tranquil spa is a sacred space for relaxation and rejuvenation. Services include massages, facials, body treatments and infrared sauna. Massages start at $60 and facials start at $100. Owner and lead esthetician Kelly Temple also operates a second loft location just a few blocks away. ⊠ *1522 Bull St., Victorian District* ☎ *912/559–1616, 912/446–1522* ⊕ *www.templedayspasavannah.com.*

# Chapter 5

# STARLAND DISTRICT, THOMAS SQUARE, AND MIDTOWN

Updated by
Jessica Leigh Lebos

● Sights    🍴 Restaurants    🛏 Hotels    ● Shopping    🍸 Nightlife
★★★☆☆    ★★★★★    ★☆☆☆☆    ★★★★★    ★★★★★

# NEIGHBORHOOD SNAPSHOT

## TOP EXPERIENCES

■ **Get your art on:** Starland's public murals, street art, galleries, and museums are a colorful feast for the eyes.

■ **Check out the books:** Built in 1916, the Bull Street Library is a grand example of neoclassical architecture.

■ **Have fun at First Fridays:** Join the vibrant monthly street fair featuring artists, musicians, and food trucks.

■ **Embrace the weird:** Eccentric shops like Starland Strange and Graveface Records & Curiosities keep it quirky.

■ **Party in the yard:** Constructed from old shipping containers, Starland Yard hosts a full bar, live music, and revolving food trucks.

■ **Drink local brews:** Two Tides Brewing Company concocts and serves up awesome suds, from crisp pale ales to juicy sours.

## GETTING HERE

Located immediately south of the Victorian District, the Thomas Square neighborhood—which includes the Starland District—is easily reached on foot by continuing south on Bull Street from Forsyth Park. This pedestrian-friendly corridor with restaurants, cafes, shops, and bars is packed from morning 'til the wee hours. There's plenty of free street parking, though it can be competitive on weekends.

## QUICK BITES

■ **Foxy Loxy.** Fresh pastries, tasty tacos, and authentic Texas kolaches pair anytime of day with coffee drinks and a curated selection of beer and wine. ⊠ 1919 Bull Street, Thomas Square ⊕ foxyloxycafe.com.

■ **Big Bon Bodega.** Wood-fired bagels, hot coffee, and other brunchy treats are available through lunchtime, with pop-up pizza on the weekends. ⊠ 2011 Bull St., Thomas Square ⊕ bigbonfamily.com.

■ **Yia Yia's Kitchen.** Find authentic Greek specialties like gyros, baklava, and fresh salads. ⊠ 3113 Habersham St., Midtown ⊕ yiayiasav.com.

"Midtown" in Savannah includes the charming historic neighborhoods south of Forsyth Park all the way to Derenne Avenue, including the Thomas Square Historic Streetcar District, artsy Starland, stately Ardsley Park, and the post-War residential areas surrounding Habersham Village plaza.

The most interesting dining, shopping, and adventure options are centered along the Bull Street corridor from 32nd Street to Victory Drive, though exploration a few blocks east and west is rewarded with tucked-away murals, funky stores, and hole-in-the-wall eats.

Developed in the 1880s, Thomas Square became the next "suburb" as the Victorian District filled in with families and new businesses. Architecture runs from sublime Beaux-Arts mansions to modest Craftsmen cottages, though many of these historic homes were foundering before the revitalization efforts of the 21st century. The Savannah College of Art and Design's renovation of the historic Richard Arnold School in 2009 brought renewed foot traffic to the area along Bull Street, spurring small business development in the form of cafés, galleries, shops, and bars as well as a vibrant cultural arts scene distinct from the rest of the city.

A few blocks to the south, at what was once sprawling farmland at the edge of the Thomas Square neighborhood, lies the old white dairy that gives the Starland District its name. The area's cheap real estate and funky storefronts were claimed by artists and entrepreneurs in the 1990s, and the area has exploded in recent years with public art collaborations, innovative gathering spots, unique shops, and restaurants that go far beyond the typical Savannah menus. Presiding over the corner of Bull and 41st streets is the neighborhood's pink and purple crown jewel, art supply hub Starlandia.

#  Sights

### Bull Street Library

**LIBRARY** | Even if you don't have a library card, it's worth browsing the beautiful neoclassical building built in 1916 with funding from a Carnegie grant. The grand foyer and revolving exhibits are nourishment for the senses, and the massive windowed reading lounge and third-story alcove are wonderful places to curl up with a book. ⊠ *2002 Bull St., Thomas Square* ☎ *912/652–3600* ⊕ *liveoakpl.org* ▨ *Free* ⊘ *Closed Sun.*

### First City Pride Center

**VISITOR CENTER** | Formerly known as the Savannah LGBT Center, this nexus of activism, health services, and community events is a friendly, safe space for queer folk and allies. Check in for revolving art exhibits, special lectures, and guidance toward local resources. ⊠ *1515 Bull St., Starland District* ☎ *912/304–5428* ⊕ *firstcitypridecenter.org.*

### Savannah African Art Museum

**ART MUSEUM** | Once the private collection of Savannah businessman Don Cole, this assemblage of over a thousand sculptures, artifacts, tribal costumes, carved masks, pottery, and other sacred objects from West and Central Africa is now on display for the general public in a beautifully restored yellow mansion. The museum has works and artifacts from over 180 cultures and also hosts workshops and lectures relating to African history. ⊠ *201 E. 37th St., Thomas Square* ☎ *912/721–7745* ⊕ *savannahafricanartmuseum.org* ▨ *Free* ⊘ *Closed Sun.–Tues.*

 # Restaurants

### Al Salaam Deli

**$** | **MIDDLE EASTERN** | If your taste buds seek something other than standard Southern fare, head to one of Savannah's few Middle Eastern restaurants. Owned and operated by a husband-and-wife team Meqbel and Rose Salameh Al Salaam, the restaurant is celebrated for its perfectly fried falafel, spit-roasted lamb, and hummus and baba ganoush platters. **Known for:** authentic falafel; plentiful food and low prices; take-out options. ⑤ *Average main: $11* ⊠ *2311 Habersham St., Thomas Square* ☎ *912/447–0400* ⊕ *al-salaam-deli.business.site* ⊘ *Closed Sun.*

### Ardsley Station

**$$$** | **AMERICAN** | With an approachable-but-classy atmosphere and an all-day menu full of American classics, there's something for everyone at this bustling neighborhood hotspot. Stacked burgers and sandwiches, hearty salads, and creamy pasta dishes dominate the lunch and dinner menus, while egg dishes and waffles pair up with a mimosa-laden weekend brunch. **Known for:** large plates; convivial atmosphere; caramel salted crunch cake. ⑤ *Average main: $30* ⊠ *102 E. Victory Dr., Starland District* ☎ *912/777–5888* ⊕ *ardsleystation.com.*

### Brochu's Family Tradition

**$$** | **SOUTHERN** | The new kid on the Starland block elevates Southern staples like fried chicken and oysters with high presentation and super-charged flavors. Locals flock to the spacious patio for late afternoon cocktails and house-made pickles, and the dining room buzzes with sociability and a kickin' soundtrack. **Known for:** convivial atmosphere; original craft cocktails; fancy fried chicken. $ *Average main: $19* ⊠ *2400 Bull St., Suite 8, Starland District* ⊕ *www.brochusfamilytradition.com* ☉ *Closed Mon. and Tues. No lunch.*

### Bull Street Taco

**$$** | **MEXICAN FUSION** | Every night is taco night at this bright and busy spot. Handmade tortillas, authentic recipes, and tasty vegetarian options bring delicious depth to the usual street-style taco fare. **Known for:** red-chili cauliflower taco; street-style corn on the cob; DIY taco kits to go. $ *Average main: $15* ⊠ *1608 Bull St., Thomas Square* ☎ *912/349–6931* ⊕ *bullstreettaco.com* ☉ *Closed Sun.*

### Cotton & Rye

**$$$** | **SOUTHERN** | Embodying the new Southern cuisine, Cotton & Rye offers a menu that is creative and artistic with a strong sense of tradition. You'll see classic, recognizable comfort dishes like shrimp n' grits and thick bone-in pork chops, but careful intention goes into the preparation and presentation that results in delightful sensory surprises. **Known for:** upscale take on gastropub fare; inventive, homemade desserts; patio dining. $ *Average main: $34* ⊠ *1801 Habersham St., Thomas Square* ☎ *912/777–6286* ⊕ *www.cottonandrye.com* ☉ *Closed Sun. and Mon. No lunch.*

### ★ Elizabeth on 37th

**$$$** | **AMERICAN** | This elegant turn-of-the-20th-century mansion has been feeding regional specialties to Savannah's upper crust for decades. Chef Kelly Yambor has helmed the kitchen since 1996, and she masters dishes like Georgia shrimp and Savannah red rice, a double-cut Berkshire pork chop with apple-cabbage slaw, and local grouper Celeste (with a sesame-almond crust). **Known for:** impressive wine list; top fine-dining experience in town; seven-course tasting menu option. $ *Average main: $35* ⊠ *105 E. 37th St., Thomas Square* ☎ *912/236–5547* ⊕ *elizabethon37th.net* ☉ *Closed Sun. No lunch.*

### Green Truck Neighborhood Pub

**$** | **BURGER** | **FAMILY** | Serving one of the best burgers in the state, this casual haunt draws diners from far and wide for its grass-fed beef—though vegetarians will find satisfaction with the hearty meatless patties. Everything from the coffee to the produce is

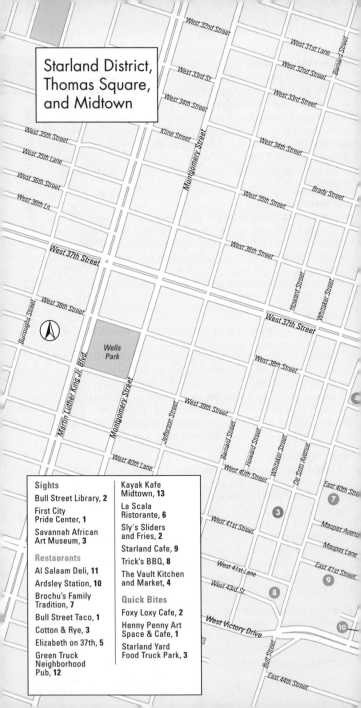

# Starland District, Thomas Square, and Midtown

West 32nd Street
West 31st Lane
West 32nd Street
Barnard Street
West 33rd St
West 33rd Street
West 34th Street
Kline Street
West 34th Street
Montgomery Street
West 35th Street
West 35th Street
West 35th Lane
Brady Street
West 36th Street
West 36th Ln.
West 36th Street
West 37th Street
Howard Street
Whitaker Street
West 38th Street
Burroughs Street
West 37th Street
Wells Park
West 38th Street
Martin Luther King Jr. Blvd
Montgomery Street
Jefferson Street
West 39th Street
Barnard Street
Howard Street
Whitaker Street
De Soto Avenue
West 40th Lane
West 40th Street
East 40th Stre
Maupas Avenu
West 41st Street
Maupas Lane
East 41st Street
West 41st Lane
West 43rd Ln.
West Victory Drive
Bull Street
East 44th Street

**Sights**

Bull Street Library, **2**

First City
Pride Center, **1**

Savannah African
Art Museum, **3**

**Restaurants**

Al Salaam Deli, **11**

Ardsley Station, **10**

Brochu's Family
Tradition, **7**

Bull Street Taco, **1**

Cotton & Rye, **3**

Elizabeth on 37th, **5**

Green Truck
Neighborhood
Pub, **12**

Kayak Kafe
Midtown, **13**

La Scala
Ristorante, **6**

Sly's Sliders
and Fries, **2**

Starland Cafe, **9**

Trick's BBQ, **8**

The Vault Kitchen
and Market, **4**

**Quick Bites**

Foxy Loxy Cafe, **2**

Henny Penny Art
Space & Cafe, **1**

Starland Yard
Food Truck Park, **3**

**KEY**

- **1** Sights
- **1** Restaurants
- **1** Quick Bites

W. 31st St.

East Henry Ln.

East Anderson Street

31st Ct.

East 31st Street

East Anderson Lane

Whitaker Street

Bull Street

**1**

**1** East 31st Lane

Drayton Street

Abercorn Street

Lincoln Street

East 32nd Street

Habersham Street

East 32nd St

**1**

Price Street

East 33rd Street

East 34th Street

**2**

East 33rd Street

Bull Street

East 34th Lane

East 35th Street

East 34th Lane

East 34th Street

**2**

Thomas Park

East 35th Lane

Abercorn Street

**3**

East 34th Lane

**2**

East 36th Street

East 35th Street

Lincoln Street

East 35th Lane

East 36th Lane

East 36th Street

East 35th Lane

East 36th Street

Plant Street

Ware Street

**5**

**6**

**3**

East 37th Street

East 36th Ln.

Drayton Street

Hamilton Court

East 38th Street

East 37th Street

East 39th Street

East 38th Street

Abercorn Street

Lincoln Street

Habersham Street

**11**

Price Street

East 39th Street

East Broad Street

East 40th Street

**12**

East 41st Lane

East 41st Street

Maupas Avenue

East 42nd Street

East Victory Drive

0           1,000 ft

0           250 m

**13**

locally sourced, and even the ketchup is made in house. **Known for:** great beer selection; homemade ketchup and pimento cheese; locally sourced beef. $ *Average main: $13* ⊠ *2430 Habersham St., Thomas Square* ☎ *912/234–5885* ⊕ *greentruckpub.com* ⊘ *Closed Sun.*

### Kayak Kafe Midtown

**$$ | VEGETARIAN |** This palm-shaded eatery is the sister restaurant to the original downtown location and hands down the best spot for vegetarian and vegan options in the city. There's also more than enough on the menu to keep a meat eater happy—consider the fried chicken tacos or the chicken-and-goat-cheese enchiladas. **Known for:** hearty salads; excellent brunch; outdoor seating. $ *Average main: $15* ⊠ *5002 Paulsen St., Midtown* ☎ *912/349–4371* ⊕ *eatkayak.com.*

### La Scala Ristorante

**$$$$ | ITALIAN |** This richly decorated, renovated mansion houses one of the finest dining experiences outside of downtown with grand flourishes like antique furniture, a piano bar, and a chapel space upstairs surrounded by stained glass. White-tablecloth settings match the traditional menu of Italian favorites—the herbed risotto is recommended as a first course, followed by the tagliatelle vongole. **Known for:** nice outdoor patio; excellent wine list; complimentary valet parking. $ *Average main: $46* ⊠ *119 E. 37th St., Thomas Square* ☎ *912/238–3100* ⊕ *lascalasavannah.com* ⊘ *Closed Sun. and Mon.*

### Sly's Sliders and Fries

**$ | AMERICAN | FAMILY |** Tiny burgers get gourmet treatment and are paired with generous portions of perfectly crispy skinny fries at this local favorite. Try the Mr. Chow, which comes with a fried egg and extra bacon, or the Lil Sandy with pulled pork; vegetarians can chow down on the Shroomwich, featuring three kinds of marinated fungi. **Known for:** smoked brisket sliders; delicious skinny fries; awesome canned beer selection. $ *Average main: $4* ⊠ *1710 Abercorn St., Thomas Square* ☎ *912/239–4219* ⊕ *slysslidersandfries.com.*

### Starland Cafe

**$$ | CAFÉ |** Housed in a brightly painted two-story house, this legendary lunch spot is the restaurant that started the neighborhood's renaissance. From the fresh-pressed vegetarian Greek panini (brimming with crispy asparagus, hummus, marinated artichokes, feta, tomato, pesto, and house aioli) to the generously portioned Kitchen Sink Salad (dates, raisins, artichokes, apples, grapes, crunchy rice noodles, tomatoes, and onion), it's hard to go wrong with a menu that prioritizes freshness and locally sourced greens. **Known for:** bustling weekday lunch crowd; famous tomato Thai soup; iced Earl Grey tea. ⑤ *Average main: $16* ⊠ *11 E. 41st St., between Bull and Drayton Sts., Starland District* ☎ *912/443–9355* ⊕ *thestarlandcafe.com* ⊗ *Closed weekends. No dinner.*

### Tricks BBQ

$ | **BARBECUE** | You can usually smell the delicious aroma before you see the line snaking around this outdoor pit stop right off Victory Drive. Using mouthwatering smoke techniques and a secret golden mustard sauce recipe, Tricks serves up to-go containers of the finest ribs around. **Known for:** pork ribs; lamb dinners; chicken legs. ⑤ *Average main: $10* ⊠ *2601 Bull St., Starland District* ☎ *912/436-7338* ⊕ *instagram.com/tricksbbq* ⊗ *Closed Sun. and Mon.*

### The Vault Kitchen and Market

$$ | **ASIAN FUSION** | An anchor on the Bull Street Corridor, this former bank features a varied menu of Asian fusion and sushi delights. The bright and bustling space, which honors its financial past in clever design choices and menu descriptions, welcomes visitors with flavors from Laos, Japan, and beyond, including melt-in-your-mouth miso salmon. **Known for:** industrial-chic interior; chicken clay pot with Thai green eggplant and rice; unique sushi rolls. ⑤ *Average main: $18* ⊠ *2112 Bull St., Starland District* ☎ *912/201–1950* ⊕ *thevaultkitchen.com.*

## ☕ Coffee and Quick Bites

### ★ Foxy Loxy Cafe

$ | **CAFÉ** | A full-service coffee shop featuring lovingly-crafted lattes and a Tex-Mex menu, Foxy Loxy is the always-busy hangout for students, artists, and entrepreneurs. Order a horchata and take your laptop out to the courtyard, where a koi pond, acoustic music, and Saturday night s'mores parties at the firepit invite folks to lounge in the open air. **Known for:** beautifully crafted drinks; authentic kolache pastries; strong Wi-Fi. ⑤ *Average main: $5* ⊠ *1919 Bull St., Starland District* ☎ *912/401–0543* ⊕ *foxyloxycafe. com* ⊗ *No dinner.*

### Henny Penny Art Space & Cafe

$ | **CAFÉ** | **FAMILY** | From the same owners as Foxy Loxy and the Coffee Fox, this wide-open, family-oriented café offers a place for kids to explore the art project of the day while parents enjoy some caffeine. The menu also includes vegan donuts, grab-and-go sandwiches, and the in-house bakery's famous kolaches. **Known for:** good pastries and treats; fun place with big tables for kids to work at; sells Leopold's ice cream. ⑤ *Average main: $6* ⊠ *1514 Bull St., Thomas Square* ☎ *912/328–5497* ⊕ *hennypennycafe.com.*

Starland Yard is a festive foodie haven.

### Starland Yard Food Truck Park

$ | **AMERICAN** | **FAMILY** | Rotating food trucks means that menus revolve weekly at this literal playground constructed out of old shipping containers. Two permanent fixtures are a well-stocked central bar and Pizzeria Vittoria, whose piping hot oven manned by award-winning chef Kyle Jacovino churns out the neighborhood's best pizza. **Known for:** amazing pizza; fun, lively atmosphere; many food varieties. ⑤ *Average main: $11* ⊠ *2411 De Soto Ave., Starland District* ☎ *912/417–3001* ⊕ *starlandyard.com* ⊗ *No lunch Mon.–Wed.*

## 🍸 Nightlife

### Colleagues & Lovers

**COCKTAIL BARS** | Intrepid explorers reaching further south into Habersham Village will find this artfully decorated cocktail lounge with a cadre of expert mixologists and a diverse clientele—the trip is worth it for the martini lovers. Artisanal flatbreads, pastas, and salads come from the kitchen, and pizza Wednesdays are a local tradition. ⊠ *4523 Habersham St., Savannah* ☎ *912/999–6582* ⊕ *www.colleaguesandloverssavannah.com.*

### Late Air

**WINE BAR** | Featuring natural wines from regions around the world by the glass or bottle, this fun, funky wine lounge is revitalizing nightlife in Ardsley Park. Chef Juan Stephenson pairs the wine list with a revolving menu of small plates that keep refined palates busy into the night. ⊠ *2805 Bull St., Starland District* ☎ *912/231–3971* ⊕ *lateairwine.com.*

### Lone Wolf Lounge

**PUB** | Offering the warm vibe of a down-home, 1970s-era watering hole with an expertly crafted cocktail menu, Lone Wolf prides itself as an anti-hipster hangout far from the madding crowd. Choose from a refreshing mix of high- and low-brow beverages, from a cold Schlitz for a couple bucks to a house cocktail made by some of Savannah's best bartenders for under $10. Toss back a shot of Fernet Branca or sip a Zippah, an invigorating crisp mix of gin, absinthe, and lemon with a touch of earthiness. A mix of townies, students, and neighborhood folks gather around the wood-paneled bar and booths as well as the sumptuous Cobra Room, open sporadically for karaoke. ⊠ *2429 Lincoln St., Thomas Square* ⊕ *lonewolfsav.com.*

### Moodright's

**BARS** | Offering an old-school dive vibe without the grime, Moodright's is a sweet place to gather for a game of pool, a few rounds of duckpin bowling (like traditional bowling, but with smaller pins) or to just nurse your favorite beer in one of the comfy vinyl booths. Monday is Bingo Night, and if you're intrigued by the duckpin bowling, check out the pros on Wednesday league nights. ⊠ *2424 Abercorn St., Thomas Square* ☎ *912/335–7276* ⊕ *moodrights.com.*

### Sobremesa Wine Lounge

**WINE BAR** | This lovely neighborhood wine bar features a revolving list of wines by the glass, gorgeous charcuterie boards, and indulgent desserts. Savannah locals Guinn and Ryan combine the relaxed conviviality of Portugal and Spain with Southern hospitality. ⊠ *2312 Abercorn St., Thomas Square* ☎ *912/220–3217* ⊕ *www.sobremesasav.com.*

### Water Witch Tiki

**COCKTAIL BARS** | If you're seeking to sink into gorgeous cocktails with complex garnishes and wicker chairs upholstered in jungle prints, this is your oasis. Wear your loudest Hawaiian shirt and sip electrifying concoctions served in fabulous tiki mugs. ⚠ **There's a steep charge if you don't return the glassware.** ⊠ *2220 Bull St., Starland District* ☎ *912/201–3164* ⊕ *waterwitchtiki.com.*

### The Wormhole

**LIVE MUSIC** | With cheap drinks and a stage that's always occupied by local bands, comedians, and occasional special guests, the Wormhole cultivates a proud dive vibe. No pretensions or fancy craft cocktails here, just a bar stool with your name on it. There's also a full kitchen offering burgers and other bar snacks until the wee hours. ⊠ *2307 Bull St., Starland District* ☎ *912/349–6770* ⊕ *wormholebar.com.*

# 🛍 Shopping

## ANTIQUES

### ★ Picker Joe's Antique Mall & Vintage Market

**ANTIQUES & COLLECTIBLES** | A haven for lovers of architectural salvage, vintage treasures, mid-century furniture, and antique decor, Picker Joe's offers 10,000 square feet of discovery. A consistent receiver of local awards, the shop's many booths are carefully tended and offer a true variety of quality finds for pickers of all walks of life. ⊠ *217 E. 41st St., Thomas Square* ☎ *912/239–4657* ⊕ *pickerjoes.com.*

## ART SUPPLIES

### ★ Starlandia Art Supply

**CRAFTS** | The electric purple facade on the corner greets visitors as they enter on Bull Street from Victory Drive, signifying you've found the funkiest, artsiest neighborhood in Savannah. Inside, you'll find all manner of craft supplies, paints, canvases, markers, fabric swatches, tools, books, local art for sale, and fabulous treasures you never knew you needed. ⊠ *2438 Bull St., Starland District* ☎ *912/417–4561* ⊕ *starlandiasupply.com.*

## CLOTHING

### Blank Canvas Showroom

**CLOTHING** | High fashion meets affordability at this colorful showroom featuring original, unique pieces from up-and-coming designers, some fresh from the Savannah College of Art and Design. Many lines are produced in-house, offering something for every wardrobe that is sure to turn heads. ⊠ *1815 Bull St., Starland District* ☎ *347/661-8947* ⊕ *blankcanvasshowroom.com.*

### Vintage Vortex Savannah

**SECOND-HAND** | Imagine wandering around your cool aunt's enormous closet and being allowed to try on anything you like—that's how much fun a shopping trip to The Vintage Vortex is. Formerly known as Gypsy World, the spacious storefront brims with treasures for all genders, like vintage zoot suits, fur stoles, rhinestone accessories, pillbox hats, and frocks in every color of the rainbow. ⊠ *2413 Bull St., Starland District* ☎ *912/335–2620* ⊕ *vintagevortexsav.com.*

## GIFTS

### Cosmic Corner

**SOUVENIRS** | Stock up on crystals, runes, candles, incense, and other magical supplies for your sacred space at this celestial haven tucked away near the railroad tracks. You can also schedule astrological and tarot readings, chakra cleansings, and Reiki sessions with gifted professionals, or just gab with like-minded souls as you fill your basket. ⊠ *305 E. 38th St., Thomas Square* ☎ *912/421–0426* ⊕ *cosmiccornersavannah.com.*

### ★ Graveface Records & Curiosities

**MUSIC** | This longtime anchor of Starland is a huge part of the area's enticingly artsy, bizarre reputation. Vinyl heads will love digging through the bins of old and new records, some freshly pressed by the Graveface record label. There's also the wicked apparel and delightfully creepy taxidermy exhibits—yes, stuffed animals, and not the cuddly kind—that make this a must for any visit to the neighborhood. ⊠ *5 W. 40th St., Starland District* ☎ *912/335-8018* ⊕ *linktr.ee/graveface.*

### Starland Strange and Bazaar

**SOUVENIRS** | Hip, radical, weird, adorable—if there were an easy way to classify this store's style, it wouldn't be called strange. Follow artist JuLu's wildly painted stairs to find Starland-specific merch and hilariously irreverent stickers like Elvis Jesus, plus a menu of ice cream cones you can snack on while you shop. ⊠ *17 W. 41st St., Starland District* ☎ *912/452–0106* ⊕ *starlandstrange-andbazaar.com.*

### Superbloom

**SOUVENIRS** | Part gift shop, part café, Superbloom is a cheerfully eclectic space serving up marvelous, nutritious drinks along with locally made crafts. Browse screen-printed tea towels, ultra-modern affordable jewelry, hand-crafted beauty products, and more. This is the place to support local artists and artisans! ⊠ *2418 Desoto Ave., Starland District* ⊕ *superbloomsav.com.*

## 🎭 Performing Arts

### ART GALLERIES

#### Sulfur Studios + ARTS Southeast

**PERFORMANCE VENUES** | This community art center and lively nexus houses working artists, dynamic events, and revolving exhibitions. It's a must during First Fridays, when visitors can wander the labyrinthine warren of studios featuring textiles, painting, sculpture, performances and more. This is also the headquarters of ARTS

Southeast, a non-profit that sponsors installations around the city. ✉ *2301 Bull St., Starland District* ☎ *912/231–7105* ⊕ *sulfurstudios. org.*

## FESTIVALS AND SPECIAL EVENTS

### First Fridays in Starland

**FESTIVALS | FAMILY |** This creative, collaborative event takes place on the first Friday evening of each month throughout the Starland neighborhood. The family-friendly event features food trucks, music, art receptions, exhibits, and open studios. Check out their Instagram page for more information. ✉ *2301 Bull St., Starland District* ⊕ *instagram.com/starlandfirstfridays.*

# 🏃 Activities

## BASEBALL

### Savannah Bananas

**BASEBALL & SOFTBALL | FAMILY |** Witness the international sensation—the Savannah Bananas have changed baseball forever with bright yellow uniforms, new rules, and unabashed sense of fun. A Bananas game is more than an athletic event: it's entertainment and camaraderie, with plenty of activities for the kids, dancing players, and lots of banana-themed snacks. Craft beers and all-you-can-eat passes make this a favorite local pastime. ✉ *1401 E. Victory Dr., Daffin Park* ☎ *912/712–2482* ⊕ *thesavannahbananas. com.*

## COOKING CLASSES

### Chef Darin's Kitchen Table

**COLLEGE | FAMILY |** After making a name for himself in the local dining scene, Chef Darin created his own cooking school in 2015 with hands-on classes for cooks of all levels. The state-of-the-art facility includes a kitchen stocked with five KitchenAid dual fuel ranges and a double wall oven as well as Savannah's only local kitchen shop. Class subjects range from Lowcountry comfort food to Pan Asian cuisine. ✉ *2514 Abercorn St., Suite 140, Thomas Square* ☎ *912/704–6882* ⊕ *chefdarin.com* 🍽 *From $90.*

## TENNIS

### Daffin Park Tennis Complex

**TENNIS |** There are three hard courts and six clay courts at the Daffin Park Tennis Complex, located near Grayson Stadium and surrounded by live oaks. The facilities are often used for league play; reservations are suggested. ✉ *1001 E. Victory Dr., Midtown* ☎ *912/351–3851* ⊕ *savannahga.gov/813/Tennis-Program.*

# MOON RIVER DISTRICT, THUNDERBOLT, AND THE ISLANDS

Updated by
Chantel Britton

⊙ Sights    🍴 Restaurants    🛏 Hotels    🛍 Shopping    🍸 Nightlife
★★★★★    ★★★☆☆    ★★☆☆☆    ★★☆☆☆    ★★☆☆☆

# NEIGHBORHOOD SNAPSHOT

## TOP EXPERIENCES

■ **Cross Moon River:** Even though it's not wider than a mile, the spot from the famous Johnny Mercer song is best shared with a huckleberry friend.

■ **Paddle among the marshes:** Kayaking through the golden spartina grass reveals serene views and a world of wildlife.

■ **Hike the path of bootleggers:** An old moonshine still lies in the woods just off Skidaway Island State Park's Big Ferry Trail.

■ **Drive back in time:** The oak-lined road to the tabby ruins of Wormsloe State Historic Site dates back to Georgia's oldest settlers.

■ **Hear a big "boom!":** Cannon and musket firings are part of the regular programming at Old Fort Jackson.

■ **Learn to say "okra" in Gullah Geechee:** The Pin Point Heritage Museum chronicles the language, lifestyle, and traditions of this unique culture.

## GETTING HERE

All of these neighborhoods are best reached by car as public transportation is sparse or not available at all. From downtown Savannah, head east on Victory Drive, aka Highway 80 E; the City of Thunderbolt lies on both sides as you come to the Bull River Bridge. Continue on this road to find Wilmington and Whitemarsh islands. The Moon River District, including Sandfly and Isle of Hope, can be reached via Skidaway Road.

## QUICK BITES

■ **Flying Fish Bar & Grill.** Fried shrimp and ahi tuna bites hit the spot on the way home from the beach. ⌧ 7906 US-80, Wilmington Island ⊕ flyingfish-savannah.com.

■ **Auspicious Baking Company.** There's a reason you always see a line for the most heavenly crois-sants and pastries for miles; avail-able for takeout Friday through Sunday. ⌧ 7360 Skidaway Rd, Sand-fly ⊕ auspicious-bakingco.com.

■ **Basil's Pizza and Deli.** Traditional pizzas, subs, and calzones are served up in a friendly atmosphere. ⌧ 216 Johnny Mercer Blvd., Wilmington Island ⊕ basilson-line.com.

Drive out of Savannah's downtown and you'll find one-of-a-kind marsh views and stunning sunset vistas. Thunderbolt, bordering Savannah's east side and the Wilmington River, is a lush bedroom community and historic fishing village that's home to Bonaventure Cemetery and delicious seafood spots like Tubby's Tank House. Head farther east on U.S. 80 and discover Wilmington Island, a cozy neighborhood on the Wilmington River. Historic Fort Pulaski and Oatland Island Wildlife Center are nearby.

Experience marshside tranquility in the Moon River District, named after the tune that made Savannah native Johnny Mercer famous. The area includes the Sandfly, Isle of Hope, and Skidaway Island neighborhoods, and is an off-the-beaten-path stop for outdoor adventurers and history buffs.

Learn about Gullah Geechee culture at the former oyster cannery that is now the Pin Point Heritage Museum, explore the area by water with various kayak outfitters, and sip a handcrafted cocktail on the dock at The Wyld Dock Bar. See beautiful coastal homes on Isle of Hope, a historic community flanked by the Herb and Skidaway rivers. Wormsloe Historic Site on Skidaway Road is known for its picturesque "oak allee" drive. Carry on to Skidaway Island and enjoy a nature walk at Skidaway Island State Park.

## ◎ Sights

### ★ Bonaventure Cemetery

**CEMETERY** | The largest and most famous of Savannah's municipal cemeteries, Bonaventure spreads over 100 acres and sits on a bluff above the Wilmington River. Once a sprawling plantation, the land became a private cemetery in 1846 and was established as a public cemetery in 1907. An emblematic destination for visitors, the evocative landscape is one of lush natural beauty transposed against an elegant, eerie backdrop of lavish marble headstones,

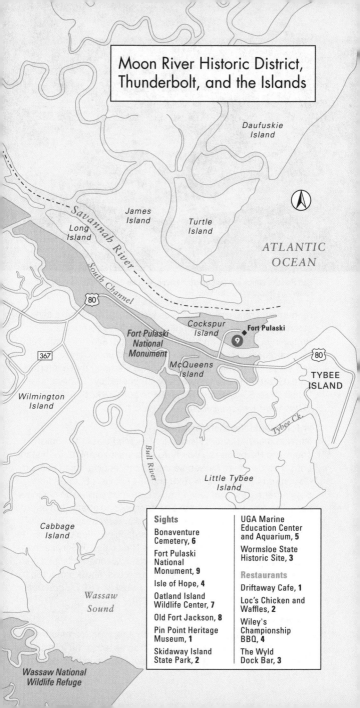

# Moon River Historic District, Thunderbolt, and the Islands

*Daufuskie Island*

*James Island*

*Turtle Island*

**ATLANTIC OCEAN**

*Savannah River*

*Long Island*

*South Channel*

80

*Cockspur Island* ◆ **Fort Pulaski**

**9**

*Fort Pulaski National Monument*

367

*McQueens Island*

80

**TYBEE ISLAND**

*Wilmington Island*

*Tybee Ck.*

*Bull River*

*Little Tybee Island*

*Cabbage Island*

*Wassaw Sound*

*Wassaw National Wildlife Refuge*

| Sights | UGA Marine Education Center and Aquarium, **5** |
|--------|--------|
| Bonaventure Cemetery, **6** | Wormsloe State Historic Site, **3** |
| Fort Pulaski National Monument, **9** | Restaurants |
| Isle of Hope, **4** | Driftaway Cafe, **1** |
| Oatland Island Wildlife Center, **7** | Loc's Chicken and Waffles, **2** |
| Old Fort Jackson, **8** | Wiley's Championship BBQ, **4** |
| Pin Point Heritage Museum, **1** | The Wyld Dock Bar, **3** |
| Skidaway Island State Park, **2** | |

Fort Pulaski, which sits on Cockspur Island, was built in the 19th century and was in service through the Civil War.

monuments, and mausoleums as well as sweeping oaks and blooming camellia trees. John Muir reportedly camped at Bonaventure in 1867 on his legendary "thousand-mile walk," and local photographer Jack Leigh, novelist and poet Conrad Aiken, and singer-songwriter Johnny Mercer are among those interred here. Great tours of the cemetery are offered by "Bonaventure Don." ⊠ *330 Bonaventure Rd., Thunderbolt* ☏ *912/651–6843* ⊕ *bonaventurehistorical.org.*

### ★ Fort Pulaski National Monument

**MILITARY SIGHT** | **FAMILY** | Named for Casimir Pulaski, the Polish count and Revolutionary War hero, this must-see sight for history buffs was designed by Napoléon's military engineer and built on Cockspur Island between 1829 and 1847. Robert E. Lee's first assignment after graduating from West Point was as an engineer here. The fort was thought to be impervious to attack, but as weapons advanced, it proved penetrable. During the Civil War, the fort fell after bombardment by newfangled rifled cannons. The restored fortification, operated by the National Park Service, has moats, drawbridges, massive ramparts, towering walls, and an informative visitors center. Trails, picnic areas, and a protected bird refuge surround the park. ⊠ *101 Fort Pulaski Road, Thunderbolt* ☏ *912/219–4233* ⊕ *nps.gov/fopu* 🎟 *$10.*

### Isle of Hope

**TOWN** | In 1736, General James Oglethorpe, who founded the colony of Georgia, parceled out 1,500 acres along the Intracoastal Waterway on the condition that the owners would help defend the city. The northernmost tract, today known as the Isle of Hope, was bequeathed to Henry Parker, who became the first acting governor in 1752. In the 1840s, the island had become a popular community for summer homes and, by 1875, the terminus for the Savannah, Skidaway, and Seaboard railroads, three major transit routes that transported travelers from far up the east coast and across the South. Today, the horseshoe-shaped island provides sweeping views and cool breezes from almost any point along the bluff, as well as an array of beautiful, historic homes. ⊠ *Moon River District*.

### Oatland Island Wildlife Center

**ZOO | FAMILY** | A few miles east of the Historic District, this wildlife preserve and educational center is one of the best family outings around. Home to a variety of animal habitats spread along a 2-mile path through pristine maritime forest, it feels more like a nature walk than a trip to the zoo as you're as likely to see wild otters and red-tailed hawks as you are the permanent residents. Several coastal habitats are represented, including the wetlands that are home to alligators, herons, and cranes. Bobcats, wolves, bison, armadillos, and assorted birds of prey live in large exhibits, and a butterfly garden flutters with colorful pollinators. Call or visit the website for reservations and/or additional information. ■**TIP→ Be sure to wear comfortable shoes.** ⊠ *711 Sandtown Rd., Oatland Island* ☎ *912/395–1212* ⊕ *oatlandisland.org* ⊡ *$5*.

### Old Fort Jackson

**MILITARY SIGHT** | The oldest standing fort in Georgia was garrisoned in the War of 1812 and was the Confederate headquarters for the river batteries. Surrounded by a tidal moat, the brick fort guards Five Fathom Hole, the 18th-century deep-water port in the Savannah River. Inside you'll see exhibits that highlight the life of a soldier in the 19th century. Blacksmithing demonstrations, traditional music programs, and battle reenactments—including live cannon and musket firings—are among the attractions. ⊠ *1 Fort Jackson Rd., Thunderbolt* ☎ *912/232–3945* ⊕ *www.chsgeorgia. org/OFJ* ⊡ *$10*.

### Pin Point Heritage Museum

**HISTORY MUSEUM** | The culturally rich community surrounding this museum lived in relative isolation for nearly 100 years before modern development reached Skidaway Island. Residents of Pin Point are Gullah/Geechee descendants of first-generation freed slaves from Ossabaw Island. Founded in 1890 on the banks of Moon River, this fishing community has a deep connection to the water. Many residents once worked at the A. S. Varn & Son oyster and crab factory, which has been transformed into this interactive

The Pin Point Heritage Museum tells the history of the Gullah Geechee community descended from former enslaved people.

museum to honor the life, work, and history of the community. ✉ *9924 Pin Point Ave., Moon River District* ☎ *912/355–0064* ⊕ *chsgeorgia.org/phm* ⊘ *Closed Sun.–Wed.*

### Skidaway Island State Park

**STATE/PROVINCIAL PARK** | Winding trails through maritime forest and along the Intracoastal Waterway invite hikers, naturalists, and wildlife seekers into a 588-acre world of natural beauty and history. Pack a picnic to explore saw palmettos and the old moonshine still, or reserve a camping spot to marvel at the night sky over the Skidaway Narrows. RV hookups, group shelter, and cabins available. ✉ *Skidaway Island State Park, 52 Diamond Causeway, Moon River District* ☎ *912/598–2300* ⊕ *gastateparks.org/SkidawayIsland* 🎫 *Parking $5.*

### UGA Marine Education Center and Aquarium

**AQUARIUM** | **FAMILY** | On the grounds of the former Modena Plantation, the University of Georgia runs this aquarium with revolving exhibits about the state's coastal wildlife and ecosystems. Kids love the touch tanks featuring creatures from tidal creeks, the ocean beaches, and the open waters of the continental shelf up-close. The sea turtles are especially popular. Pack a picnic lunch and enjoy the fresh air after visiting the aquarium, and don't miss the nearby nature trails and ADA-approved salt marsh boardwalk. ✉ *30 Ocean Science Circle, Moon River District* ✛ *8 miles south of Savannah* ☎ *912/598–2496* ⊕ *gacoast.uga.edu/uga-aquarium* 🎫 *$7* ⊘ *Closed Sun.*

## Wormsloe State Historic Site

**MILITARY SIGHT** | In 1736, General James Oglethorpe gave 500 acres to Noble Jones, who was required to build a small fort to protect Savannah from an attack up the Skidaway River. Wormsloe is the only property in Georgia remaining in the hands of descendants of the original owners. Over the years, the land was used to produce cotton, as well as fruits, vegetables, and silk. In later years it served as a dairy farm and rice mill. Many of the 400 oaks planted along the 1½-mile entry in 1891 still stand proud today—you might recognize them from the movie *Forrest Gump*. Today, you can tour the tabby fort ruins, wander around the historic cemetery, and take in colonial plantation reenactments. ⊠ *7601 Skidaway Rd., Moon River District* ☎ *912/353–3023* ⊕ *www. gastateparks.org/wormsloe* ⊠ *$11.25.*

 **Restaurants**

## Driftaway Cafe

**$$ | SEAFOOD** | In the heart of the historic Sandfly neighborhood lies this "casual coastal" eatery where folks from the surrounding islands come to unwind. Choose from small dishes like firecracker shrimp tacos, turkey club wrap, or tuna tataki salad for lunch or dinner; larger entrées like grilled mahi mahi and pan-seared scallops are available after 5 pm. **Known for:** weekend brunch; extensive draft beer selection; live music on the weekends. ⑤ *Average main: $15* ⊠ *7400 Skidaway Rd., Suite D, Moon River District* ☎ *912/303-0999* ⊕ *driftawaycafe.com.*

## Loc's Chicken and Waffles

**$ | AMERICAN** | Tucked in a strip mall in Savannah's Sandfly neighborhood, this unassuming spot is an affordable and satisfying option for all-day breakfast and lunch. In addition to the juicy chicken and waffles, they also serve up an array of fluffy omelets and classic handhelds. **Known for:** golden Belgian waffles; sweet strawberry butter; crispy fried catfish filets. ⑤ *Average main: $10* ⊠ *7360 Skidaway Rd., Suite D1, Moon River District* ☎ *912/692–1114* ⊕ *locschickenandwaffles.com.*

## ★ Wiley's Championship BBQ

**$ | BARBECUE** | Tucked away in a strip mall on the way out to Tybee Island, this highlight of the local barbecue scene began with legendary pit master Wiley McCrary, who passed away in 2018. His recipes live on in the small space that's intimate and friendly; the staff is like long-lost family. **Known for:** slow-cooked barbecue staples; BBQ sampler feeds two people and lets you sample just about everything they make; Extra-Tingly Better Than Sex BBQ sauce. ⑤ *Average main: $14* ⊠ *4700 U.S. 80 E., Moon*

*River District* ☎ *912/201–3259* ⊕ *wileyschampionshipbbq.com* ♥ *Closed Sun.*

### ★ The Wyld Dock Bar

**$$ | SEAFOOD |** Enjoy elevated fish-shack food with yacht-rock vibes at this former marina where many of the patrons arrive by water. Order at the counter for a fresh catch of the day prepared perfectly; pair it with flavorful sides like crispy chicharrones and skillet okra. **Known for:** unparalleled marsh views; outdoor seating; local seafood. $ *Average main: $17* ✉ *2740 Livingston Ave., Moon River District* ☎ *912/692–1219* ⊕ *thewylddockbar.com* ♥ *Closed Mon.*

## 🍸 Nightlife

### BARS AND NIGHTCLUBS

### Molly McGuire's

**BARS |** Tucked away in a strip mall, this shady oasis offers indoor and outdoor bars, trivia nights, and live music on Fridays. A full menu and creative cocktail lineup make it a great place to gather with friends, watch the big game, or just while away the evening. ✉ *216 Johnny Mercer Blvd., #1, Wilmington Island* ☎ *912/898–0852* ⊕ *mollymcguiressavannah.com.*

### Tubby's Tank House

**BARS | FAMILY |** If you're looking to catch the big game or just enjoy a few beers on the covered deck, Tubby's is a fun spot to pass the time. By day, it's a seafood haven with a family vibe; after dark and during football season, the indoor and outdoor bars fill up with friendly locals and visitors cheering on their favorite pro and college teams. ✉ *2909 River Dr., Thunderbolt* ☎ *912/354–9040* ⊕ *www.tubbysthunderbolt.com.*

## 🛍 Shopping

### Cents and Sensibility

**ANTIQUES & COLLECTIBLES |** With a clever name inspired by a Jane Austen novel, this consignment shop vends fine furniture and unique antiques. Find an evolving assortment of mid-century movables, original artwork, and timeless tchotchkes in their showroom. ✉ *7360 Skidaway Rd., Suite E-4, Moon River District* ☎ *912/897–4961* ⊕ *www.centssensibility.com.*

### Savannah Bee Co. Showroom and Bee Garden

**SPECIALTY STORE |** The home base of this sweet international brand is always buzzing. All of Savannah Bee Company's honey varietals, body care products, gifts, and more are available in this spacious

1733 WORMSLO

showroom, and the enclosed indoor hive makes it possible to see the busy bees at work. Guided tours include donning a beekeeper's hat and veil and venturing out to the garden for an immersive experience. The whole family can sample the latest honey of the season, and those 21 and over can catch a "buzz" with mead tastings. ⊠ *211 Johnny Mercer Blvd., Wilmington Island* ☎ *912/629–0908* ⊕ *savannahbee.com.*

# 🏃 Activities

## BOATING AND FISHING

### Miss Judy Charters

**FISHING** | The legendary Captain Judy Helmey has headed up her charter fishing company for decades, and nobody knows the hidden honey holes better (locals swear by her weekly fishing report). Her 10-boat fleet offers packages ranging from 3-hour sightseeing tours to 14-hour deep-sea fishing expeditions, with plenty of delightful tales included. Expect to catch redfish, trout, and flounder in close waters and mackerel and barracuda on the open sea. ⊠ *124 Palmetto Dr., Wilmington Island* ☎ *912/897–4921* ⊕ *missjudycharters.com* 🖃 *From $350 for 3 hours of inshore fishing; from $1,000 for 4 hours of offshore fishing.*

### Moon River Kayak Tours

**KAYAKING** | Setting out from either Wilmington or Skidaway islands, Moon River Kayak offers a different experience than many of the tours originating on Tybee Island. Paddling the marshes of Skidaway Narrows and Johnny Mercer's Moon River gives you a more inland perspective, rich with sightings of spectacular birds like ospreys and eagles. Be sure to bring your binoculars. ⊠ *Hogan's Marina, 36 Wilmington Island Rd., Wilmington Island* ☎ *912/898–1800* ⊕ *bullriver.com* 🖃 *From $55.*

### ★ Savannah Canoe and Kayak

**KAYAKING** | Leading you through inlets and tidal creeks, Savannah Canoe and Kayak employs highly skilled guides that provide expert instruction for newbies and challenges for seasoned paddlers. You'll also learn about the history of these historic waterways and visit lesser-known spots, including hidden creeks and Little Tybee. Half-day tours start at $75 for three hours. ⊠ *414 Bonaventure Rd., Thunderbolt* ☎ *912/341–9502* ⊕ *savannahcanoeandkayak.com* 🖃 *From $75.*

# TYBEE ISLAND

Updated by
Summer Bozeman

| ◎ Sights | 🍴 Restaurants | 🛏 Hotels | 🛍 Shopping | 🍸 Nightlife |
|---|---|---|---|---|
| ★★★★☆ | ★★★★☆ | ★★★☆☆ | ★★★★☆ | ★★★★☆ |

# NEIGHBORHOOD SNAPSHOT

## TOP EXPERIENCES

■ **Water adventures:** The beautiful golden marshes surrounding provide the perfect setting for kayaking and stand-up paddleboarding.

■ **Dolphin cruises:** Various tour companies offer short trips to see dolphins frolicking and most guarantee a close-up sighting.

■ **Georgia's tallest lighthouse:** The 178 steps to the top of the Tybee Island Light Station lead you to one of the best views in the Lowcountry.

■ **Local seafood:** Georgia is known for its sweet, wild Georgia shrimp, and restaurants here serve it in abundance.

■ **Toast the sunset:** While most of Tybee's beaches face the east, you can settle in on a patio or porch facing the marsh to the west and sip as the sun goes down.

■ **Meet the wildlife:** The Tybee Island Marine Science Center offers the opportunity to greet protected loggerhead sea turtles, which nest on the beach in the summertime.

## GETTING HERE

Tybee Island is a little less than 30 miles from the airport by car; traffic through downtown Savannah will make it about a 45-minute trip. If you're coming by car, Savannah and Tybee Island are accessible via Interstates 95 and 16. Be aware that all parking on Tybee is metered seven days a week, but meters are electronic and accept credit/debit cards. If you download the convenient app Park TYB, it will alert you when your meter is about to expire and you can re-up right from your phone.

## QUICK BITES

■ **Tybean Coffee Bar.** Enjoy breakfast burritos, lattes, teas, and a Numi matcha at this beachy cottage. ⊠ *1213 US Hwy 80 E, Tybee Island* ⊕ *tybeancoffeebar.com.*

■ **The Sugar Shack.** A Tybee tradition since 1971, it offers cones, ice cream sandwiches, coffees, candies, and more. ⊠ *301 1st St., Tybee Island* ⊕ *tybeesugarshack.com.*

The farthest barrier island off of Savannah's coast, Tybee Island is a quirky beach town full of art and eclectic energy. The Euchee people were the first to live here and named the island after their word for "salt," but these days, the island is chock-full of seafood restaurants, independent motels, and souvenir shops—most of which sprang up during the 1950s and haven't changed much since.

Swimsuits and flip-flops are acceptable attire anywhere on the island. Tybee is hyper-local with almost no chain businesses and has a vibe like it's the beach town of your childhood that time forgot. Fun-loving locals still host big annual parties like fall's Pirate Festival and spring's Beach Bum Parade. February's Tybee Run Fest—the modern iteration of the more than 20-year-old Tybee Marathon—brings over 1,000 runners to the iconic pier and pavilion. Tybee Island's entire expanse of taupe sand is divided into three public beach stretches: North Beach, the Pier and Pavilion, and the South End. Beach activities abound, including swimming, boating, fishing, sea kayaking, and parasailing. Newer water sports have gained popularity, including kiteboarding and stand-up paddleboarding. Don't leave town without taking a dolphin tour, an hour-long boat ride just off the coast to see families of dolphins feeding and frolicking near the jetties and shrimp boats. They're so used to the boats that they get very close, thrilling the kids and making for great photos and video to share with friends.

## ◉ Sights

### Tybee Island Light Station and Museum
**LIGHTHOUSE | FAMILY |** Considered one of North America's most beautifully renovated lighthouses, the Tybee Light Station has been guiding Savannah River mariners since 1736. It's not the first lighthouse built on this site; the original was constructed on orders of General James Oglethorpe in 1732. You can walk up 178 steps for amazing views at the top. The lightkeeper's cottage houses a small theater showing a video about the lighthouse. The nearby museum is in a gun battery constructed for the

Spanish-American War. ⊠ *30 Meddin Dr., Tybee Island* ☎ *912/786–5801* ⊕ *www.tybeelighthouse.org* ⊠ *$10* ۞ *Closed Tues.*

★ **Tybee Island Marine Science Center**
**SCIENCE MUSEUM | FAMILY |** Don't miss the Tybee Island Marine Science Center's interesting exhibit on Coastal Georgia, which houses local wildlife ranging from Ogeechee corn snakes to American alligators. Schedule one of two guided walks along the beach and marshes if you're interested in the flora and fauna of the Lowcountry. There is also a "Turtle Talk," which consists of a classroom discussion and hands-on workshop. ■TIP➔ **Arrive early, as parking near the center can be competitive in the busier months.** ⊠ *37 Meddin Dr., Tybee Island* ☎ *912/786–5917* ⊕ *www. tybeemarinescience.org* ⊠ *$10* ۞ *Closed Mon.–Tues.*

**Tybee Island Pier and Pavilion**
**MARINA/PIER |** This is Tybee's "grand strand," the center of the summer beach action. Anchored by a 700-foot pier that is sometimes host to summer concerts, this stretch of shoreline is your best bet for people-watching and beach activities. Just off the sand at the bustling intersection of Tybrisa Street and Butler Avenue, a cluster of watering holes, souvenir shops, bike shacks, and oyster bars makes up Tybee's main business district. There are public restrooms at the Pier and at 15th and Tybrisa Streets. The pier is popular for fishing and is also the gathering place for fireworks displays. ■TIP➔ **There's metered street parking as well as two good-sized lots. Both fill up fast during the high season, so arrive early.** ⊠ *Tybrisa St. at Butler Ave., Tybee Island* ☎ *912/652–6780.*

## 🏖 Beaches

**North Beach**
**BEACH |** Tybee Island's North Beach is an all-in-one destination for beachgoers of every age. Located at the mouth of the Savannah River, the scene is generally low-key and is a great vantage point for viewing the cargo ships making their way to the Port of Savannah. A large, metered parking lot gives you convenient access to the beach, Fort Screven, and the adjacent Tybee Island Lighthouse and Museum, a 178-step lighthouse with great views of the surrounding area. The North Beach Grill, located in the parking lot, is perfect for an ice-cold beverage or bite to eat. To get here from Highway 80, turn left on Campbell Street and follow the signs to the Tybee Island Lighthouse. ■TIP➔ **The local police are notorious for parking tickets, so make sure not to let your meter run over.** **Amenities:** food and drink; lifeguard; parking (fee); toilets. **Best for:** solitude; sunrise; swimming; walking. ⊠ *Meddin Dr. at Gulick St., north of 1st St., Tybee Island.*

You'll learn all about coastal wildlife, including alligators, at the Tybee Island Marine Science Center.

### South Beach

**BEACH** | If your idea of a good beach day involves empty stretches of sand, unobstructed views, plenty of privacy, and the sound of crashing waves, then you should test the waters at the south end. As its name suggests, the south end is located at the southern tip of the island where Tybee's Back River meets the Atlantic Ocean. ⚠ **Riptides and strong currents are prevalent here, so use extreme caution when swimming and obey all signage.**

At low tide, the waters recede to expose a stunning system of sandbars that are great for shelling and spotting sea life. Check the tides to make sure you don't get stranded on the sandbars. This is one of Tybee's prettiest beaches, and is worshipped by locals for its seclusion. There are no restaurants in the immediate vicinity, so it's a good idea to bring a cooler packed with snacks and beverages. Parking is tough—just two very small metered lots. In high season, arrive on the early or the late side, when crowds are thinner. **Amenities:** parking (fee). **Best for:** sea kayaking; sunset; walking; windsurfing. ⊠ *Butler Ave., at 19th St., Tybee Island.*

## 🍴 Restaurants

### A-J's Dockside

**$$** | **SEAFOOD** | This island bar and grill resembles a fish camp that was expanded time and time again to accommodate its growing clientele. Colorful and laid-back, the ambience is characteristic

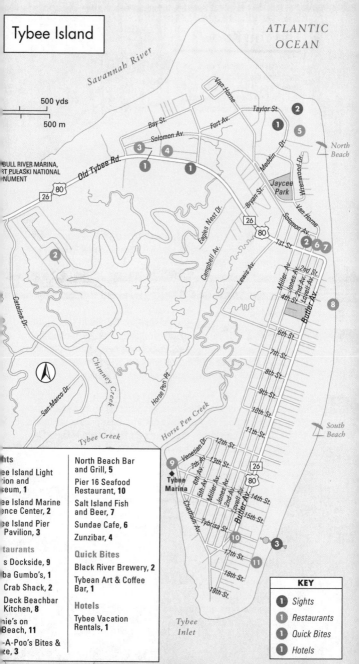

# Tybee Island

*ATLANTIC OCEAN*

*Savannah River*

500 yds
500 m

BULL RIVER MARINA,
FORT PULASKI NATIONAL
MONUMENT

Taylor St.

Van Horne

Fort Av.

Bay St.

Solomon Av.

Old Tybee Rd.

Meddin Dr.

North
Beach

Jaycee
Park

Bryan St.

Eagles Nest Dr.

Campbell Av.

Solomon Av.

1st St.

Lewis Av.

Miller Av.
Jones Av.
2nd St.
2nd Av.
Lovell Av.
Butler Av.

4th St.

5th St.

7th St.

8th St.

9th St.

10th St.

Chimney Creek

Horse Pen Pt.

San Marco Dr.

Catalina Dr.

Tybee Creek

Horse Pen Creek

11th St.

12th St.

Venetian Dr.

7th Av.
6th Av.
Miller Av.
Jones Av.
Lovell Av.
2nd Av.
Butler Av.

13th St.

14th St.

15th St.

Tybrisa Av.

Chatham Av.

17th St.

18th St.

19th St.

South
Beach

Tybee
Marina

Tybee
Inlet

**Sights**

Tybee Island Light
Station and
Museum, **1**

Tybee Island Marine
Science Center, **2**

Tybee Island Pier
and Pavilion, **3**

**Restaurants**

... s Dockside, **9**

...ba Gumbo's, **1**

... Crab Shack, **2**

... Deck Beachbar
... Kitchen, **8**

...nie's on
...Beach, **11**

...-A-Poo's Bites &
...ze, **3**

North Beach Bar
and Grill, **5**

Pier 16 Seafood
Restaurant, **10**

Salt Island Fish
and Beer, **7**

Sundae Cafe, **6**

Zunzibar, **4**

**Quick Bites**

Black River Brewery, **2**

Tybean Art & Coffee
Bar, **1**

**Hotels**

Tybee Vacation
Rentals, **1**

| KEY | |
|---|---|
| **1** | Sights |
| **1** | Restaurants |
| **1** | Quick Bites |
| **1** | Hotels |

## Did You Know?

Tybee Island, a popular vacation spot since the 1800s, is home to three miles of beaches. The 2010 film *The Last Song*, starring Miley Cyrus and Liam Hemsworth, was filmed here.

You can have a Lowcountry boil with shrimp, corn, and smoked sausage at The Crab Shack, one of Tybee's most popular restaurants.

of Tybee Island itself, which perhaps explains why it is a favorite among locals, and the food, mostly fresh seafood, is simple and delicious. **Known for:** spacious patio overlooking the marsh; great spot to watch the sunset; live entertainment Friday–Sunday. $ *Average main: $17* ⊠ *1315 Chatham Ave., Tybee Island* ☎ *912/786–5434* ⊕ *ajsdocksidetybee.com.*

### Bubba Gumbo's
$ | **SEAFOOD | FAMILY** | Watch boats pass and the sun set over Lazaretto Creek while enjoying fried oysters, steamed shrimp, hush puppies, and Lowcountry boil. Fitting right in to Tybee's laid-back beach bum vibe, this seafood shack welcomes boaters, local surfers, and visitors alike inside an unfussy dining room or on the ample porch. **Known for:** scenic views; casual atmosphere; fresh-caught seafood. $ *Average main: $10* ⊠ *1 Old Tybee Rd., Tybee Island* ☎ *912/786–4445* ⊕ *www.tybeebubbags.com* ☾ *No lunch Sun.–Thurs.*

### The Crab Shack
$$ | **SEAFOOD | FAMILY** | "Where the elite eat in their bare feet" is the motto of this laid-back eatery tucked away on a side street just over the bridge to Tybee Island. The beer is cold, the vibe is relaxed, and items like the Lowcountry boil—a huge plate of shrimp, corn on the cob, and smoked sausage—are delicious. **Known for:** scenic views; family-friendly environment; resident felines and alligators. $ *Average main: $15* ⊠ *40 Estill Hammock Rd., Tybee Island* ☎ *912/786–9857* ⊕ *www.thecrabshack.com.*

### The Deck Beachbar and Kitchen

**$$ | SEAFOOD |** By Anthony Debreceny, the restaurateur behind downtown Savannah's The Collins Quarter and The Fitzroy, this is the only restaurant on Tybee Island where you can walk straight from your table onto the sand. The cuisine is casual and approach-able with elevated takes on fish tacos, a pulled-pork banh mi, and more, served alongside refreshing craft cocktails and local beer offerings. **Known for:** seafood staples like peel-and-eat shrimp and fresh oysters; great location as the only restaurant directly on the beach; free covered parking while dining in. $ *Average main: $18* ✉ *Beachside Colony, 404 Butler Ave., Tybee Island* ☎ *912/328–5397* ⊕ *www.thedecktybee.com* ☽ *Closed Tues. and Wed.; closed from Nov.–Feb.*

### Fannie's on the Beach

**$ | SEAFOOD |** A great place to grab a bite after a long day pow-er-lounging on the beach, this beachside eatery is a favorite with locals and visitors alike. The menu lists simple favorites like sand-wiches, burgers, and fried seafood, but all are prepared exceed-ingly well. **Known for:** great views of the ocean from the third-story deck; live music Wednesday to Saturday; creative pizzas. $ *Average main: $13* ✉ *1613 Strand Ave., Tybee Island* ☎ *912/786–6109* ⊕ *www.fanniesonthebeach.com* ☽ *Closed Tues.*

### ★ Huc-A-Poo's Bites & Booze

**$$ | AMERICAN | FAMILY |** Drink and eat like the locals do at this eccentric, come-as-you-are spot. With walls covered in vintage signs, records, and various trash and treasure, guests enjoy a great breeze on a large porch or in the screened-in restaurant as they tuck into slices or 18-inch stone-baked pies loaded with tan-talizing ingredients and unique combinations; the beer is ice-cold and best enjoyed in pitchers, and the prices can't be beat. **Known for:** authentic island relaxation; live music on the weekends; lively game nights during college football season. $ *Average main: $15* ✉ *1213 E. Hwy. 80, Tybee Island* ☎ *912/786–5900* ⊕ *www. hucapoos.com.*

### North Beach Bar and Grill

**$ | SEAFOOD | FAMILY |** Between the historic Tybee Island Lighthouse and North Beach lies one of the island's most colorful, Caribbe-an-inspired eateries. The menus feature local and sustainable seafood, including delectable crab cakes and the fresh citrus shrimp salad, along with lots of family-friendly options. **Known for:** laid-back patio seating; seafood fritters; beachside convenience. $ *Average main: $13* ✉ *33 Meddin Dr., Tybee Island* ☎ *912/786–4442* ⊕ *www.northbeachbarandgrill.net* ☽ *Closed Tues.*

### Pier 16 Seafood Restaurant

**$$$ | AMERICAN |** With two tiers of outdoor dining decks, Pier 16 makes the most of Tybee's island sunshine. Cuisine is slightly elevated above standard beachside fare, but still includes staples like fish or shrimp tacos, crab-stuffed mushrooms, and various oyster preparations. **Known for:** fried and steamed seafood as well as regional favorite dishes; prime location near the head of Tybrisa Street; wine selection. $ *Average main: $28 ⊠ 1601 Inlet Ave., Tybee Island ☎ 912/472–4326 ⊕ www.pier16tybeeisland.com.*

### Salt Island Fish and Beer

**$$ | SEAFOOD | FAMILY |** This casual eatery specializes in fresh takes on typical beach food, like smoked fish dip made with the local catch, a mahi mahi banh mi, shrimp bruschetta, and blue crab poutine. You can still get your favorites, though, as the innovative menu also includes standards like beer-battered flounder and fisherman's stew served over jasmine rice. **Known for:** weekday happy-hour specials; unique sides; fresh, eclectic menu. $ *Average main: $20 ⊠ 101 Lovell Ave., Tybee Island ☎ 912/499–4279 ⊕ www.saltislandfb.com ⊙ Closed Tues.*

### ★ Sundae Cafe

**$$ | AMERICAN |** Tucked into an unassuming strip mall off the main drag on Tybee Island, this gourmet restaurant is a diamond in the rough. Locals and tourists alike enjoy the diverse menu, fresh seafood, and brilliant food combinations—don't miss the unique seafood "cheesecake" starter, consisting of shrimp and crabmeat over greens with a hint of Gouda. **Known for:** generous portions at reasonable prices; tucked-away location; reservations recommended. $ *Average main: $19 ⊠ 304 1st St., Tybee Island ☎ 912/786–7694 ⊕ www.sundaecafe.com ⊙ Closed Sun.*

### Zunzibar

**$$ | FUSION |** Evolved from the Historic District express sandwich shop, Zunzibar is a rainbow-colored respite from anything that brings you down. It's bright and open air, and features a variety of cocktails and refreshing beverages alongside bar bites like Peri-Peri cheese dip and mustafa curry hot wings that fit perfectly alongside the original dishes and sandwiches that brought them to the national stage. **Known for:** unique flavors; cashless payment; island breezes. $ *Average main: $16 ⊠ 1115 Hwy 80 E., Tybee Island ☎ 912/472–4902 ⊕ www.zunzibar.com.*

## A Side of Tybee Almost Gone 🛏

You may hear some wild stories about Tybee Island: that it is a veritable Margaritaville, a kitschy resort area right out of the 1950s, or a hideout for eccentric beach bums. All the rumors are true, but that doesn't mean the island hasn't changed some over the years. If you want to keep in the traditional Tybee vibe, check out **Mermaid Cottages** (⊕ mermaidcottages. com), which rents a variety of funky, colorful bungalows—with names like the Crabby Pirate and Cantaloupe Cottage. They are a trip back to nostalgic beach communities of old and a fun way to experience the pleasures of life on the island.

## ☕ Coffee and Quick Bites

### Back River Brewery

**$$ | AMERICAN |** Tybee Island's only microbrewery features an array of craft beers from dark lager to fruity and floral sours with characteristically Tybee-sounding names, like "Move Beach, Get Out the Whale Juicy IPA" and "Hurricane Season Sour." The brewery also provides fresh and tasty snacks served alongside their frosty mugs, including dishes like a watermelon and cantaloupe salad, seasonal veggie wraps, and an Auspicious Bakery–made pretzel served with Back River Brewery beer cheese. The space is small but cozy, and still provides enough room for a live music setup, performed on Fridays and Saturdays. **Known for:** small plates; approachable beer varieties; convenient location. ⑤ *Average main: $15* ⊠ *402 1st St., Upper, Tybee Island* ☎ *912/472–4660* ⊕ *www. backriverbrewery.com.*

### Tybean Art & Coffee Bar

**$ | CAFÉ |** This funky mini-gallery and coffee shop has an extensive menu of espresso drinks, frappes, smoothies, matchas, and teas alongside scones, muffins, and other grab-and-go baked goods. Peruse the unique art pieces and gifts while the barista crafts your drink, then enjoy it outside on the deck. **Known for:** cheerful staff; located near numerous small boutiques and galleries; funky and artistic atmosphere. ⑤ *Average main: $9* ⊠ *1213 Old U.S. Hwy. 80, Tybee Island* ☎ *912/224–5227* ⊕ *www.tybeanartandcoffeebar. com.*

## 🛏 Hotels

**Tybee Vacation Rentals**

**$ | HOUSE |** If renting a five-star beach house, a pastel island cottage, or a waterfront condo in a complex with a pool and tennis courts is your coastal-Georgia dream stay, check out Tybee Vacation Rentals. **Pros:** a variety of accommodations available; perfect for self-catering; pool and tennis courts in complex. **Cons:** two-night minimum; conveniences can vary depending on location of property; properties fill up fast. $ *Rooms from: $129* ✉ *1010 Hwy. 80 E., Tybee Island* ☎ *912/786–5853, 855/651–1840* ⊕ *www. tybeevacationrentals.com* 🛏 *250+ houses* ⦿ *No Meals.*

## 🎭 Performing Arts

### FESTIVALS AND SPECIAL EVENTS

**Tybee Island Pirate Fest**

**FESTIVALS | FAMILY |** Swashbucklers and wenches descend on Tybee Island in early October for the Pirate Fest. Don your best pirate-theme costumes for the Buccaneer Ball at the Crab Shack to kick off the weekend's festivities. Saturday is the popular Pirate Victory Parade, where Butler Avenue becomes a sea of ships filled with buccaneers tossing beads and booty. Venture over to the Thieves' Market, where vendors from across the country peddle their pirate wares and arts and crafts. Fun for the whole family, the festival includes magicians, puppet shows, and storytellers. Live entertainment rounds out the experience with concert headliners like Vince Neil and Quiet Riot. ✉ *Strand Ave., between Tybrisia St. and 17th Pl., Savannah* ⊕ *tybeepiratefest.com.*

## 🏃 Activities

### BIKING

**Tim's Bike, Beach & Disc Golf**

**BIKING |** Filled with ocean-view trails, Tybee Island offers a bike-friendly environment and rentals at half the cost of down-town. Tim's Beach Gear rents bikes for adults and kids, as well as pull-behind carriers and jogging strollers. The shop offers free delivery and pickup on the island. Daily rates are $12 and include helmets and cup holders. And talk about one-stop shopping: umbrellas, beach chairs, towels, and games like disc golf, bocce ball, and horseshoes are also available. ✉ *1101 U.S. Hwy. 80, Tybee Island* ☎ *912/786–8467* ⊕ *www.timsbeachgear.com.*

Tybee residents are tied to the water; almost every house along Tybee Creek has a wooden dock.

## BOATING AND FISHING

### Captain Derek's Dolphin Adventure Tours

**BOAT TOURS** | Known as a habitat for bottlenose dolphins, Tybee Island is a place for a dolphin-sighting cruise. Captain Derek's daytime cruises offer beautiful views of the marshes and beach as well as landmarks like the Cockspur Island Lighthouse, and dolphins will often playfully leap through the boats so closely you could almost reach out and touch them (but please don't). Sunset cruises provide an even more picturesque view of the landscape and shoreline, and private charters are also available. Seeing dolphins isn't absolutely guaranteed but it's rare not to, and if you don't see any on your tour, Captain Derek's offers a free ticket to try again. ⊠ *3 Old Hwy. 80, Tybee Island* ☎ *912/658–2322* ⊕ *tybeedolphinadventure.com* ✉ *From $28.*

### Sea Kayak Georgia

**KAYAKING** | Owned by professional paddlers and instructors Marsha Henson and Ronnie Kemp, Sea Kayak Georgia provides gear, tours, and courses for beginners and advanced kayakers alike, not to mention stand-up paddleboard rentals and the unique experience of teacher-led stand-up paddleboard yoga. Seasoned guides and naturalists lead half-day salt-marsh paddle tours. ⊠ *1102 U.S. Hwy. 80, Tybee Island* ☎ *912/786–8732* ⊕ *www.seakayakgeorgia. com* ✉ *Tours from $50.*

### ★ Sundial Charters

**BOAT TOURS** | Captain Rene Heidt and her team of skippers know the backwaters and secret sandbars of Tybee Island and Little Tybee like the natives they are. If dancing with dolphins, taking in glorious sunsets, and searching for giant sharks' teeth is on your agenda, booking an outing with Sundial is a sure bet. ⊠ *1615 Chatham Ave, Savannah* ☎ *912/786–9470* ⊕ *www.sundialcharters. com* ✉ *Starting at $240 for a three-hour tour.*

### Tybee Jet Ski & Watersports

**JET SKIING** | For those who enjoy more fast-paced activities, little compares to the rush of jet skiing on the island waterways or riding the swells of the beach. Tybee Jet Ski & Watersports rents Jet Skis/waverunners, and their shop offers everything you need for sea kayaking excursions. Ninety-minute guided tours of the coastal marshes and tidal streams, Little Tybee Island, or the historic Cockspur Island Lighthouse can also be arranged. ⊠ *1 Old Hwy. 80, Tybee Island* ☎ *912/707–8062* ⊕ *tybeejetski.com* ✉ *Jet Ski rentals from $99, kayak rentals from $35 for a half-day, kayak tours from $38.*

## WATER SPORTS

### East Coast Paddleboarding

**WATER SPORTS** | With its tidal creeks and small waves, Tybee Island is the perfect place to learn stand-up paddleboarding. Beginners can take a two-hour flat-water introductory class, or learn the art of paddle surfing in 90 minutes. Private and group classes are also available, as are paddleboard rentals. Tours of Little Tybee and Horsepen Creek include a lesson and gear and give paddlers the opportunity to see coastal wildlife. ⊠ *Inlet Ave., Tybee Island* ☎ *912/484–3200* ⊕ *eastcoastpaddleboarding.com* ✉ *Classes from $100.*

# SOUTHSIDE, GATEWAY, AND GREATER SAVANNAH

Updated by
Chantel Britton

⊙ Sights    🍴 Restaurants    🛏 Hotels    🛍 Shopping    🍸 Nightlife

★★★★★    ★★★☆☆    ★★★☆☆    ★★☆☆☆    ★★☆☆☆

# NEIGHBORHOOD SNAPSHOT

## TOP EXPERIENCES

■ **Eat on the water:** Every meal at Love's Seafood and Steaks comes with a view of the Ogeechee River.

■ **Paddle among the cypress trees:** Ogeechee Riverkeeper leads stunning canoe and kayak trips.

■ **Stop and smell the roses:** There's always something blooming at the Coastal Georgia Botanical Gardens.

■ **Walk along an ancient waterway:** The trails of the historic Savannah-Ogeechee Barge Canal date back to the 1820s.

■ **Play a round of golf:** Tee up at the city-owned Bacon Park Golf Course or one of the nearby private clubs.

■ **Sit in a B-17 Bomber:** The Mighty Eighth Museum boasts a fully restored WWII fighter plane—except for the engine, of course.

## GETTING HERE

The neighborhoods of Southside Savannah—including Georgetown, Vernonburg, and Windsor Forest—are reached by car using the Truman Parkway or following Abercorn Street until it becomes GA-204. The area where GA-204 meets I–95 is known as the Gateway. Public transit runs to here, but check schedules.

## PLANNING YOUR TIME

These areas offer plentiful outdoor recreation in the rivers and marshes but not much in the way of shopping or nightlife. Plan your visit for daylight hours, and definitely bring bug spray!

## QUICK BITES

■ **Flacos House.** Super fresh tacos, burritos, and other Mexican favorites are served in to-go containers, but you can still eat inside. ⊠ 7 *Fort Argyle Rd., Georgetown.*

■ **Krispy Kreme.** If you've never had a hot glazed donut from this famous Southern chain, you must treat yourself. ⊠ 11506 *Abercorn St., Southside.*

■ **Spanky's Southside.** This is the place to satisfy a hankering for the original crispy chicken fingers without going downtown. ⊠ 308 *Mall Way, Southside.*

Miles away from the downtown crowds, Savannah's Southside offers natural beauty and off-the-beaten-path sights. You'll also find the city's suburban shopping malls and great deals on chain hotel and motel rooms where Interstate 95 meets GA Highway 204, known as the Gateway.

The tannin-rich Ogeechee, Little Ogeechee and Vernonburg Rivers flow through these neighborhoods, offering a bevy of water-related opportunities like kayaking, meals with a view, and one of the nicest RV parks around. The southside is also the home of Georgia Southern University's Savannah campus. The area is close to Savannah/Hilton Head Airport and about 20 minutes from downtown.

## ◉ Sights

### Coastal Georgia Botanical Gardens
**GARDEN | FAMILY** | In 1890, Mrs. Herman B. Miller planted three clumps of Japanese timber bamboo near her farmhouse 15 miles south of Savannah. As the bamboo took to the warm Southern climate, it spread to what now stands today at the Bamboo Farms at the Coastal Georgia Botanical Gardens. The gardens, deeded to the University of Georgia in 1983 for research and cultivation, now boast a 4-acre bamboo maze, a children's garden, and stunning seasonal formal and shade gardens including beds of iris and daffodil bulbs and the wonderful camellia trail in late winter/early spring. The annual Christmas lights event glimmers with fun for the whole family. ⊠ *2 Canebrake Rd., Savannah* ☎ *912/921–5460* ⊕ *coastalbg.uga.edu* ⊡ *$5* ⊙ *Closed Mon.*

### Fort McAllister
**MILITARY SIGHT** | You can find this Civil War–era fort overlooking the Ogeechee River just south of Savannah in the quiet, quaint town of Richmond Hill. Among the best examples of a restored Confederate fortification, this stronghold includes a museum, signal tower, and mortar battery, among others. Campsites and cottages are available for overnight stays, and you can rent a canoe or a kayak for a tranquil time on the water. ⊠ *3894 Fort McAllister Rd., Southside* ☎ *912/727–2339* ⊕ *gastateparks.org/FortMcAllister* ⊡ *$9.75.*

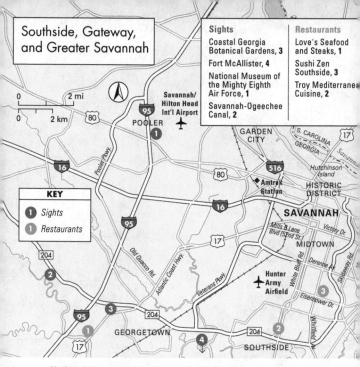

Southside, Gateway,
and Greater Savannah

| Sights | Restaurants |
|---|---|
| Coastal Georgia Botanical Gardens, **3** | Love's Seafood and Steaks, **1** |
| Fort McAllister, **4** | Sushi Zen Southside, **3** |
| National Museum of the Mighty Eighth Air Force, **1** | Troy Mediterranean Cuisine, **2** |
| Savannah-Ogeechee Canal, **2** | |

KEY

**1** Sights

**1** Restaurants

## National Museum of the Mighty Eighth Air Force

**MILITARY SIGHT** | Members of the "Greatest Generation" formed the famous World War II squadron called the Mighty Eighth in Savannah in 1942. Within a month, they answered the call to arms and shipped out to the United Kingdom as part of the Allied Forces. Flying in Royal Air Force planes, the Mighty Eighth was the largest Army Air Force unit during World War II and played a major role in defeating the Nazis. Exhibits at this museum begin with the prelude to World War II and the rise of Adolf Hitler, and continue through Desert Storm. You can see vintage aircraft, fly a simulated bombing mission with a B-17 crew, test your skills as a waist gunner, and view interviews with courageous World War II vets. The museum also has three theaters, a chapel, an art gallery, and a 7,000-volume library. ⊠ *175 Bourne Ave., Pooler* ☎ *912/748–8888* ⊕ *mightyeighth.org* ⊠ *$12* ⊗ *Closed Mon.*

## Savannah-Ogeechee Canal

**TRAIL** | In 1824, officials chartered a project to use African American and Irish laborers to dig a 16-mile canal between the Savannah and Ogeechee rivers—by hand. Although it was once used to float lumber and other commodities via a series of tidal locks, only the small portion between Highway 204 and the Ogeechee River remains open to the public. Take the tow path toward the river,

Only a small portion of Savannah-Ogeechee Canal, which was dug by hand in 1824, is still open to the public.

and you might see hawks, owls, snakes, and other wildlife; just don't touch the crumbling bricks. Be sure to stop into the on-site museum to chat with Connie the Canoe Lady. If the museum is closed, you can leave the admission fee in the honor box; better yet, PayPal a donation to ✉ *socsconnection@gmail.com.* ✉ *681 Fort Argyle Rd., Southside* ☎ *912/748–8068* ⊕ *www.savanna-hogeecheecanal.org* ⌕ *$5* ⊙ *Museum closed Mon. and Tues.*

## 🍴 Restaurants

### Love's Seafood and Steaks

**$$$** | **SEAFOOD** | **FAMILY** | Four generations own and operate this charming, family-owned coastal eatery located on the banks of the bucolic Ogeechee River. Suitable for a lunchtime meal or a special occasion dinner, Love's serves up perfectly prepared regional dishes like Lowcountry boil, fried green tomatoes, and its famous bone-in catfish. **Known for:** Lowcountry boil; spectacular sunsets; ability to accomodate large groups. ⑤ *Average main: $26* ✉ *6817 Chief of Love Rd., Southside* ☎ *912/925–3616* ⊕ *lovessea-food.com* ⊙ *Closed Mon.–Wed.*

### Sushi Zen Southside

**$$** | **JAPANESE** | If you've had your fill of Southern cuisine, head to this quality spot in a strip mall for award-winning sushi, daily specialty rolls, and grilled meat and noodle dishes. The longtime fixture has been around since 1998. **Known for:** cooked food as good as the sushi; intimate space; creative ingredient combinations.

## International Eats

Savannah's food offerings run deeper than just traditional Southern cooking. If it's the islands you crave, head to the Southside of Savannah for a meal at **Sweet Spice** (⌧ 5515 Waters Ave., Southside ☎ 912/335–8146); they serve up traditional favorites like jerk chicken and curried goat.

**La Canasta Panaderia** (⌧ 1545 E. Montgomery Crossroad., Southside ☎ 912/352–4800) is the place for authentic Mexican pastries, carne asada, and big plates of beans and rice. The flan is out of this world!

For Korean flavors, make your way to **Kim Chi II** (⌧ 149 E. Montgomery Cross Rd., Southside ☎ 912/227–2025). Try the fiery *kimchi banchan* or the bubbling-hot pork-and-tofu stew.

$ *Average main: $17* ⌧ *1100 Eisenhower Dr., #4B, Southside* ☎ *912/303–0141* ⊕ *sushizensav.com* ⊘ *Closed Sun. No lunch Sat. and Mon.*

### Troy Mediterranean Cuisine

**$$ | GREEK |** Don't let the strip mall location fool you; this spacious restaurant offers authentic Greek and Italian specialties with romantic ambience. The pita bread is soft and pillowy, perfect for the creamy hummus and baba ganoush, and entrées like falafel platters and the merlot-braised lamb shank come in hearty, generous portions. **Known for:** lemon-chicken soup; gyro platter; lamb chops. $ *Average main: $20* ⌧ *10510 Abercorn St, Suite D., Southside* ☎ *912/921–5117* ⊕ *troymediterraneancuisine.com.*

## 🛍 Shopping

### FOOD

### ★ Byrd Cookie Company

**FOOD |** Founded in 1924, this internationally renowned family-owned and -operated gourmet food company specializes in benne (sesame seed) wafers, trademark Savannah cookies (notably key lime), and other house-made sweets and crackers, all sold in decorative tins. Although you'll find locations around the city, the Waters Avenue flagship Byrd's Famous Cookies store sells picture tins of Savannah and the entire line of Byrd's gourmet foodstuffs, including condiments and dressings. Free cookie and cracker samples come with every visit. ⌧ *6710 Waters Ave., Southside* ☎ *912/355–1716* ⊕ *byrdcookiecompany.com.*

## MARKETS

### Keller's Flea Market

**MARKET** | Pickers and bargain hunters descend upon Keller's every weekend to peruse the offerings of over 400 vendors, who proffer kitschy souvenirs, antiques, collectibles, cars, clothing, fresh produce, sweet treats and everything in between. Keep an eye out for the 15-foot-tall black-and-white cow statue out front—you can't miss it. ⊠ *5901 Ogeechee Rd., Southside* ☎ *912/927–4848* ⊕ *kellersfleamarket.com* ☉ *Closed weekdays.*

## 🏃 Activities

### CAMPING

#### Red Gate Campground and RV Resort

**$ | PERMANENT CAMP** | RV travelers enjoy a glorious "glamping" experience at this luxurious campground minutes outside the city. **Pros:** beautiful environment; friendly community; spacious sites. **Cons:** outside the city; active train tracks nearby Red Gate; limited bathrooms and showers. ⑤ *Rooms from: $55* ⊠ *136 Red Gate Farms Trail, Southside* ☎ *912/272–8028* ⊕ *redgatecampground. com* 🛏 *21 hook-ups* ⦿ *No Meals.*

### GOLF

#### Bacon Park Golf Course

**GOLF** | Completely renovated in 2014, Savannah's municipal golf club offers two courses shaded by live oaks and Spanish moss: the 18-hole Donald Ross and the 9-hole Legends Course. Located on Savannah's Southside, Bacon Park is the best bang for your golfing buck in the area, with discounts for military, seniors, and juniors. ⊠ *1 Shorty Cooper Rd., Southside* ☎ *912/354–2625* ⊕ *baconparkgolf.com* 🏷 *Legends Course from $32, Donald Ross from $54* 🏌 *Legends Course: 9 holes, 3,091 yards, par 36; Donald Ross Course: 18 holes, 6,418 yards, par 71.*

#### Crosswinds Golf Club

**GOLF** | This 18-hole championship course features parkland-style play close to Savannah/HHI International Airport, 12 miles from downtown Savannah. Crosswinds has a reputation for being exceedingly well maintained; a 9-hole executive course is available, as is a driving range. ⊠ *232 James Blackburn Dr., Savannah* ☎ *912/966–1909* ⊕ *crosswindsgolfclub.com* 🏷 *Championship Course from $50, Executive Course from $31* 🏌 *Championship Course: 18 holes, 6,748 yards, par 72; Executive Course: 9 holes, 1,126 yards, par 27.*

### Henderson Golf Club

GOLF | Located 15 miles from downtown, Henderson Golf Club might not be Savannah's biggest course, but its abundance of natural beauty makes it a draw for locals and visitors alike. This lush municipal course is close to Gateway and surrounded by live oaks and wandering wetlands. Cart rental is included in the price. ⊠ *1 Al Henderson Dr., Southside* ☎ *912/920–4653* ⊕ *henderson-golfclub.com* ✉ *$45 weekdays, $49 weekends* ⅄ *18 holes, 6,700 yards, par 71.*

### Southbridge Golf Club

GOLF | Nestled within one of Savannah's most exclusive private housing communities, Southbridge is a popular Bermuda grass course designed by Rees Jones. This course is great for all skill levels; discounted rates are available. ⊠ *415 Southbridge Blvd., Southside* ☎ *912/651–5455* ⊕ *southbridgegolfclub.com* ✉ *$60 Fri.–Sun. and holidays, $55 Mon.–Thurs.* ⅄ *18 holes, 6,922 yards, par 72.*

## KAYAKING

### Ogeechee Riverkeeper

KAYAKING | As stewards, watchdogs, and nature lovers, the Ogeechee Riverkeeper fosters deep appreciation for this 294-mile blackwater river with day-trips, educational programs, and tourist recommendations. Efforts to keep this waterway clean doubled down in 2011 after a massive fish kill caused by industry upstream; these days the green water sparkles, though vigilance remains necessary. Although the organization does not rent kayaks, it does provide free maps of the area and can help put you in touch with local guides. Several companies in the Thunderbolt or Moon River districts rent kayaks. ⊠ *785 King George Blvd., Suite 102, Southside* ☎ *866/942–6222* ⊕ *ogeecheeriverkeeper.org* ✉ *Free maps.*

## TENNIS

### Bacon Park Tennis Club

TENNIS | This complex is one of two staffed facilities operated by the City of Savannah. Call in advance to reserve one of the 16 lighted asphalt courts. ⊠ *6262 Skidaway Rd., Southside* ☎ *912/351–3850* ⊕ *www.savannahsportscouncil.com/facilities/bacon-park-tennis.*

### Lake Mayer Park

TENNIS | FAMILY | These eight lighted hard courts are available at no charge. Reservations are always recommended. ⊠ *1850 E. Montgomery Crossroads, Southside* ☎ *912/652–6780* ⊕ *savannahsportscouncil.com/facilities/lake-mayer-community-park.*

# Chapter 9

# HILTON HEAD AND THE LOWCOUNTRY

Updated by
Melissa Bigner

| ⊙ Sights | 🍴 Restaurants | 🛏 Hotels | ⬤ Shopping | 🍸 Nightlife |
|---|---|---|---|---|
| ★★★★☆ | ★★★★☆ | ★★★★☆ | ★★★★☆ | ★★★★☆ |

# WELCOME TO HILTON HEAD AND THE LOWCOUNTRY

## TOP REASONS TO GO

★ **Beautiful beaches:** Swim, soak up the sun, take a walk and collect shells, or ride your bike along the 12 miles of beaches on Hilton Head Island.

★ **Golfing paradise:** With more than 26 challenging courses, Hilton Head has earned an international reputation as a top destination for golfers.

★ **Outdoor activities:** Visitors to Hilton Head can stay busy by enjoying land activities, such as tennis, cycling, and horseback-riding, or water activities, such as kayaking, fishing, and boating.

★ **Family fun:** This semi-tropical island has been a family-friendly resort destination for decades, thanks to its vast array of lodgings, a variety of amazing restaurants, and a laid-back vibe—all making for an ideal vacation.

★ **Beaufort:** This small coastal town offers large doses of heritage and culture; it's worth the day trip to experience the unique beauty and history of the area.

Hilton Head is just north of South Carolina's border with Georgia. The 42-square-mile island is shaped like a foot, hence the reason locals often describe places as being at the "toe" or "heel" of Hilton Head. This part of South Carolina is best explored by car, as its points of interest are spread across a flat coastal plain that is a mix of wooded areas, marshes, and sea islands. The more remote areas are accessible only by boat.

**1 Hilton Head Island.** One of the Southeast coast's most popular tourist destinations, Hilton Head is famous for activities like golf and tennis. The island's natural beauty attracts flocks of retirees and families alike, all looking to spend time outdoors and take in the sights that make the Lowcountry so unique. Bluffton is located on the mainland, just before you cross the bridge onto the island.

**2 Beaufort.** This charming town is a destination in its own right, with a lively dining scene, cute bed-and-breakfasts, and many historic and picturesque places to enjoy.

**3 Daufuskie Island.** A scenic ferry ride from Hilton Head, Daufuskie Island is a beautiful place to explore; visitors can delight in the nearly deserted beaches and strong Gullah culture.

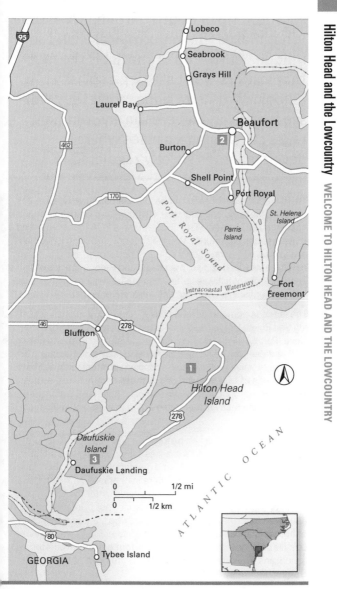

Hilton Head Island is an incredibly beautiful resort town that anchors the southern tip of South Carolina's coastline. What makes this semitropical island so unique? At the top of the list is the fact that visitors won't see large, splashy billboards or neon signs. What they will see is an island where the environment takes center stage, a place where development is strictly regulated.

There are 12 miles of sparkling beaches, amazing world-class restaurants, top-rated golf courses—Harbour Town Golf Links annually hosts the RBC Heritage Golf Tournament, a PGA Tour event—and a thriving tennis community. Wildlife abounds, including loggerhead sea turtles, alligators, snowy egrets, wood storks, and great blue heron, as well as dolphins, manatees, and various species of fish. There are lots of activities offered on the island, including parasailing, charter fishing, kayaking, and other water sports.

The island is home to several private gated communities, including Sea Pines, Hilton Head Plantation, Shipyard, Wexford, Long Cove, Port Royal, Indigo Run, Palmetto Hall, and Palmetto Dunes. Within these, you'll find upscale housing (some of it doubling as vacation rentals), golf courses, shopping, and restaurants. Sea Pines is one of the most famous of these communities, as it is known for the iconic candy-cane-stripe Hilton Head Lighthouse. There are also many areas on the island that are not behind security gates.

Hilton Head also has a rich history. The first people to live here were the Escamacus and Yemassee tribes. Hilton Head's first English settler arrived in 1717 and created the island's first plantation. By 1860, 24 plantations were in operation on Hilton Head, all existing off the labor of enslaved people. After the Civil War, much of the land was confiscated from former plantation owners and given to formerly enslaved people, who created a collection of homes that came to be known as Mitchelville. It was America's first self-governing community of formerly enslaved African Americans. Their descendants make up the heart of the region's Gullah community today.

# Planning

## When to Go

The high season follows typical beach-town cycles, with June through August and holidays year-round being the busiest and most costly. Mid-April, during the annual RBC Heritage Golf Tournament, is when rates tend to be highest. Thanks to the Low-country's mostly moderate year-round temperatures, tourists are ever-present. Spring is the best time to visit, when the weather is ideal for tennis and golf. Autumn is almost as active for the same reason.

To get the best deal, it's imperative that you plan ahead, as the choicest locations can be booked six months to a year in advance. To get a good deal during the winter season, when the crowds fall off, enlist a booking agency for room reservations. Villa rental companies often offer snowbird rates for monthly stays during the winter season. Parking is always free at the major hotels, but valet parking can cost extra; smaller properties have free parking, too, but no valet service.

### FESTIVALS

#### Hilton Head Island Gullah Celebration

**ARTS FESTIVALS | FAMILY |** This annual showcase of Gullah life through arts, music, and theater is held at a variety of locations throughout Hilton Head and the Lowcountry each February. ⊠ *539 William Hilton Pkwy., Hilton Head Island* 🕾 *843/255–7303* ⊕ *www.gullahcelebration.com.*

## Planning Your Time

No matter where you stay on Hilton Head Island, spend your first day relaxing on the beach or hitting the links. After that, you'll have time to visit some of the area's attractions, including the Coastal Discovery Museum or the Sea Pines Forest Preserve. There are plenty of dining opportunities and activities to keep guests of all ages entertained for several days. For those staying longer than a weekend, some worthy day trips include visits to Old Town Bluffton, historic Beaufort, or the city of Savannah.

# Getting Here and Around

## AIR

Most travelers use the Savannah/Hilton Head International Airport, less than an hour from Hilton Head, which is served by American Airlines, Allegiant, Avelo, Breeze, Delta, Frontier, JetBlue, Silver, Southwest, Sun Country Airlines, and United. Hilton Head Island Airport is served by American Airlines, Delta, and United. There are a variety of transportation services available, including rental cars and taxi cabs.

**CONTACTS Hilton Head Island Airport.** (HHH). ⊠ *120 Beach City Rd., North End* ☎ *843/255–2950* ⊕ *hiltonheadairport.com.* **Savannah/ Hilton Head International Airport.** ⊠ *400 Airways Ave., Northwest* ☎ *912/964–0514* ⊕ *savannahairport.com.*

## BOAT AND FERRY

As an island, Hilton Head is a paradise for boaters and has docking available at several different marinas and harbors.

**BOAT DOCKING INFORMATION Harbour Town Yacht Basin.** ⊠ *Sea Pines, 149 Lighthouse Rd., South End* ☎ *843/363–8335* ⊕ *seapines.com.* **Safe Harbor Skull Creek Marina.** ⊠ *1 Waterway La., North End* ☎ *843/681–8436* ⊕ *www.shmarinas.com/locations/safe-harbor-skull-creek.* **Shelter Cove Harbour & Marina.** ⊠ *Shelter Cove, 1 Shelter Cove La., Mid-Island* ☎ *866/661–3822* ⊕ *www.sheltercovehiltonhead.com.*

## CAR

Driving is the best way to get onto Hilton Head Island. Off Interstate 95, take Exit 8 onto U.S. 278 East, which leads you through Bluffton (where it's known as Fording Island Road) and then to Hilton Head. Once on Hilton Head, U.S. 278 forks: on the right is William Hilton Parkway, and on the left is the Cross Island Parkway. If you take the Cross Island (as the locals call it) to the south side where Sea Pines and many other resorts are located, the trip will take 10 to 15 minutes. If you take William Hilton Parkway, the trip will take about 30 minutes. Be aware that at check-in and checkout times on Friday, Saturday, and Sunday, traffic on U.S. 278 can slow to a crawl.

■ TIP → **Be careful of putting the pedal to the metal, particularly on the Cross Island Parkway. It's patrolled regularly.**

Once on Hilton Head Island, signs are small and blend in with the trees and landscaping, and nighttime lighting is kept to a minimum. The lack of streetlights can make it difficult to find your way at night, so be sure to get good directions, and keep your smart phone charged.

### TAXI

There are several regional taxi services available for transportation to and from the airports. Rideshare apps such as Uber and Lyft are also popular among travelers on Hilton Head; just be sure to notify drivers if you are staying in a gated community.

**CONTACTS Diamond Transportation.** ⊠ *Hilton Head Island* ☎ *843/247–2156* ⊕ *hiltonheadrides.com.* **Yellow Transportation HHI.** ⊠ *Hilton Head Island* ☎ *843/686–6666* ⊕ *www. yellowtransportationhhi.com.*

### TRAIN

Amtrak gets you as close as Savannah, Georgia, or Yemassee, South Carolina.

## Rain in Hilton Head 👁

Don't be discouraged when you see a weather forecast during the summer months saying there's a 30% chance of rain for Hilton Head. It can be an absolutely gorgeous day, and suddenly a storm will pop up late in the afternoon. That's because on hot sunny days, the hot air rises up into the atmosphere and mixes with the cool air, causing the atmosphere to become unstable, thereby creating thunderstorms. These storms move in and out fairly quickly, and they can bring welcome respite from the summer heat. Pack a light jacket or a portable poncho.

**CONTACTS Savannah Amtrak Station.** ⊠ *2611 Seaboard Coastline Dr., Savannah* ☎ *800/872–7245* ⊕ *www.amtrak.com/stations/sav.*

# Hotels

Hilton Head is known as one of the best vacation spots on the East Coast, and its hotels are a testimony to its reputation. The island is awash in regular hotels and resorts, not to mention beachfront and golf-course-view private villas, cottages, and luxury homes. You can expect the most modern conveniences and world-class service at the priciest places. Clean, updated rooms and friendly staff are everywhere—this is the South, after all.

⇨ *Hotel and restaurant reviews have been shortened. For full listings, visit Fodors.com. Hotel prices are for two people in a standard double room in high season, excluding service charges and tax. Restaurant prices are for a main course at dinner, excluding sales tax.*

| What It Costs in U.S. Dollars | | | |
|---|---|---|---|
| $ | $$ | $$$ | $$$$ |
| **HOTELS** | | | |
| under $150 | $151–$225 | $226–$300 | over $300 |
| **RESTAURANTS** | | | |
| under $15 | $16–$25 | $25–$35 | over $35 |

# Restaurants

The number of fine-dining restaurants on Hilton Head is extraordinary, given the size of the island. Because of the proximity to the ocean and the small farms on the mainland, most locally owned restaurants are still heavily influenced by the catch of the day and seasonal harvests. Many advertise early-bird menus, so sometimes getting a table before 6 can be a challenge. During the height of the summer season, reservations are a good idea, though in the off-season you may need them only on weekends. Beaufort's restaurant scene is excellent as well, providing an array of dining options sure to satisfy visitors hungry for local flavor and hospitality.

# Tours

With all there is to explore on Hilton Head, it's no surprise there are a multitude of tours that allow guests to see the island up-close from experienced local guides. Whether you're interested in eco-tours that focus on wildlife such as dolphins and birds or want to learn more about historical landmarks and the cultural heritage of the Gullah people, specialized tours are available for groups of all ages. Naturally, many tours are water-based—from small boats to sailboats to kayaks—and take off from any of the marinas, with Harbour Town and Shelter Cove being among the most popular areas for sunset cruises and family-friendly dolphin-watching adventures. But unique tours can be found islandwide, like discovering sea turtle nests on the beach through the Coastal Discovery Museum or riding horseback through the Sea Pines Nature Preserve.

### Captain Mark's Dolphin Cruises
**BOAT | FAMILY |** Captain Mark hosts dolphin-watching nature cruises, sport crabbing, and sunset cruises out of Shelter Cove Marina. ⊠ *Shelter Cove Marina, 9 Harbourside La., Mid-Island* ☎ *843/785–4558* ⊕ *www.cruisehiltonhead.com.*

### Gullah Heritage Trail Tours

**GUIDED TOURS** | **FAMILY** | More than a bus tour, this local outfit offers an experiential look at the local culture that emerged from enslaved Africans in the Lowcountry, including visits with locals and a one-room schoolhouse. Tours leave from the Coastal Discovery Museum. ⊠ *Coastal Discovery Museum, 70 Honey Horn Dr., North End* ☎ *843/681–7066* ⊕ *www.gullaheritage.com.*

### Live Oac Outdoor Adventure Co.

**ECOTOURISM** | **FAMILY** | This full-service outfitter offers dolphin and eco-tours, fishing charters, sunset cruises, boat rentals, and a whole host of water sport activities from tubing and wakeboarding to kneeboarding and water-skiing. Private charters and boating excursions are led by experienced, professional guides. Reservations are required. ⊠ *Hilton Head Harbor, 43A Jenkins Rd., North End* ☎ *843/384–1414* ⊕ *www.liveoac.com.*

### Low Country Nature Tours

**BOAT** | **FAMILY** | Based at Shelter Cove Marina, this outfit led by Captain Scott Henry offers private educational birding and dolphin-watching tours on comfortable six-passenger boats. Advance reservations are required. ⊠ *Shelter Cove Marina, 1 Shelter Cove La., Mid-Island* ☎ *843/683–0187.*

## Visitor Information

Brochures and maps can be found at nearly all grocery stores and shopping centers on the island, with a host of informative kiosks located at tourist areas. Every resort and hotel has knowledgeable staff ready to help guests. The Sea Pines Resort Welcome Center also provides a wealth of information.

**CONTACTS Hilton Head Island-Bluffton Chamber of Commerce and Visitor and Convention Bureau.** ⊠ *1 Chamber of Commerce Dr., Mid-Island* ☎ *843/785–3673* ⊕ *www.hiltonheadchamber.org.*

## Hilton Head Island

Hilton Head Island is known far and wide as a vacation destination that prides itself on its top-notch golf courses and tennis programs, world-class resorts, and beautiful beaches. But the island is also steeped in American history. It has been home to Native American tribes, European explorers and settlers, soldiers from the Revolutionary War and the Civil War, and plantation owners profiting off the forced labor of enslaved Africans, whose descendants make up today's Gullah community.

More than 10,000 years ago, the island was inhabited by Paleo-Indians. From 8,000 to 2,000 BC, Native American tribes of the Cusabo lived on the island; a shell ring made from their discarded oyster shells from that period can be found in the Sea Pines Nature Preserve.

The recorded modern history of the island goes back to the early 1500s, when Spanish explorers sailing coastal waters came upon the island and found settlements belonging to the Yemassee people. Over the next 200 years, the island was controlled at various times by the Spanish, the French, and the British. In 1663, Captain William Hilton claimed the island for the British crown (and named it for himself), and established indigo, rice, and corn plantations, forcing hundreds of enslaved people to live and labor on them.

During the Revolutionary War, the British harassed islanders and burned plantations. During the War of 1812, British troops again burned plantations, but the island recovered from both wars. During the Civil War, Union troops took Hilton Head in 1861 and freed the more than 10,000 enslaved people on the island. Mitchelville, one of the country's first self-governed settlements of freed Black people, was created. Because there was no bridge to Hilton Head, its formerly enslaved people, called "Gullah," subsisted on agriculture and the seafood-laden waters.

Over the years, much of the former plantation land was sold at auction. Then, in 1949 and 1950, General Joseph Fraser purchased a total of 18,000 acres, much of which would eventually become various communities, including Hilton Head Plantation, Palmetto Dunes, and Spanish Wells. The general bought another 1,200 acres, which his son, Charles, used to develop Sea Pines. The first bridge to the island was built in 1956, and modern-day Hilton Head was born.

What makes Hilton Head so special now? An emphasis on development that also preserves the environment means that, despite its growth over the past half-century, the island is still a place that values its history and natural beauty, and welcomes people from around the world with its hospitality and authenticity.

## GETTING HERE AND AROUND

Hilton Head Island is 19 miles east of Interstate 95. Take Exit 8 off Interstate 95 and then U.S. 278 east, directly to the bridges. If you're heading to the southern end of the island, your best bet to save time and avoid traffic is the Cross Island Parkway.

During the Hilton Head Island Gullah Celebration, you can learn more about the culture so essential to this region.

# ◉ Sights

Your impression of Hilton Head depends on where you stay when you visit the island. The oldest and best known of Hilton Head's developments, Sea Pines, occupies 4,500 thickly wooded acres. It's not wilderness, however; among the trees are three golf courses, tennis clubs, riding stables, and shopping plazas. A free trolley shuttles visitors around the resort. Other well-known communities are Palmetto Dunes and Port Royal Plantation.

### Audubon Newhall Preserve

**TRAIL | FAMILY |** There are walking trails, a self-guided tour, a pond, and eight distinct areas to explore on this 50-acre preserve located off Palmetto Bay Road. Native plant life is tagged and identified in the pristine forest, and many species of birds can also be found here. ⊠ *55 Palmetto Bay Rd., off Cross Island Pkwy., South End* ⊕ *www.hiltonheadaudubon.org* ▨ *Free.*

### Ben Ham Images

**ART GALLERY |** The extraordinary black-and-white large format photography of Ben Ham includes many stirring Lowcountry landscapes. ⊠ *210 Bluffton Rd., Bluffton* ☎ *843/815–6200* ⊕ *www. benhamimages.com/lowcountry.*

## Island Gators

The most famous photo of Hilton Head's original developer, Charles Fraser, ran in the *Saturday Evening Post* in 1962. It shows him outfitted with a cane and straw hat, with an alligator on a leash.

What you will learn if you visit the Coastal Discovery Museum, where the old photograph is blown up for an interpretive board on the island's early history, is that someone else had the gator by the tail (not shown) so that it would not harm Fraser or the photographer.

These prehistoric creatures are indeed indigenous to this subtropical island. Alligators can be found among the many ponds and lagoons in Sea Pines and islandwide. Spotting a live gator on the banks of a lagoon is a possibility while riding your bike or playing golf. But no matter where you happen to see these intriguing reptiles, do not feed them or attempt to get near them as they are fast and can be aggressive. Having respect for the gators in their natural habitat means keeping a safe distance, especially when children or small pets are involved.

### ★ Coastal Discovery Museum

**TRAIL | FAMILY |** Located on the grounds of the former Honey Horn Plantation, this interactive museum features a butterfly enclosure, programs for children, and guided walks of the 68-acre property that includes historic buildings and barns, marsh front boardwalks, and a wide variety of magnificent trees, such as live oaks, magnolias, and one of the state's largest Southern red cedars. A Smithsonian Affiliate, the museum hosts a variety of temporary exhibits that focus on a range of interesting historic topics and artistic mediums. Animal tours, history tours, and kayak tours are also available and should be booked in advance. Informative and inspiring, the Coastal Discovery Museum lets visitors experience the Lowcountry up close. ⊠ *70 Honey Horn Dr., off Hwy. 278, North End* ☎ *843/689–6767* ⊕ *www.coastaldiscovery.org* ⊠ *Free; donation suggested; most tours and programs are individually priced.*

### ★ Harbour Town

**CITY PARK | FAMILY |** Located within the Sea Pines Resort, Harbour Town is a charming area centered on a lighthouse and marina that's filled with interesting shops and restaurants. White gravel paths and rows of red rocking chairs add to its small-town feel, and families are attracted to the large playground and live entertainment underneath the centuries-old Liberty Oak during

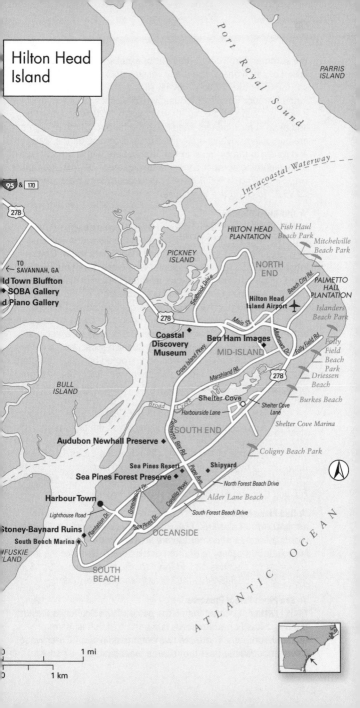

the summer. Stroll down the pier for excellent views of Daufuskie Island or catch one of the many vessels docked there and set sail for adventure. Rising above it all is the landmark candy-cane-stripe Harbour Town Lighthouse, which visitors can climb to enjoy a view of Calibogue Sound. (It was built in 1970 as an attraction and beacon for mariners heading to the harbor.) Summer nights are particularly lovely here, with a breeze coming off the water and music in the air; soak in the atmosphere with a drink at one of the welcoming outdoor bars and seating areas. ⊠ *149 Lighthouse Rd., South End* ☎ *866/305–9814* ⊕ *harbourtownlighthouse.com/* ⊠ *$6.25 to climb the lighthouse.*

## ★ Old Town Bluffton

**TOWN | FAMILY** | In 1996, Old Town Bluffton was designated a National Register Historic District town thanks to the 80-some historic churches and cottages that still stand there today. Originally inhabited by the Yemassee people, who were driven out by the first English settlers, the town's later population of slaveholders played a key role in South Carolina's secession. By the late 1990s, though, Old Bluffton had become the quirky cousin of Hilton Head, with its well-worn bungalows populated by art galleries and antique shops. Today, historic homes and houses of worship still flank oak-lined streets dripping with Spanish moss, but now they intermingle with newly constructed tin-roofed buildings designed and laid out to preserve the small-town vibe. Anchored by Promenade Street, the modern section hops with trendy bars, restaurants, and shops. Grab a sandwich to go from the Downtown Deli (⊠ *1223 May River Rd.*) and head to the Calhoun Street Public Dock for a picnic looking over the May River. (Instagrammers and photographers should aim for sunset.) While there, check out the beautiful grounds of the historic Church of the Cross (⊠ *110 Calhoun St.*). To buy fresh shellfish off the dock, visit Bluffton Oyster Company (⊠ *63 Wharf St.*) at the end of Wharf Street. ⊠ *May River Rd. and Calhoun St., Bluffton* ⊕ *www.oldtownbluffton.com.*

## ★ Red Piano Gallery

**ART GALLERY** | Sculptures, Lowcountry landscapes, and eccentric works by scores of contemporary artists can be found at this large, upscale gallery in Bluffton that's been a staple of the local art scene for decades. ⊠ *Old Town Bluffton, 40 Calhoun St., Suite 201, Bluffton* ☎ *843/842–4433* ⊕ *redpianoartgallery.com.*

## ★ Sea Pines Forest Preserve

**TRAIL | FAMILY** | Located within the gates of the Sea Pines Resort, the Sea Pines Forest Preserve is made up of 605 acres of protected wilderness. There are two entrances: one off Greenwood Drive, about a mile past the resort's main gate, has a parking

The Stoney-Baynard Ruins contain what is left of Braddock's Point Plantation after it was burned down in 1869.

area; the other is located off Lawton Drive. Walking, biking, and horse-riding paths take you past a stocked fishing pond, a waterfowl pond, a 4,000-year-old Native American shell ring, a wildflower field, wetland boardwalks, picnic areas, and boat docks. Nature tours, boat tours, fishing expeditions, and wagon tours are available through Sea Pines and can be booked in advance. Nearby Lawton Stables offers a unique experience to explore the forest via a guided horseback tour. ⊠ *The Sea Pines Resort, Greenwood Dr., South End* ☎ *843/671–1343 CSA office to call for permits for fishing or group outings, 843/671–2586 Lawton Stables, contact for tours on horseback* ⊕ *seapines.com* 🖃 *$9 per car; free for those staying at Sea Pines.*

### SOBA Gallery

**ART GALLERY** | Located in Old Town Bluffton, this bungalow-turned-gallery houses the Society of Bluffton Artists (SOBA) and showcases the work of its local painters, sculptors, and photographers. ⊠ *8 Church St., Bluffton* ☎ *843/757–6586* ⊕ *www. sobagallery.com.*

### Stoney-Baynard Ruins

**HISTORIC SIGHT | FAMILY** | This historic site contains the remains of four structures once part of Braddock's Point Plantation. John "Saucy Jack" Stoney forced enslaved people to build the plantation in the 1790s; it was eventually bought by William Baynard in 1840. Union troops occupied the plantation home during the Civil War, and the home was burned in 1869. The 6-acre site, which includes the ruins of the main house, the plantation overseer's house, and a house used by enslaved people, was listed on the National Register of Historic Places in 1994. Now located within the Sea Pines Resort, Baynard Ruins Park has a small parking area as well as trails and interpretative signs that describe the historical and archaeological significance of the area. If you are staying in Sea Pines, you can ride your bike to the site and explore at your leisure. Guided tours are also available through Sea Pines. ⊠ *Plantation Dr., near the intersection of Marsh and Plantation roads, South End* ⊕ *seapines.com.*

## Sand Dollars ⊕

Hilton Head Island's beaches hold many treasures, including starfish, sea sponges, and sand dollars. Note that it is strictly forbidden to pick up any live creatures on the beach, especially live sand dollars. How can you tell if they are alive? Live sand dollars are brown and fuzzy and will turn your fingers yellow and brown. You can take sand dollars home only if they're white. Soak them in a mixture of bleach and water to remove the scent once you get home.

## ⊕ Beaches

Hilton Head boasts some of the most accessible beaches in the Lowcountry. Two—Coligny Beach Park and Islanders Beach Park—offer free beach wheelchair rentals (with a $25 refundable deposit). Once on the beach, know a delightful stroll could end with an unpleasant surprise if you don't put your towels, shoes, and other earthly possessions far from the waterline. Tides on the island can fluctuate as much as 7 feet. Be sure to check the tide chart before venturing out to the beach for the day.

### Alder Lane Beach

**BEACH** | **FAMILY** | A great place for solitude during the winter—and popular with families during the summer season—this beach has hard-packed sand at low tide, making it ideal for walking. It's accessible from the Marriott Grande Ocean Resort. **Amenities**: lifeguards; parking; showers; toilets. **Best for**: swimming; walking. ⊠ *2 Woodward Ave., off South Forest Beach Dr., South End.*

### Burkes Beach

**BEACH** | This beach is usually not crowded, mostly because it is a bit hard to find, and it's a 10-minute walk from parking (at Chaplin Community Park, 35 Cast Net Drive). However, it's a nature-lover's hideaway on an otherwise bustling island. Amenities include seasonal lifeguards (who also offer umbrella and chair rentals),

Sand sculptures are a frequent sight on Hilton Head's beaches.

an outdoor rinse station, and restrooms (in the park). October through March off-leash dogs are welcome; outside of that window, they are permitted with restrictions. At sunrise, birds and deer bring the adjacent marsh to life. ■ **TIP→ Time a visit around low tide—the marsh flooding during high tide can cut off access.** **Amenities**: parking; restrooms; rinse station; seasonal rentals and lifeguards. **Best for**: dog walking; solitude; sunrise; swimming; windsurfing. ⊠ *60 Burkes Beach Rd., off William Hilton Pkwy., Mid-Island* ⊕ *hiltonheadislandsc.gov/parks/BurkesBeach.*

### ★ Coligny Beach Park
**BEACH | FAMILY |** The island's most popular public beach is a lot of fun, but during high season it can get very crowded. It has a splash pad fountain that delights little children, plus bench swings, sometimes a beach-toy borrowing bin, and umbrellas and chaise lounges for rent. If you have to go online, there's also Wi-Fi access. **Amenities**: clean showers and toilets; food and drink relatively close; free parking; lifeguards. **Best for**: families; partiers; swimming; windsurfing. ⊠ *1 Coligny Circle, at Pope Ave. and South Forest Beach Dr., South End* ⊕ *hiltonheadislandsc.gov/parks/ColignyBeach.*

### ★ Driessen Beach
**BEACH | FAMILY |** A good destination for families, Driessen Beach Park has a playground, clean shower and restrooms, and a charming path to the beach that's part boardwalk, part sandy path, part beach matting. It's often peppered with people flying kites, making it colorful and fun. **Amenities**: metered parking; seasonal

lifeguards and rentals; showers; toilets. **Best for**: sunrise; surfing; swimming; walking. ⊠ *64 Bradley Beach Rd., off William Hilton Pkwy., Mid-Island* ⊕ *hiltonheadislandsc.gov/parks/DriessenBeach.*

### Fish Haul Beach Park

**BEACH | FAMILY** | While it's not ideal for swimming because of the many sharp shells on the sand and in the water, this secluded public beach is a terrific spot for a walk, bird-watching, or shell-and shark tooth–hunting. It is not on the Atlantic Ocean, but rather on Port Royal Sound. Bonus: It neighbors historic Mitchelville, the site of the first Civil War-era community that was built and self-governed entirely by formerly enslaved people. **Amenities**: parking; showers; toilets. **Best for**: solitude; sunrise; walking. ⊠ *124 Mitchelville Rd., North End* ⊕ *hiltonheadislandsc.gov/parks/ FishHaulBeach.*

### Folly Field Beach Park

**BEACH | FAMILY** | Located next to Driessen Beach, Folly Field Beach Park is a treat for families. Though it can get crowded in high season, it's still a wonderful spot for a day of sunbathing and swimming. The best waves for surfing anywhere on the island break here. **Amenities**: boardwalk; parking; seasonal lifeguards and rentals; showers; toilets. **Best for**: sunrise; surfing; swimming; walking. ⊠ *55 Starfish Dr., off Folly Field Rd., Mid-Island* ⊕ *hilton-headislandsc.gov/parks/FollyFieldBeach.*

### Islanders Beach Park

**BEACH | FAMILY** | Featuring a boardwalk, a playground, a picnic pavilion, parking, and outdoor showers and restrooms, Islander Beach Park is a great spot for families looking to spend the day at the beach. When you think of a classic family beach experience, this is the place for it. **Amenities**: lifeguards (seasonal); parking; showers. **Best for**: swimming. ⊠ *94 Folly Field Rd., off William Hilton Pkwy., North End.*

##  Restaurants

### A Lowcountry Backyard Restaurant

**$$ | SOUTHERN | FAMILY** | This unassuming little restaurant located off Palmetto Bay Road in a little outdoor shopping center (the Village Exchange) serves excellent seafood dishes with Southern flavor in a laid-back setting with indoor and outdoor seating. Don't ignore the full bar that serves South Carolina moonshine. **Known for:** funky atmosphere; excellent shrimp and grits; fun for kids and families. ⑤ *Average main: $20* ⊠ *The Village Exchange Shopping*

*Center, 32 Palmetto Bay Rd., South End* ☎ *843/785–9273* ⊕ *www. hhbackyard.com* ☽ *Closed Sun.*

### Black Marlin Bayside Grill

**$$$ | SEAFOOD |** This busy waterside restaurant specializing in seafood platters and smaller bites like lobster and fish tacos is open for lunch and dinner every day, and brunch on the weekend. Located in Palmetto Bay Marina, the Black Marlin has indoor and outdoor seating, as well as family-style meals available for take-out. **Known for:** a hopping happy hour; its outdoor watering hole, Hurricane Bar; weekend oyster roasts during winter. Ⓢ *Average main: $26* ⊠ *86 Helmsman Way, South End* ☎ *843/785–4950* ⊕ *www.blackmarlinhhi.com.*

### ★ Captain Woody's

**$$ | SEAFOOD | FAMILY |** If you're looking for a fun, casual, kid-friendly seafood restaurant, this vibrant joint offers creamy crab bisque, oysters on the half shell, and a sampler platter that includes crab legs, shrimp, and oysters. Open daily for lunch and dinner, plus a Sunday brunch, Captain Woody's has indoor and outdoor seating, as well as live music weekly. **Known for:** grouper sandwiches, including the buffalo grouper, grouper melt, and grouper Reuben; lively atmosphere; good happy hour. Ⓢ *Average main: $25* ⊠ *14 Executive Park Rd., South End* ☎ *843/785–2400* ⊕ *www.captain-woodys.com.*

### Charlie's Coastal Bistro

**$$$$ | FRENCH |** This second-generation family-owned culinary landmark has been serving French cuisine with a Lowcountry flair since 1982. The name changed in recent years (from Charlie's L'Etoile Verte) but the rest remains true to the spot's origin. **Known for:** extensive wine list (more than 500 bottles); varying seafood entrées offered nightly; fine dining in a relaxed atmosphere. Ⓢ *Average main: $35* ⊠ *8 New Orleans Rd., Mid-Island* ☎ *843/785– 9277* ⊕ *www.charliesgreenstar.com* ☽ *Closed Sun. No lunch Sat.*

### The Crazy Crab

**$$ | SEAFOOD | FAMILY |** With two locations on Hilton Head, the Crazy Crab has been a longtime institution thanks to its quality seafood and friendly environment. Don't miss the she-crab soup and crab cakes. **Known for:** picturesque views; ample seating; she-crab soup and fried seafood platters. Ⓢ *Average main: $23* ⊠ *104 William Hilton Head Pkwy., North End* ☎ *843/681–5021 Jarvis Creek location, 843/363–2722 Harbour Town location* ⊕ *www. thecrazycrab.com.*

## The Shrimp Boat Tradition

Watching shrimp trawlers coming into the home port at sunset, mighty nets raised and trailed by an entourage of hungry seagulls, is a cherished Lowcountry tradition. The shrimping industry has been an integral part of the South Carolina economy for nearly a century, but farm-raised imported shrimp has had a big impact on the market and has caused the number of shrimpers to dwindle across the state.

The season for fresh-caught shrimp is May to December. People can support local fishermen by buying only certified, local wild shrimp from stores or from the shrimpers directly. In restaurants, look for the "Certified Wild American Shrimp" logo or ask your server if they use local seafood.

On Hilton Head, try Benny Hudson Seafood for local shrimp straight from the dock (⊠ 175 Squire Pope Road), or visit South End Seafood (⊠ 18 Executive Park Road) for the same. In Bluffton, the Bluffton Oyster Company (⊠ 63 Wharf Street) has been selling fresh oysters, clams, crabs, and shrimp since 1899. Gay Fish Company on Saint Helena Island or Sea Eagle Market in Beaufort are other local businesses that are keeping the tradition alive in South Carolina.

### Frankie Bones

$$$ | **ITALIAN** | The early '60s theme here appeals to an older crowd that likes the traditional Italian dishes on the early dining menu, but younger patrons who order flatbread pizzas and small plates can be found at the bar area. Reservations are accepted at both the Hilton Head and Bluffton locations, and you can buy housemade marinara and Bolognese sauces, meat rubs, and spice blends to go. **Known for:** cool twists on traditional dishes; drinks for dessert, like a key lime colada martini and house-made limoncello; the 24-ounce "Godfather Cut" prime rib. $ *Average main:* $30 ⊠ 1301 Main St., North End ☎ 843/682–4455 ⊕ www. frankieboneshhi.com.

### Harold's Country Club Bar & Grill

$ | **AMERICAN** | Not the "country club" you might expect, Harold's is a remodeled gas station in the little town of Yemassee, just east of Interstate 95 in northern Beaufort County. There's a Southern-centric down-home buffet every Thursday, and Saturday steak nights require you reserve your cut before you show for supper. (Think of it like booking a table, only you're booking … meat?) Seating is family-style in one of the large, kitschy dining rooms.

**Known for:** great live entertainment; kitschy dining rooms; a worthy stop on your way in or out of town. $ *Average main: $15* ✉ *97 U.S. 17A, Yemassee* ✛ *30 mins north of Beaufort* ☎ *843/589–4360* ⊕ *www.haroldscountryclub.com* ⊗ *Closed Sun.–Wed.*

### Hinoki

**$$ | JAPANESE |** Slip into a peaceful oasis through a tunnel of bamboo at Hinoki, which has arguably the best sushi on the island. Try the Hilton Head roll, which is whitefish tempura and avocado; the Hinoki roll with asparagus, spicy fish roe, tuna and avocado; or the amazing tuna sashimi salad with spicy mayo, cucumbers, onions, salmon roe, and crabmeat. **Known for:** super-fresh sushi with more than 50 menu items; extensive sake menu; udon noodle dishes and bento boxes. $ *Average main: $20* ✉ *Orleans Plaza, 37 New Orleans Rd., South End* ☎ *843/785–9800* ⊕ *hinokihhi.com* ⊗ *Closed Sun. No lunch Mon. and Sat.*

### Kenny B's French Quarter Cafe

**$$ | AMERICAN | FAMILY |** Surrounded by Mardi Gras memorabilia, owner Kenny himself cooks up jambalaya, gumbo, and muffaletta sandwiches at this family-run, Cajun-inspired restaurant that has been serving locals and tourists since 1999. The extensive menu also features Southern staples such as crab cakes and shrimp and grits. **Known for:** colorful Mardi Gras decor; no reservations, so be prepared to wait; beignets like they're made in New Orleans. $ *Average main: $20* ✉ *Circle Center, 1534 Fording Island Rd., South End* ☎ *843/785–3315* ⊕ *www.eatatkennybs.com* ⊗ *Closed Mon. and Tues.*

### ★ Michael Anthony's Cucina Italiana

**$$$$ | ITALIAN |** This restaurant has a convivial spirit, and its innovative pairings and plate presentations are au courant. Expect fresh, top-quality ingredients, simple yet elegant sauces, and waiters who know and care about the food and wine they serve. **Known for:** cooking demonstrations; on-site market with fresh pasta; wine tastings. $ *Average main: $45* ✉ *Orleans Plaza, 37 New Orleans Rd., Suite L, South End* ☎ *843/785–6272* ⊕ *www.michael-anthonys.com* ⊗ *Closed Sun. and Mon. No lunch.*

### Mi Tierra

**$ | MEXICAN |** This traditional Mexican restaurant has tile floors, colorful sombreros, and paintings of chili peppers hanging on the walls. Don't forget to order the guacamole and bean dip with your margarita and try the *enchiladas suizas*, tortillas filled with chicken and topped with green tomatillo sauce, sour cream, and avocado. **Known for:** authentic Mexican comfort food; signature dish: arroz con camarones—butterfly shrimp sautéed with garlic butter and vegetables; daily specials and affordable kids' menu. ⑤ *Average main: $15 ⊠ 130 Arrow Rd., South End* ☎ *843/342–3409* ⊕ *www. mitierrahiltonhead.com.*

## One Hot Mama's

**$$** | **BARBECUE** | **FAMILY** | This barbecue joint has an upbeat atmosphere, multiple flat-screen TVs, and an outdoor patio with a big brick fireplace. With baby back ribs, award-winning pulled pork sandwiches, great burgers, and a fun kids' menu, you should expect to bring your appetite to One Hot Mama's. **Known for:** it's in the "Barmuda Triangle" (other bars are just steps away); award-winning wings with sauces like strawberry-jalapeño; brisket stroganoff. ⑤ *Average main: $23 ⊠ 7A-1 Greenwood Dr., South End* ☎ *843/682–6262* ⊕ *onehotmamas.com.*

## ★ Red Fish

**$$$** | **CONTEMPORARY** | Appealing to locals and tourists alike, the menu at upscale Red Fish features classic seafood dishes, mouthwatering apps, and delicious desserts. The contemporary restaurant's wine cellar is filled with some 1,000 bottles, and there's also a retail wine shop. **Known for:** award-winning burger; fabulous service; outdoor fireplace. ⑤ *Average main: $32 ⊠ 8 Archer Rd., South End* ☎ *843/686–3388* ⊕ *www.redfishofhilton-head.com* ☾ *No lunch.*

## Santa Fe Cafe

**$$$** | **AMERICAN** | The sights, sounds, and aromas of New Mexico greet you here: Native American rugs, Mexican ballads, steer skulls and horns, and the smell of chilies and mesquite on the grill. Listen to *guitarra* music in the rooftop cantina, enjoy the adobe fireplaces on chilly nights, or dine under the stars. **Known for:** rooftop cantina with a cozy fireplace and live music; signature grouper served with chipotle Parmesan au gratin; one of the island's best margaritas. ⑤ *Average main: $28 ⊠ 807 William Hilton Pkwy., Mid-Island* ☎ *843/785–3838* ⊕ *santafehhi.com* ☾ *Closed Sun. and Mon.*

## Skull Creek Boathouse

**$$** | **SEAFOOD** | **FAMILY** | Soak up the salty atmosphere in this complex of dining areas where almost every table has a stunning view of the water. Outside is a third dining area and a bar called the Marker 13 Buoy Bar, where Adirondack chairs invite you to sit back, listen to live music, and catch the sunset. **Known for:** an adjacent outdoor Sunset Landing beer garden; tasty sandwiches and po'boys with a Southern twist; sushi, ceviche, and carpaccio from the Dive Bar. ⑤ *Average main: $25 ⊠ 397 Squire Pope Rd., North End* ☎ *843/681–3663* ⊕ *www.skullcreekboathouse.com.*

### Truffles Cafe

**$$$** | **MODERN AMERICAN** | **FAMILY** | When a restaurant keeps its customers happy for decades, there's a reason, and in the case of Truffles, it's the consistently good service and excellent food. Popular entrées include grilled salmon with a mango-barbecue glaze and the chicken pot pie. **Known for:** wide-ranging, crowd-pleasing menu with plenty of seafood; very popular with locals; on-site market with thoughtful gifts. ⑤ *Average main: $27* ✉ *Sea Pines Center, 71 Lighthouse Rd., South End* ☎ *843/671–6136* ⊕ *www. trufflescafe.com.*

### WiseGuys

**$$$** | **STEAK HOUSE** | The red-and-black decor is modern and sophisticated at this lively restaurant on the north end of the island. The food is a spin on the classics, from seafood to steak, and the shared plate menu is on point. **Known for:** a delightful crème brûlée flight and deep-fried bread pudding; extensive wine list and cocktail menu; charred rib-eye steak entrée. ⑤ *Average main: $32* ✉ *1513 Main St., North End* ☎ *843/842–8866* ⊕ *wiseguyshhi.com* ⊘ *No lunch.*

## 🛏 Hotels

### Beach House Hilton Head Island

**$$$$** | **RESORT** | **FAMILY** | Located along one of the island's busiest stretches of sand, this resort is within walking distance of Coligny Plaza's shops and restaurants. **Pros:** central location cannot be beat; spacious rooms; hoppin' bar and restaurant. **Cons:** in summer the number of kids raises the noise volume; small front desk can get backed up; not a spot for a quiet getaway. ⑤ *Rooms from: $450* ✉ *1 S. Forest Beach Dr., South End* ☎ *843/785–5126 hotel staff, 855/474–2882 reservations* ⊕ *www.beachhousehhi.com* ⇥ *202 rooms* ❍ *No Meals.*

### ★ The Inn & Club at Harbour Town

**$$$$** | **HOTEL** | This European-style boutique hotel located within the Sea Pines Resort pampers guests with British service and a dose of Southern charm—butlers are on hand anytime, and the kitchen delivers around the clock. **Pros:** the staff spoils you from arrival to checkout; ideal location, walking distance to golf and tennis; complimentary valet parking. **Cons:** it's a drive to the beach; two-day minimum on most weekends; less appealing for families. ⑤ *Rooms from: $750* ✉ *The Sea Pines Resort, 7 Lighthouse La., South End* ☎ *843/363–8100* ⊕ *www.seapines.com/accommodations/inn-club* ⇥ *60 rooms* ❍ *No Meals.*

## ★ Montage Palmetto Bluff

$$$$ | **B&B/INN** | A 30-minute drive from Hilton Head, the Low-country's most luxurious resort sits on 20,000 acres that have been transformed into a perfect replica of a small Southern town, complete with its own clapboard church. **Pros:** 18-hole May River Golf Club on-site; tennis/bocci/croquet complex has an impressive retail shop; the river adds both ambience and boat excursions. **Cons:** the mock Southern town is not the real thing; isolated from the amenities of Hilton Head; escaping in luxury is priced accordingly. ⑤ *Rooms from: $800* ✉ *477 Mount Pelia Rd., Bluffton* ☎ *843/706–6500 resort, 855/264–8705 reservations* ⊕ *www. montagehotels.com/palmettobluff* ⌁ *50 cottages, 75 inn rooms* ⦿ *No Meals.*

## Omni Hilton Head Oceanfront Resort

$$$$ | **RESORT** | **FAMILY** | At this beachfront hotel with a Caribbean sensibility, the spacious accommodations range from studios to two-bedroom suites. **Pros:** lots of outdoor dining options; well suit-ed for both families and couples; packages are often good deals, and many include breakfast, bottles of wine, or outdoor cabana massages. **Cons:** wedding parties can be noisy; pricey; noise travels through room walls. ⑤ *Rooms from: $490* ✉ *23 Ocean La., Palmetto Dunes, Mid-Island* ☎ *843/842–8000* ⊕ *www.omnihilton-head.com* ⌁ *323 rooms* ⦿ *No Meals.*

## Palmera Inn and Suites

$$$$ | **HOTEL** | **FAMILY** | This property located just off William Hilton Parkway has private balconies and full kitchens in each suite. **Pros:** one of the island's most reasonably priced lodgings; parking and Wi-Fi are free; good place for an extended stay. **Cons:** doesn't have an upscale feel; more kids means more noise, especially around the pool area; going to the beach or to dinner requires a drive. ⑤ *Rooms from: $359* ✉ *12 Park La., South End* ☎ *843/686–5700* ⊕ *www.palmerainnandsuites.com* ⌁ *156 suites* ⦿ *No Meals.*

## Sonesta Resort Hilton Head Island

$$$$ | **RESORT** | **FAMILY** | Set in a luxuriant garden that always seems to be in full bloom, the Sonesta Resort is the centerpiece of the Shipyard private community, which means guests have access to its amenities, such as golf and tennis. **Pros:** wonderful on-site spa; spacious rooms; beach access. **Cons:** crowded during summer; service is sometimes impersonal; doesn't have the views of com-peting resorts. ⑤ *Rooms from: $422* ✉ *Shipyard Plantation, 130 Shipyard Dr., South End* ☎ *843/842–2400* ⊕ *www.sonesta.com/ hiltonheadisland* ⌁ *340 rooms* ⦿ *No Meals.*

### The Westin Hilton Head Island Resort and Spa

$$$$ | **RESORT** | **FAMILY** | A circular drive winds around a sculpture of long-legged marsh birds as you approach this beachfront resort inside Port Royal. **Pros:** the beach here is absolutely gorgeous; pampering spa; access to the Port Royal Golf & Racquet Club. **Cons:** lots of groups in the off-season; crowds during summer can back up the check-in process; on-site Carolina Room restaurant gets mixed reviews. $ *Rooms from: $505* ⊠ *Port Royal Plantation, 2 Grass Lawn Ave., North End* ☏ *843/681–4000* ⊕ *www.marriott. com/hotels/hotel-information/restaurant/hhhwi-the-westin-hilton- head-island-resort-and-spa* ↴ *416 rooms* ❒ *No Meals.*

## PRIVATE VILLA RENTALS

Hilton Head has thousands upon thousands of villas, condos, and private homes for rent. In fact, homes outnumber hotel rooms nearly two-to-one. Villas and condos seem to work particularly well for families with children, since they offer more space and privacy than a hotel room. Often these vacation homes cost less per day than hotels of the same quality and provide more home-like amenities such as full kitchens, laundry, and room for bikes and outdoor gear.

While using online booking sites such as VRBO or Airbnb is a decent option, using a reputable local rental agency has many advantages.

Villas and condos are primarily rented by the week, Saturday to Saturday. It pays to make sure you understand exactly what you're getting before making a deposit or signing a contract.

■ TIP→ **Before calling a vacation rental company, make a list of the amenities you want.**

Ask for pictures of each room and ask when the photos were taken. If you're looking for a beachfront property, ask exactly how far it is to the beach. Make sure to ask for a list of all fees, including those for parking, cleaning, pets, security deposits, and utility costs. Finally, get a written contract and a copy of the refund policy.

## RENTAL AGENTS

**Resort Rentals of Hilton Head Island by Vacasa.** This company represents some 500 homes and villas, including many located inside the gated communities of Sea Pines, Palmetto Dunes, and Shipyard. Others are in North and South Forest Beach and the Folly Field area. Most of the properties are privately owned, so decor and amenities can vary. ✉ *32 Palmetto Bay Rd., Suite 1B, Mid-Island* ☎ *800/845–7017* ⊕ *www.vacasa.com/usa/South-Carolina/Hilton-Head-Island.*

### ★ The Sea Pines Resort

**$$$** | **RESORT** | **FAMILY** | The vast majority of the overnight guests at the Sea Pines Resort rent one of the more than 400 villas, condos, and beach houses through the resort itself. **⑤** *Rooms from: $264* ✉ *32 Greenwood Dr., South End* ☎ *843/785–3333, 866/561–8802* ⊕ *seapines.com/vacation-rentals* ⟿ *400 villas and houses* ¶⊘ *No Meals.*

## 🍸 Nightlife

As with many island destinations, there is no shortage of places to unwind and have a drink after dark on Hilton Head. The bars and restaurants cater to a diverse crowd—old and young, locals and tourists, casual and upscale—and the result is you can always find a place with fabulous views and friendly people for a fun night out.

### Big Bamboo Cafe

**BARS** | This South Pacific–themed bar and restaurant features live music, a great selection of craft beers and cocktails, and a lunch and dinner menu serving up tasty tacos and burgers. Located on the second story in Coligny, there's indoor and outdoor seating. ✉ *Coligny Plaza, 1 N. Forest Beach Dr., South End* ☎ *843/686–3443* ⊕ *www.bigbamboocafe.com.*

### Comedy Magic Cabaret

**COMEDY CLUBS** | Several nights a week this lounge brings top-flight comedic talent to Hilton Head. There's a light menu of appetizers and sandwiches, plus a full bar. General admission tickets are $44.50 per person. ■**TIP**→ **Book ahead online because the shows sell out fairly quickly.** ✉ *South Island Square, 843 William Hilton Pkwy., South End* ☎ *843/681–7757* ⊕ *www.comedymagiccabaret.com.*

### ★ The Jazz Corner

**LIVE MUSIC** | The elegant supper-club atmosphere at this popular spot makes it a wonderful setting in which to enjoy an evening of jazz, swing, or blues. There's a special martini menu, an extensive wine list, and a late-night menu. ■**TIP**→ **The club fills up quickly, so make reservations.** ✉ *The Village at Wexford, 1000 William Hilton Pkwy., Suite C-1, South End* ☎ *843/842–8620* ⊕ *www.thejazzcorner.com.*

### ★ The Salty Dog Cafe

**BARS | FAMILY |** The popular Salty Dog Cafe has been drawing crowds for more than 30 years with its lively atmosphere and outdoor bar and seating area overlooking scenic Braddock Cove at South Beach Marina. They serve breakfast, lunch, and dinner, and guests can sit inside or outside and enjoy items such as crab dip, fish sandwiches, fried shrimp, and Jake's hush puppies. Adults can relax with a cocktail from the extensive drink menu, and kids can hop over to the Salty Dog Ice Cream Shop located next door. Don't forget to bring home a T-shirt with the trendy Salty Dog Cafe logo at the nearby store. ⊠ *South Beach Marina, 232 S. Sea Pines Dr., South End* ☎ *843/671–2233* ⊕ *saltydog.com/dine/cafe.html.*

### ★ Reilley's Plaza

**GATHERING PLACE |** Dubbed the "Barmuda Triangle" by locals, the little cluster of bars and restaurants located just off Sea Pines Circle is a fun spot to grab a drink, eat wings and burgers, watch a game, or meet up with friends in the various outdoor areas. Reilley's Grill & Bar is the area's cornerstone, with a big outdoor bar, seating area, and delicious food. Elsewhere, the Boardroom is open late with live music; One Hot Mama's has tasty wings and burgers; MidiCi Italian Kitchen has wooden tables and open-air seating; and Brother Shucker's Bar & Grill serves up fun with raw oysters, vodka specials, and trivia nights. ⊠ *Reilley's Plaza, 7D Greenwood Dr., South End* ⊕ *www.reilleyshiltonhead.com.*

## 🎟 Performing Arts

### Arts Center of Coastal Carolina

**PERFORMANCE VENUES |** Locals love the theater productions at this arts hub that strives to enrich the community through performing and visual arts. The nonprofit supports youth education programs and showcases the works of more than 150 local artists in its Walter Greer Gallery. ⊠ *14 Shelter Cove La., Mid-Island* ☎ *843/686–3945* ⊕ *www.artshhi.com.*

### Hilton Head Symphony Orchestra

**CONCERTS |** With nearly 100 musicians, the Hilton Head Symphony Orchestra is a fully professional ensemble devoted to bringing world-class music to the Lowcountry. In addition to year-round performances, the orchestra supports a host of youth programs, including an international piano competition. ⊠ *First Presbyterian Church, 540 William Hilton Pkwy., Mid-Island* ☎ *843/842–2055* ⊕ *www.hhso.org.*

# 👜 Shopping

Hilton Head is a great destination for those who love shopping, with plenty of small businesses that carry everything from locally made gifts and specialty items to upscale clothing and casual island wear. Multiple open-air shopping centers can be found throughout the island too. And the Tanger Outlets feature nearly 100 stores in Bluffton.

## GIFTS

### Harbour Town Lighthouse Gift Shop

**SPECIALTY STORE | FAMILY |** Located at the top of the iconic red-and-white Harbour Town Lighthouse, this shop sells tasteful South Carolina–themed gifts and nautical souvenirs. ⊠ *The Sea Pines Resort, 149 Lighthouse Rd., South End* ☎ *866/305–9814* ⊕ *www.harbourtownlighthouse.com/shop.*

### Markel's Card & Gift Shop Inc.

**SPECIALTY STORE |** The helpful and friendly staff at Markel's is known for wrapping gifts with giant bows. You'll find unique Lowcountry gifts, including hand-painted wineglasses and beer mugs, lawn ornaments, baby gifts, greeting cards, and more. ⊠ *1008 Fording Island Rd., Bluffton* ☎ *843/815–9500* ☙ *Closed Sun.*

### Pretty Papers & Gifts

**SPECIALTY STORE |** This is the go-to local spot for wedding invitations, fine stationery, and gifts since 1983. ⊠ *The Village at Wexford, 1000 William Hilton Pkwy., Suite E7, Mid-Island* ☎ *843/341–5116* ⊕ *www.prettypapershhi.com* ☙ *Closed Sun.*

### ⭐ Salty Dog T-Shirt Factory

**SOUVENIRS | FAMILY |** You can't leave Hilton Head without a Salty Dog T-shirt, so hit this factory store for the best deals. The trendy T-shirts are hard to resist, and there are lots of options for kids and adults in various colors and styles. ⊠ *67 Arrow Rd., South End* ☎ *843/842–6331* ⊕ *www.saltydog.com.*

### The Storybook Shoppe

**BOOKS | FAMILY |** This charming, whimsical children's bookstore has a darling reading area for little ones as well as educational toys for infants to teens. ⊠ *Old Town Bluffton, 41 Calhoun St., Bluffton* ☎ *843/757–2600* ⊕ *www.thestorybookshoppe.com* ☙ *Closed Sun.*

## JEWELRY

### Forsythe Jewelers

**JEWELRY & WATCHES |** This is the island's leading jewelry store, offering pieces by famous designers. ⊠ *The Shops at Sea Pines*

Center, 71 Lighthouse Rd., South End ☎ 843/671–7070 ⊕ www.
forsythejewelers.biz ⊘ Closed Sun.

## SHOPPING CENTERS

### Coligny Plaza

**MALL | FAMILY |** Things are always humming at this shopping center,
which is within walking distance of the most popular public beach
on Hilton Head. Coligny Plaza has more than 50 shops and restaurants, including unique clothing boutiques, souvenir shops, and
a Piggly Wiggly grocery store. Don't miss Skillets for breakfast,
Frozen Moo for ice cream, and Frosty Frog for drinks outdoors.
⊠ Coligny Circle, 1 N. Forest Beach Dr., South End ☎ 843/842–
6050 ⊕ colignyplaza.com.

### ★ Harbour Town

**SHOPPING CENTER | FAMILY |** Located within the Sea Pines Resort,
Harbour Town is a picture-perfect little area with plenty of shops
that appeal to visitors young and old. S. M. Bradford Co., Currents,
and Fashion Court specialize in upscale clothing, while Knickers
and Harbour Town Surf Shop carry outdoor wear. Kids and families
will enjoy the Cinnamon Bear Country Store and Hilton Head
Toys. ⊠ The Sea Pines Resort, 149 Lighthouse Rd., South End
☎ 866/561–8802 ⊕ seapines.com/recreation/harbour-town.

### ★ Old Town Bluffton

**NEIGHBORHOOD | FAMILY |** Charming Old Town Bluffton features local
artist galleries, antiques, shops, and restaurants. ⊠ Downtown
Bluffton, May River Rd. and Calhoun St., Bluffton ☎ 843/706–4500
⊕ www.visitbluffton.org.

### Shelter Cove Towne Centre

**MALL | FAMILY |** This sprawling development is equal parts outdoor
shopping village and park. Set up like a "town center," Towne
Centre's stores are anchored by chains like Belk and Talbots and
also populated by charming local spots like Spartina 449 and the
Palmetto Running Company. There's also a Kroger grocery store,
several restaurants and bars, and a barre studio. Shelter Cove
Community Park is a spacious outdoor area that offers beautiful
marsh views. ⊠ 40 Shelter Cove La., Mid-Island ⊕ www.shelter-
covetownecentre.com.

### Shops at Sea Pines Center

**SHOPPING CENTER |** Clothing, fine gifts and jewelry, and a selection
of local crafts and antiques can be found at this quaint open-air
shopping center located in the Sea Pines Resort. Don't miss By
Hand, Ink, a charming independent book store. ⊠ 71 Lighthouse
Rd., South End ☎ 843/363–6800 ⊕ www.theshopsatseapi-
nescenter.com.

### South Beach Marina Village

**SHOPPING CENTER | FAMILY** | Built to resemble a New England fishing village, this quaint area in Sea Pines Resort's Harbour Town is home to the Salty Dog Cafe (and the café's shop that sells the island's signature Salty Dog T-shirts), plus a selection of other souvenirs and logo'd items. There are several other little shops in South Beach, in addition to an ice cream spot and seafood restaurants. ⊠ *South Beach Marina Village, 232 S. Sea Pines Dr., South End.*

### Tanger Outlets

**OUTLET | FAMILY** | There are two separate sections to this popular shopping center: Tanger Outlet I has more than 40 upscale stores, as well as eateries like Olive Garden, Panera Bread, and Longhorn Steakhouse. Tanger Outlet II has Banana Republic, the Gap, and Nike, along with dozens of other stores that offer great discounts for shoppers. ⊠ *1414 Fording Island Rd., Bluffton* ☎ *843/837–5410,* ⊕ *www.tangeroutlet.com/hiltonhead.*

### The Village at Wexford

**SHOPPING CENTER | FAMILY** | Upscale shops, including Lilly Pulitzer and Le Cookery, as well as several fine-dining restaurants can be found in this established shopping area. There are also some unique gift shops and luxe clothing stores, such as Currents, Evelyn & Arthur, Island Child, and John Bailey Clothier. ⊠ *1000 William Hilton Pkwy., Hilton Head Island* ⊕ *villageatwexford.com.*

## 🏃 Activities

Hilton Head Island is a mecca for the sports enthusiast and for those who just want a relaxing walk or bike ride on the beach. There are 12 miles of beaches, 26 public golf courses, more than 50 miles of public bike paths, and more than 300 tennis courts. There are also tons of water sports, including kayaking and canoeing, parasailing, fishing, sailing, and much more.

### BICYCLING

More than 50 miles of public paths crisscross Hilton Head Island, and pedaling is popular along the firmly packed beach. The island keeps adding more to its network of boardwalks, which is great as it's such a safe alternative for kids. Bikes with wide tires are a must if you want to ride on the beach. They can also save you a spill should you hit loose sand on the trails.

■ **TIP→ For a map of trails, visit** ⊕ *www.hiltonheadislandsc.gov.*

Bicycles from beach cruisers to mountain bikes to tandem bikes can be rented either at bike stores or at most hotels and resorts.

Many can be delivered to your hotel, along with helmets, baskets, locks, child carriers, and whatever else you might need.

### Hilton Head Bicycle Company

**BIKING | FAMILY |** This local outfit rents bicycles, e-bikes, helmets, and more. ⊠ *112 Arrow Rd., South End* ☎ *843/686–6888* ⊕ *www. hiltonheadbicycle.com.*

### Pedals Bicycles

**BIKING | FAMILY |** Rent beach bikes for adults and children, adult trikes, bike trailers, childseats, e-bikes, bike baskets, beach carts, umbrellas, chairs, and more from this local operation, in business since 1981. ⊠ *71 Pope Ave. A, South End* ☎ *888/699–1039* ⊕ *www.pedalsbicycles.com.*

### South Beach Bike Rentals

**BIKING | FAMILY |** Rent bikes, helmets, tandems, and adult tricycles at this spot in Sea Pines Resort's Harbour Town. ⊠ *South Beach Marina, 230 S. Sea Pines Dr., Sea Pines, South End* ☎ *843/671–2453* ⊕ *southbeachbikerentals.com* ⌕ *Delivery to Sea Pines, Shipyard Plantation, Coligny, and North and South Forest Beach Drive. No delivery to Palmetto Dunes.*

## CANOEING AND KAYAKING

Canoeing or kayaking is one of the most delightful ways to commune with nature and experience the beauty of the Lowcountry's unique ecosystem. Paddle through Hilton Head's tidal creeks and estuaries and try to keep up with the dolphins.

### ★ Outside Hilton Head

**BOATING | FAMILY |** Boats, canoes, kayaks, and paddleboards are available for rent from this local outfitter that has set the standard for outdoor adventures in the Lowcountry for decades. Outside Hilton Head also offers nature tours, surf camps, tubing, and dolphin-watching excursions as well as private charters and activities for kids and families. For those questing after shark's teeth and shells, they are your best bet as their tours hit spots that are accessible by boat only. ⊠ *Shelter Cove Marina, 50 Shelter Cove La., Mid-Island* ☎ *843/686–6996* ⊕ *www.outsidehiltonhead.com.*

## FISHING

Although anglers can fish in these waters year-round, in April things start to crank up and in May most boats are heavily booked. May is the season for cobia, especially in Port Royal Sound. In the Gulf Stream you can hook king mackerel, tuna, wahoo, and mahi-mahi. ■TIP→ **A fishing license is necessary if you are fishing from a beach, dock, or pier. Licenses aren't necessary on charter fishing boats because they already have their licenses.**

### Bay Runner Fishing Charters

**FISHING | FAMILY** | With more than 50 years of experience fishing these waters, Captain Miles Altman takes anglers out for deep-sea fishing trips lasting three to eight hours. ⊠ *Shelter Cove Marina, 1 Shelter Cove La., Mid-Island* ☎ *843/290–6955* ⊕ *www. bayrunnerfishinghiltonhead.com.*

### Bulldog Fishing Charters

**FISHING | FAMILY** | A second-generation fishing captain, Captain Christiaan offers his guests 4-, 6-, 8-, and 10-hour fishing tours on his 32-foot boat, the *Bulldog*. May through October he offers sunset trips that turn into evening shark-fishing adventures. ⊠ *1 Hudson Rd., departs from docks at Hudson's Seafood House on the Docks, North End* ☎ *843/422–0887* ⊕ *bulldogfishingcharters. com.*

### Capt. Hook Party Fishing Boat

**FISHING | FAMILY** | For those looking for a fun time out on the water with friends and family, deep-sea fishing tours are available on this large party boat. Public and private offshore fishing charters are also available. The friendly crew can teach kids how to bait hooks and reel in fish. ⊠ *Shelter Cove Marina, 1 Shelter Cove La., Mid-Island* ☎ *843/785–1700* ⊕ *www.captainhookhiltonhead.com.*

### Fishin' Coach Charters

**FISHING | FAMILY** | Captain Dan Utley offers a variety of inshore fishing tours on his 22-foot boat to catch redfish and other species year-round. ⊠ *C.C. Haigh Jr. Boat Landing, 2 William Hilton Pkwy., North End* ☎ *843/368–2126* ⊕ *www.fishincoach.com.*

### Hilton Head Charter Fishing

**FISHING | FAMILY** | Captain Jeff Kline offers offshore, sport-fishing adventure trips and four-hour family trips on a quartet of 26- to 35-foot boats: the *Gullah Gal, True Grits, Gale Warning,* and *Gale Force.* ⊠ *Shelter Cove Marina, 1 Shelter Cove La., Mid-Island* ☎ *843/422–3430* ⊕ *www.hiltonheadislandcharterfishing.com.*

### Integrity Charters

**FISHING | FAMILY** | The 38-foot Hatteras Sportfisher charter boat *Integrity* offers offshore and near-shore fishing expeditions with U.S. Coast Guard–licensed Master Captain Mike Russo. ⊠ *Broad Creek Marina, 18 Simmons Rd., South End* ☎ *843/422–1221* ⊕ *www.integritycharterfishing.com.*

### Palmetto Lagoon Charters

**FISHING | FAMILY** | Captain Trent Malphrus takes groups for half- or full-day excursions to the region's placid saltwater lagoons. Redfish, bluefish, flounder, and black drum are some of the most common fish they hook. ⊠ *Shelter Cove Marina, 1 Shelter Cove*

*La., Mid-Island* ☎ *843/301–4634* ⊕ *www.palmettolagooncharters. com.*

**Stray Cat Charters**

**FISHING | FAMILY** | Whether you want to fish inshore or go offshore into the deep blue to catch fish such as cobia and snapper, Captain Jim Clark offers options for charters on his 37-foot double engine-powered catamaran, *The Stray Cat.* ⊠ *2 Hudson Rd., North End* ☎ *843/683–5427* ⊕ *www.straycatcharter.com.*

## GOLF

Hilton Head is nicknamed "Golf Island" for good reason: the island itself has 26 championship courses (public, semiprivate, and private), and the outlying area has 16 more. Each offers its own packages, some of which are great deals. Almost all charge the highest greens fees in the morning and lower fees as the day goes on. Lower rates can also be found in the hot summer months. It's essential to book tee times in advance, especially in the busy spring and fall months; resort guests and club members get first choices. Most courses can be described as casual-classy, so you will have to adhere to certain rules of the greens.

■**TIP**➔ **The dress code on island golf courses does not permit blue jeans, gym shorts, or jogging shorts. Men's shirts must have collars.**

### ★ The RBC Heritage PGA Tour Golf Tournament

**GOLF** | The most internationally famed golf event on Hilton Head Island is the RBC Heritage presented by Boeing, held mid-April at Harbour Town Golf Links. For more than 50 years, this PGA tournament has drawn flocks of fans and spectators to the island for a weeklong celebration of golf and tradition. ⊠ *The Sea Pines Resort, 2 Lighthouse La., South End* ⊕ *www.rbcheritage.com.*

## BLUFFTON GOLF COURSES

There are several beautiful golf courses in Bluffton, which is just on the mainland before you cross the bridges onto Hilton Head Island. These courses are very popular with locals and can often be more affordable to play than the courses on Hilton Head.

**Crescent Pointe Golf Club**

**GOLF** | An Arnold Palmer Signature Course, Crescent Pointe is fairly tough, with somewhat narrow fairways and rolling terrain. There are numerous sand traps, ponds, and lagoons that make for demanding yet fun holes. Some of the par 3s are particularly challenging. The scenery is magnificent, with large live oaks, pine-tree stands, and rolling fairways. Additionally, several holes have spectacular marsh views. ⊠ *Crescent Pointe, 1 Crescent Pointe, Bluffton* ☎ *843/706–2600* ⊕ *crescentpointegc.com/golf* 🖃 *$55* 🏌 *18 holes, 6,773 yards, par 71.*

### Eagle's Pointe Golf Club

GOLF | This Davis Love III–designed course is one of the area's most playable, thanks to its spacious fairways and large greens. There are quite a few bunkers and lagoons throughout the course, which winds through a natural woodlands setting that attracts an abundance of wildlife. ⊠ *Eagle's Pointe, 1 Eagle's Pointe Dr., Bluffton* 🕾 *843/757–5900* ⊕ *eaglespointegc.com* 🖾 *$59* 🏌 *18 holes, 6,780 yards, par 71.*

### The May River Golf Club

GOLF | This 18-hole Jack Nicklaus signature course at the posh Montage Palmetto Bluff resort has several holes along the banks of the scenic May River and will challenge all skill levels. The greens are Champion Bermuda grass, and the fairways are covered by Paspalum, the latest eco-friendly turf. Caddy service is always required. ⊠ *Palmetto Bluff, 477 Mount Pelia Rd., Bluffton* 🕾 *855/377–3198* ⊕ *www.montagehotels.com/palmettobluff/experiences/golf* 🖾 *$315* 🏌 *18 holes, 7,171 yards, par 72.*

### Old South Golf Links

GOLF | There are many scenic holes overlooking marshes and the intracoastal waterway at this Clyde Johnson–designed course. It's a public course, but that hasn't stopped it from winning awards. It's reasonably priced, just over the bridge from Hilton Head, and reservations are recommended. ⊠ *50 Buckingham Plantation Dr., Bluffton* 🕾 *843/785–5353* ⊕ *www.oldsouthgolf.com* 🖾 *$70* 🏌 *18 holes, 6,772 yards, par 72.*

## GOLF COURSES

### Arthur Hills and Robert Cupp Courses at Palmetto Hall

GOLF | There are two prestigious courses at the Palmetto Hall Country Club: Arthur Hills and Robert Cupp. Arthur Hills is a player favorite, with its trademark undulating fairways punctuated with lagoons and lined with moss-draped oaks and towering pines. Robert Cupp is a very challenging course but is great for the higher handicappers as well. Rates range greatly (from $65 up to $190) depending on the time of day and time of the year. ⊠ *Palmetto Hall, 108 Fort Howell Dr., North End* 🕾 *843/342–2582* ⊕ *www.palmettohallcc.com* 🖾 *$100* 🏌 *Arthur Hills: 18 holes, 6,257 yards, par 72. Robert Cupp: 18 holes, 6,025 yards, par 72* ☞ *See Palmetto Hall's website for seasonal specials.*

### Country Club of Hilton Head

GOLF | Although it's part of a country club, the semiprivate course is open for public play. A well-kept secret, it's rarely too crowded. This 18-hole Rees Jones–designed course offers a more casual environment than many of the other golf courses on Hilton

Head. ✉ *Hilton Head Plantation, 70 Skull Creek Dr., North End* ☎ *843/681–2582* ⊕ *www.clubcorp.com/Clubs/Country-Club-of-Hilton-Head* ✉ *$125* 🏌 *18 holes, 6,543 yards, par 72.*

### Golden Bear Golf Club at Indigo Run

**GOLF** | Located in the upscale Indigo Run community, Golden Bear Golf Club is the only one on the island that golf legend Jack Nicklaus designed. The course's natural woodlands setting offers easygoing rounds. It requires more thought than muscle, and you will have to earn every par you make. Though fairways are generous, you may end up with a lagoon looming smack ahead of the green on the approach shot. ✉ *Indigo Run, 72 Golden Bear Way, North End* ☎ *843/689–2200* ⊕ *www.clubcorp.com/Clubs/Golden-Bear-Golf-Club-at-Indigo-Run* ✉ *$99* 🏌 *18 holes, 6,643 yards, par 72.*

### ★ Harbour Town Golf Links

**GOLF** | Considered by many golfers to be one of those must-play-before-you-die courses, Harbour Town Golf Links is extremely well known because it has hosted the RBC Heritage PGA Golf Tournament every spring for more than 50 years. Designed by Pete Dye, the layout is reminiscent of Scottish courses of old. The 18th hole lies along the marsh and waterway, driving toward the Harbour Town Lighthouse. The Sea Pines Resort also has two other incredible courses—Heron Point by Pete Dye and Atlantic Dunes by Davis Love III—that make the complex a great destination for any golfer. ✉ *The Sea Pines Resort, 11 Lighthouse La., South End* ☎ *843/842–8484* ⊕ *seapines.com/golf* ✉ *$350* 🏌 *18 holes, 7,101 yards, par 71.*

### ★ Robert Trent Jones at Palmetto Dunes

**GOLF** | One of the island's most popular layouts, this course's beauty and character are accentuated by the 10th hole, a par 5 that offers a panoramic view of the ocean (one of only two on the entire island). There are two other golf courses located within the Palmetto Dunes Oceanfront Resort (a George Fazio course and an Arthur Hills course), and packages are available to play all three. ✉ *Palmetto Dunes Oceanfront Resort, 7 Robert Trent Jones La., North End* ☎ *888/909–9566* ⊕ *www.palmettodunes.com* ✉ *$180* 🏌 *18 holes, 7,005 yards, par 72.*

## GOLF SCHOOLS

### The Golf Learning Center at the Sea Pines Resort

**GOLF** | The well-regarded golf academy offers hourly private lessons by PGA-trained professionals and one- to two-day clinics to help you perfect your game. ✉ *The Sea Pines Resort, 100 N. Sea Pines Dr., South End* ☎ *843/785–4540* ⊕ *www.seapines.com/golf/learning-center.*

### Palmetto Dunes Golf Academy

**GOLF** | There's something for golfers of all ages at this academy: instructional videos, daily clinics, and multiday schools. Lessons are offered for ages three and up, and there are breakout programs for women. Free demonstrations are held with Doug Weaver, former PGA Tour pro and director of instruction for the academy. Mondays they offer a free demo clinic. ⊠ *Palmetto Dunes Oceanfront Resort, 4 Queens Folly Rd., Mid-Island* ☎ *888/909–9566 general info, 866/455–6890 private lessons* ⊕ *www.palmettodunes.com/golf/golf-instruction.*

## PARASAILING

For those looking for a bird's-eye view of Hilton Head, it doesn't get better than parasailing. Newcomers will get a lesson in safety before taking off. Parasailers are then strapped into a harness, and as the boat takes off, the parasailer is lifted about 500 feet into the sky.

### ★ H20 Sports

**HANG GLIDING & PARAGLIDING** | **FAMILY** | Check out views up to 25 miles in all directions while parasailing with this popular outdoor adventure company located out of the Harbour Town Marina in the Sea Pines Resort. They also offer sailing, kayak, and SUP (stand-up paddleboard) tours, Jet Ski and boat rentals, and a private water taxi to Daufuskie Island. Nature lovers will enjoy dolphin or alligator tours with experienced local guides. ⊠ *Harbour Town Marina, 149 Lighthouse Rd., South End* ☎ *843/671–4386* ⊕ *www.h2osports.com.*

### Sky Pirate Parasail & Watersports

**HANG GLIDING & PARAGLIDING** | **FAMILY** | Glide 500 feet in the air over the water and get an aerial view of the Lowcountry on an adventure out of Broad Creek Marina. The outfitter also offers boat rentals, tubing trips, water-skiing, and paddleboard rentals as well as dolphin eco-cruises. ⊠ *Broad Creek Marina, 18 Simmons Rd., Mid-Island* ☎ *843/842–2566* ⊕ *www.skypirateparasail.com.*

## SPAS

In keeping with its getaway status, Hilton Head's spas and wellness centers are worth the trip. From in-room services to full-blown luxury retreats, there's something for everyone.

### FACES DaySpa

**SPA** | This local institution has been pampering loyal clients for more than four decades, thanks to body therapists, stylists, and cosmetologists who really know their stuff. Choose from fabulous facials, enjoy a manicure and pedicure, or have a relaxing massage treatment in a facility that is committed to providing a safe and clean environment for all guests and staff. ⊠ *The Village at Wexford, 1000 William Hilton Pkwy., D1, South End* ☎ *843/785–3075* ⊕ *www.facesdayspa.com.*

### Heavenly Spa by Westin
**SPA** | As part of the oceanfront Westin Resort, this 8,000-square-foot luxury spa provides a range of unique treatments designed to rejuvenate the body and renew your spirit. From massages to facials to salon services, the Heavenly Spa lives up to its name by offering guests a chance to relax and unwind. A variety of specials and seasonal packages is available. ⊠ *The Westin Hilton Head Island Resort & Spa, 2 Grasslawn Ave., Port Royal Plantation, North End* ☎ *843/681–1019* ⊕ *www.westinhiltonheadspa.com.*

### Spa Montage Palmetto Bluff
**SPA** | Dubbed the "celebrity spa" by locals, this two-story facility is the ultimate pampering palace with treatments such as body wraps, facials, sensual soaks, and couples massages. Located at Montage Palmetto Bluff in Bluffton, the spa also offers a variety of other services, including pedicures, manicures, facials and other skin treatments, and a hair salon. Be sure to book appointments in advance. ⊠ *Montage Palmetto Bluff, 477 Mount Pelia Rd., Bluffton* ☎ *855/264–8705* ⊕ *www.montagehotels.com/palmettobluff/spa.*

## TENNIS
There are more than 360 tennis courts on Hilton Head. Tennis comes in at a close second (after golf) as the island's premier sport. It is recognized as one of the nation's best tennis destinations with a variety of well-maintained surfaces and a large number of coaches and professionals teaching clinics and private lessons available to players of all ages. Pickleball is also on the rise, and the Island is responding. Resorts have made room for the sport, and one public park even converted its tennis courts into those for pickleball.

■ TIP→ **Spring and fall are the peak seasons for cooler play, with numerous packages available at the resorts and through the tennis schools.**

### ★ Palmetto Dunes Tennis and Pickleball Center
**TENNIS | FAMILY** | Ranked among the best in the world, this facility at the Palmetto Dunes Oceanfront Resort has 17 clay tennis courts (four of which are lighted for night play) and 24 dedicated pickleball courts. There are lessons geared to players of every skill level given by enthusiastic staffers. ⊠ *Palmetto Dunes Oceanfront Resort, 6 Trent Jones La., Mid-Island* ☎ *888/879–2053* ⊕ *www.palmettodunes.com.*

### Port Royal Racquet Club

**TENNIS | FAMILY |** Magnolia trees dot the grounds of the Port Royal Racquet Club, which has eight clay courts and two pickleball courts. Located in the Port Royal private community, this award-winning tennis complex attracts guests with its professional staff, stadium seating, and tournament play. ✉ *Port Royal Plantation, 15 Wimbledon Court, Mid-Island* ☎ *843/686–8803* ⊕ *www.hiltonheadgolf.net/port-royal.*

### Sea Pines Racquet Club

**TENNIS | FAMILY |** This award-winning club has 20 clay courts, as well as a pro shop and instructional programs, including weekend clinics with Wimbledon champ Stan Smith. Guests of Sea Pines receive two hours of complimentary court time each day. ✉ *The Sea Pines Resort, 5 Lighthouse La., South End* ☎ *888/561–8802* ⊕ *seapines.com/tennis.*

### Van Der Meer Tennis

**TENNIS |** Recognized for its tennis instruction for players of all ages and skill levels, this highly rated facility has 37 hard courts, including seven indoor and covered courts. The center is the main training location for students attending the Van Der Meer Tennis Academy. In a separate location within Shipyard, the Van Der Meer Shipyard Racquet Club has 13 Har-Tru courts, seven hard courts (three of which are indoors), and a pro shop with a professional racquet stringer. ✉ *19 DeAllyon Ave., South End* ☎ *843/845–6138* ⊕ *www.vandermeertennis.com.*

## ZIP LINE TOURS

### ZipLine Hilton Head

**ZIP-LINING | FAMILY |** Take a thrilling tour on a zip line over ponds and marshes and past towering oaks and pines. This company offers 7 zip lines, a suspended sky bridge, a dual-cable racing zip line, and a network of six ropes courses. ✉ *33 Broad Creek Marina Way, Mid-Island* ☎ *843/681–3625* ⊕ *ziplinehiltonhead.com.*

# Beaufort

*38 miles north of Hilton Head via U.S. 278 and Rte. 170, 70 miles southwest of Charleston via U.S. 17 and U.S. 21.*

Charming homes and churches grace this town, founded in 1711 and located on Port Royal Island. Come here on a day trip from Hilton Head, Charleston, or Savannah, Georgia, to spend a quiet weekend at a B&B while you shop and stroll through the historic district. Visitors are drawn equally to the town's artsy scene and

## Pat Conroy's Beaufort Legacy 👁

Many fans of the late author Pat Conroy consider Beaufort his town because of his autobiographical novel *The Great Santini*, which was set here. He, too, considered it home base: "We moved to Beaufort when I was 15. We had moved 23 times. (My father was in the Marines.) I told my mother, 'I need a home.' Her wise reply was: 'Well, maybe it will be Beaufort.' And so it has been. I have stuck to this poor town like an old barnacle. I moved away, but I came running back in 1993."

Conroy lived on Fripp Island with his wife, author Cassandra King, for many years before he passed away in 2016. In order to honor his memory and the important role he played in introducing the Lowcountry to so many readers, the Pat Conroy Literary Center was founded in Beaufort. The nonprofit organization holds an annual literary festival with writing workshops and events, and also offers in-person tours at its downtown location. ☎ 843/379–7025 ⊕ www.patconroyliterarycenter.org.

to the area's natural bounty and outdoor activities. The annual Beaufort Water Festival, which takes place over 10 days in July, is an over 50-year-old tradition that attracts visitors every year.

More and more transplants have decided to spend the rest of their lives here, drawn to Beaufort's small-town charms, and the area is burgeoning. An authentic Southern town, its picturesque backdrops have lured filmmakers here to shoot *The Big Chill, The Prince of Tides,* and *The Great Santini,* the last two being Hollywood adaptations of best-selling books by the late author Pat Conroy. Conroy had waxed poetic about the Lowcountry in several novels and called the Beaufort area home.

Located in Northern Beaufort County, Beaufort is surrounded by sea islands, each unique in their own right, including Lady's Island, Cat Island, Dataw Island, St. Helena's Island, Harbor Island, Hunting Island, and Fripp Island.

### GETTING HERE AND AROUND

Beaufort is 25 miles east of Interstate 95, on U.S. 21. The only way to get here is by car, Greyhound bus, or boat.

Henry C. Chambers Waterfront Park is the perfect place to take a stroll along the water in Beaufort.

## ESSENTIALS

Well-maintained public restrooms are available at the Beaufort Visitors Center. A onetime arsenal, the yellow stucco fortress that houses the center is a local landmark.

**VISITOR INFORMATION Beaufort Visitors Center.** ⊠ *713 Craven St., Beaufort* ☎ *843/525–8500* ⊕ *www.beaufortsc.org.*

## TOURS

### SouthurnRose Buggy Tours

**CARRIAGE TOURS | FAMILY |** These 50-minute horse-drawn carriage tours leave from Waterfront Park and offer a historical perspective of downtown Beaufort, which is a great orientation to the charming town. ⊠ *1002 Bay St., Downtown Historic District* ☎ *843/524–2900* ⊕ *www.southurnrose.com* 🎟 *$32.*

# ◉ Sights

### Barefoot Farms

**FARM/RANCH |** Pull over for boiled peanuts, a jar of gumbo or strawberry jam, or perfect watermelons at this working farm's roadside stand on St. Helena Island. ⊠ *939 Sea Island Pkwy., St. Helena Island* ☎ *843/838–7421.*

### Beaufort National Cemetery

**CEMETERY |** Listed on the National Register of Historic Places, Beaufort National Cemetery is the final resting spot of both Union and Confederate soldiers from the Civil War. In 1987, 19 more

Union soldiers were interred here after having been discovered buried under the sands of Folly Beach. (These men had been missing in action since 1863.) The site's peaceful, well-maintained grounds make this a somber spot to commemorate the dead. ✉ 1601 Boundary St., Beaufort ☎ 843/524–3925 ⊕ www.cem. va.gov/cems/nchp/beaufort.asp.

### ★ Henry C. Chambers Waterfront Park

**CITY PARK | FAMILY |** Located off Bay Street in downtown Beaufort, Waterfront Park represents the heart of this charming coastal town. It's a great place to stroll along the river walk and enjoy the hanging bench swings. Parents enjoy the spacious park where kids can run in the grass or play on the enclosed playground with views of the Richard V. Woods swing bridge that crosses the Beaufort River. Trendy restaurants and bars overlook these seven beautifully landscaped acres that also feature a pavilion, stage, and historical markers and lead into the marina. ✉ 1006 Bay St., Beaufort ☎ 843/525–7011 ⊕ www.beaufortsc.org/listing/henry-c-chambers-waterfront-park/147.

### Highway 21 Drive In

**OTHER ATTRACTION | FAMILY |** Highway 21 Drive In is a charming throwback that's fun for the whole family. Showing a variety of classic movies and recent hits, the outdoor theater has been attracting crowds since 1978. A recent change in ownership brought on a refresh, including updates to the projection system and grooming of the grounds. What hasn't changed: the old-school concessions stand has everything from popcorn and candy to burgers and corn dogs, as well as funnel cakes and root beer floats. Even the ticket prices are a nod to another time and include double features on two screens. It's totally worth the trip for this slice of nostalgia to see "where the stars come out at night." ✉ 55 Parker Rd., Beaufort ☎ 843/846–4500 ⊕ www.hwy21drivein.com 💲 $8.

### John Mark Verdier House

**HISTORIC HOME |** Built and maintained by the forced labor of enslaved people, this 1805 Federal-style mansion has been restored and furnished as it would have been prior to a visit by Marquis de Lafayette in 1825. It was the headquarters for Union forces during the Civil War. The house museum also features historical photographs, a diorama of Bay Street in 1863, and an exhibit about the remarkable Beaufort-born Robert Smalls, who during the Civil War famously commandeered a Confederate ship to escape from slavery with his family. Run by Historic Beaufort Foundation, the museum offers docent-guided tours every half hour. ✉ 801 Bay St., Downtown Historic District ☎ 843/379–6335 ⊕ historicbeaufort.org 💲 Donations welcome ⊙ Closed Sun.

## The World of Gullah

In the Lowcountry, "Gullah" can refer to a language, a people, a culture, or all three. The 300-year-old English-based dialect is a mix of the African languages spoken by the enslaved people who were kidnapped and forcibly brought to the Carolina, Georgia, and Florida coastlines, including the Lowcountry. The new tongue was the first thing—and often the only thing—these people could claim as their own in the colonies.

This Gullah dialect still lingers, albeit less and less with each generation. Likewise, the culture haunts the region, but it, too, is fading. During the colonial period, plantation owners deliberately enslaved those West Africans who had experience growing rice. Why? In order to capitalize on their knowledge and labor, which could be put to the test in the rice fields of the Lowcountry.

Those who had basket-making skills were also enslaved because baskets were essential for agricultural purposes (to separate rice seed from the chaff, for example) and for household use. Sweetgrass, an indigenous grass named for its sweet, haylike aroma, was gathered, dried, coiled, and then sewn together with palmetto fronds. The designs then were African-born; today these ancestral patterns are still crafted by the women who sell the historical pieces throughout the Lowcountry. Museum-worthy from both artistic and heritage perspectives, the baskets of one South Carolina maker, Mary Jackson, are in the Smithsonian American Art Museum.

Today, Gullah culture is most evident (and prevalent) in the foods of the region. Rice is the staple alongside which such Lowcountry ingredients as okra, peanuts, benne (a word of African origin for sesame seeds), field peas, and hot peppers are served. Gullah food reflects the bounty of the islands, too: shrimp, crabs, oysters, fish, and such vegetables as greens, tomatoes, and corn. Many dishes are prepared in one pot, similar to the stewpot cooking that's found in West Africa.

On St. Helena Island, near Beaufort, the Penn Center is Gullah headquarters, and the nonprofit works to both preserve the culture and develop opportunities for modern-day Gullahs. Its roots run deep. In 1852 the first school for formerly enslaved African Americans was established here. Visitors can delve into the center's past further at its York W. Bailey Museum.

### The Kazoo Museum & Factory

**OTHER ATTRACTION | FAMILY |** Taking a tour of this unique kazoo museum and factory is a fun and informative experience; you even get to make your own kazoo at the end. ⊠ *12 John Galt Rd., Beaufort* ☎ *843/982–6387* ⊕ *www.thekazoofactory.com* 🖭 *$14.50* ☹ *Closed weekends.*

### Parish Church of St. Helena

**CHURCH |** The congregation of this 1724 church was established in 1712. The house of worship itself was turned into a hospital during the Civil War, and gravestones were brought inside to serve as operating tables. While on church grounds, stroll the peaceful cemetery and read the fascinating inscriptions. ⊠ *505 Church St., Beaufort* ☎ *843/522–1712* ⊕ *www.sthelenas1712.org.*

### ★ St. Helena Island

**ISLAND |** Between Beaufort and Fripp Island lies St. Helena Island, a sizable sea island that is less commercial than the other islands in the area and home to a tight-knit Gullah community. The highlight here is Penn Center, a historic school and museum that was the first school for formerly enslaved people in 1862. Visitors can also see the Chapel of Ease ruins, go to Lands End and discover Fort Fremont Historical Park, or stop by roadside farms and local restaurants. ⊠ *Rte. 21, St. Helena Island* ⊕ *www.beaufortsc.org/ area/st.-helena-island.*

## 🔼 Beaches

### ★ Hunting Island State Park

**BEACH | FAMILY |** This state park located on a barrier island 18 miles southeast of Beaufort has 5,000 acres of rare maritime forest and 4 miles of public beaches—some which are dramatically eroding. The light sand beach decorated with driftwood and the subtropical vegetation is breathtaking; it almost feels like you're in Jurassic Park. You can kayak in the tranquil saltwater lagoon, stroll the 1,120-foot-long fishing pier, and go fishing or crabbing. You can explore the grounds and exhibits of the historic 1859 Hunting Island Lighthouse (the lighthouse itself is closed for repairs). Bikers and hikers can enjoy 8 miles of trails. The Nature Center (🖭 *$8*) has exhibits, an aquarium, and tourist information. There is also a campground on the northern end that has 102 sites, but be sure to book in advance as these nearly oceanfront campsites fill up fast. **Amenities:** grills; parking; toilets. **Best for:** sunrise; swimming; walking. ⊠ *2555 Sea Island Pkwy., St. Helena Island* ☎ *843/838–2011* ⊕ *www.southcarolinaparks.com/hunting-island* 🖭 *$8.*

# 🍴 Restaurants

### Breakwater Restaurant & Bar

**$$$ | ECLECTIC |** This classy downtown restaurant offers tasting plates such as tuna crudo and fried shrimp, as well as main dishes like lamb meatloaf and filet mignon with a truffle demi-glace. The presentation is as contemporary as the decor. **Known for:** contemporary approach to Lowcountry cuisine; elegant atmosphere; local loyalty. ⑤ *Average main: $33* ✉ *203 Carteret St., Downtown Historic District* ☎ *843/379–0052* ⊕ *www.breakwatersc.com* ⊘ *Closed Sun.*

### Johnson Creek Tavern

**$$ | AMERICAN |** There are times when you just want a cold one accompanied by some raw oysters. When that's the case, head out to Harbor Island and this no-frills-just-fun hangout with inside-outside seating and lovely marsh views. **Known for:** friendly atmosphere; fresh seafood; cheap happy hour specials. ⑤ *Average main: $22* ✉ *2141 Sea Island Pkwy., Harbor Island* ☎ *843/838–4166* ⊕ *www.johnsoncreektavern.com* ⊘ *Closed Wed.*

### ★ Plums

**$ | AMERICAN |** This popular local eatery still uses family recipes for its soups, crab-cake sandwiches, and curried chicken salad. Open daily for breakfast and lunch, Plums is the perfect spot to enjoy a meal outside and to take in the beautiful views of downtown Beaufort. **Known for:** tasty raw bar; inventive burgers and sandwiches for lunch; great location on Waterfront Park. ⑤ *Average main: $12* ✉ *904 Bay St., Downtown Historic District* ☎ *843/525–1946* ⊕ *www.plumsrestaurant.com.*

### Saltus River Grill

**$$$ | SEAFOOD |** This upscale restaurant wins over diners with its sailing motifs, great cocktails, and modern Southern menu. Take in the sunset and a plate of seared sea scallops from the gorgeous outdoor seating area overlooking the waterfront park. **Known for:** signature crab bisque; raw bar with a tempting array of oysters and sushi; thoughtful wine list. ⑤ *Average main: $35* ✉ *802 Bay St., Downtown Historic District* ☎ *843/379–3474* ⊕ *www.saltusrivergrill.com* ⊘ *No lunch.*

# 🛏️ Hotels

Even though accommodations in Beaufort have increased in number, prime lodgings can fill up fast, so book online or call ahead.

### ★ Beaufort Inn

**$$$ | B&B/INN |** This 1890s Victorian inn charms with its handsome gables and wraparound verandas. **Pros:** in the heart of the historic district; beautifully landscaped space; breakfast is complimentary at two nearby restaurants. **Cons:** atmosphere in the main building may feel too dated for those seeking a more contemporary hotel; no water views; can fill up with wedding parties during spring. $ Rooms from: $280 ✉ 809 Port Republic St., Downtown Historic District ☎ 843/379–4667 ⊕ www.beaufortinn.com 🛏️ 48 rooms �’O’ Free Breakfast.

### Best Western Sea Island Inn

**$$ | HOTEL | FAMILY |** This well-maintained hotel in the heart of the historic district puts you within walking distance of many shops and restaurants. **Pros:** updated rooms; directly across from marina and an easy walk to art galleries and restaurants; breakfast included. **Cons:** air-conditioning is loud in some rooms; breakfast room can be noisy; lacks the charm of nearby B&B alternatives. $ Rooms from: $209 ✉ 1015 Bay St., Beaufort ☎ 843/522–2090 ⊕ www.sea-island-inn.com 🛏️ 43 rooms �’O’ Free Breakfast.

### City Loft Hotel

**$$$ | HOTEL |** This 1960s-era motel was cleverly transformed by its hip owners to reflect their minimalist style. **Pros:** stylish decor; use of the adjacent gym; central location. **Cons:** the sliding Asian screen that separates the bathroom doesn't offer full privacy; no lobby or public spaces; not as charming as a B&B. $ Rooms from: $249 ✉ 301 Carteret St., Downtown Historic District ☎ 843/379–5638 ⊕ www.citylofthotel.com 🛏️ 22 rooms �’O’ No Meals.

### Cuthbert House Inn

**$$$$ | B&B/INN |** This 1790 home is filled with 18th- and 19th-century heirlooms and retains the original Federal fireplaces and crown and rope molding. **Pros:** owners are accommodating; complimentary wine and hors d'oeuvres service; great walk-about location. **Cons:** history as a home to slaveholders; stairs creak; some furnishings are a bit busy. $ Rooms from: $305 ✉ 1203 Bay St., Downtown Historic District ☎ 843/521–1315 ⊕ www.cuthberthouseinn.com 🛏️ 10 rooms �’O’ Free Breakfast.

### Fripp Island Golf & Beach Resort

$$$$ | **RESORT** | **FAMILY** | On the island made famous in Pat Conroy's *Prince of Tides,* with 3½ miles of broad, white beach and unspoiled scenery, this private resort has long been known as a safe haven where kids are allowed to roam free, go crabbing at low tide, bike the trails, and swim. **Pros:** fun for all ages; the beachfront Sandbar has great frozen drinks and live music; two golf courses: Ocean Creek and Ocean Point. **Cons:** far from Beaufort; some dated decor; could use another restaurant with contemporary cuisine. ⑤ *Rooms from: $550* ⊠ *1 Tarpon Blvd., Fripp Island* ✛ *19 miles south of Beaufort* ☎ *843/838–1558* ⊕ *www. frippislandresort.com* ⌨ *180 rentals* ⦿ *No Meals.*

##  Nightlife

### Luther's Rare & Well Done

**BARS** | A late-night waterfront hangout, Luther's is casual and fun, with a young crowd watching the big-screen TVs or listening to live music. There's also a lunch and dinner menu with favorites such as Brewsky's burger and teriyaki wings, but the food's not the draw here. The decor features exposed brick, pine paneling, old-fashioned posters on the walls, a great bar area, and plenty of outdoor seating. ⊠ *910 Bay St., Downtown Historic District* ☎ *843/521–1888.*

## 🛍 Shopping

### Lulu Burgess

**JEWELRY & WATCHES** | This amazing little shop in downtown Beaufort is overflowing with colorful, quality items from funny cards and locally made jewelry to kitchen accessories and novelty goodies. Owner Nan Sutton's outgoing personality and eye for adorable gifts make shopping at Lulu Burgess a real treat. ⊠ *917 Bay St., Beaufort* ☎ *843/524–5858* ⊕ *www.luluburgess.com.*

### Rhett Gallery

**ANTIQUES & COLLECTIBLES** | This family-owned gallery sells Lowcountry art by generations of the Rhetts, including remarkable wood carvings and watercolor paintings. The historic, two-story building also houses antique maps, books, and Audubon prints. ⊠ *901 Bay St., Downtown Historic District* ☎ *843/524–3339* ⊕ *rhettgallery. com.*

#  Activities

## BICYCLING

### Lowcountry Bicycles

**BIKING | FAMILY |** If you want to rent a decent set of wheels—or need yours fixed—this affordable shop is the hub of all things bike-related in Beaufort. ✉ *102 Sea Island Pkwy., Beaufort* ☎ *843/524–9585* ⊕ *www.lowcountrybicycles.com.*

### Spanish Moss Trail

**BIKING | FAMILY |** Built along former railroad tracks, this paved trail is the Lowcountry's answer to the Rails to Trail movement. The nearly 10-mile trail (16 miles once it's eventually complete) currently connects Beaufort and Port Royal. It's open to walkers, runners, bikers, fishers, skaters, and scooters, offering great water and marsh views and providing ample opportunities to view coastal wildlife and historic landmarks. The train depot trailhead offers parking and restrooms and is located not too far from downtown Beaufort. ■**TIP→ The website offers a downloadable trail guide.** ✉ *Spanish Moss Trail Train Depot, Depot Rd., Beaufort* ⊕ *spanishmosstrail.com.*

## BOATING

### Barefoot Bubba's

**WATER SPORTS | FAMILY |** This eclectic surf shop on the way to Hunting Island rents bikes, kayaks, paddleboards, and surfboards for kids and adults and will deliver them to vacationers on the surrounding islands. They also serve ice cream. A second location on Bay Street in downtown Beaufort sells clothing and souvenirs. ✉ *2135 Sea Island Pkwy., Harbor Island* ☎ *843/838–9222* ⊕ *barefootbubbasurfshop.com.*

### ★ Beaufort Kayak Tours

**KAYAKING | FAMILY |** Tours are run by professional naturalists and certified historical guides and are designed to go with the tides, not against them, so paddling isn't strenuous. The large cockpits in the kayaks make for easy accessibility and offer an up-close observation of the Lowcountry wilds. Tours depart from various landings in the area. ✉ *Beaufort* ☎ *843/525–0810* ⊕ *www.beaufortkayaktours.com* ⊠ *$65.*

## GOLF

### Dataw Island

**GOLF |** This upscale gated island community is home to two top-rated championship golf courses. Tom Fazio's Cotton Dike golf course features spectacular marsh views, while Arthur Hills's Morgan River course has ponds, marshes, wide-open fairways, and a lovely view of the river from the 14th hole. To play these private courses, contact Dataw Island ahead of time with your request. ⊠ *100 Dataw Club Rd., Dataw Island ✛ 6 miles east of Beaufort* ☎ *843/838–8250* ⊕ *www.dataw.com/sports-golf* ▧ *From $77* ⅄. *Cotton Dike: 18 holes, 6,787 yards, par 72. Morgan River: 18 holes, 6,657 yards, par 73.*

#### Fripp Island Golf & Beach Resort

**GOLF** | This resort has a pair of championship courses. Ocean Creek was designed by Davis Love III and has sweeping views of saltwater marshes, while Ocean Point Golf Links was designed by George Cobb and runs alongside the ocean for 10 of its 18 holes. Fripp Island has been designated a national wildlife refuge, so you'll see plenty of animals, particularly marsh deer and a host of migratory birds. Be sure to book your tee times in advance since Fripp is a private island. ⊠ *300 Tarpon Blvd, Fripp Island* ☎ *843/838–1576* ⊕ *www.frippislandresort.com/golf* ⅄. *Ocean Creek: 18 holes, 6,613 yards, par 71. Ocean Point: 18 holes, 6,556 yards, par 72.*

# Daufuskie Island

*13 miles (approximately 45 minutes) from Hilton Head via ferry.*

Although Daufuskie Island is just off the coast of bustling Hilton Head, it feels like a world apart. With no bridge access, this island in the Atlantic can only be reached by boat, and the ride across the water is sure to be a memorable one, as the pristine and tranquil beauty of the Lowcountry is on full display.

Visitors will find a variety of rental accommodations available for a weekend or a weeklong stay, but many people prefer to just come for the day to explore the island and soak up the laid-back vibes. Daufuskie's past still plays a role today and noteworthy sites highlight the island's history, including an 18th-century cemetery, former slave quarters, the 1886 First Union African Baptist, two lighthouses, and the schoolhouse where Pat Conroy taught that was the setting for his novel *The Water Is Wide.*

The island's Gullah roots are integral to understanding the cultural fabric of Daufuskie, and guests can learn more about the Gullah population with a guided tour. With many unpaved roads and acres of undeveloped land, the most popular modes of transportation on the island are either a bicycle or a golf cart. Whether taking in the natural scenery, discovering lessons from history, or sipping a cocktail at Freepoint Marina, a trip to Daufuskie is an experience you'll not soon forget.

## GETTING HERE AND AROUND

The only way to get to Daufuskie is by boat. Several water taxis ferry residents and visitors alike there several times daily, with departure points spanning from Bluffton to Hilton Head and Savannah. Daufuskie Island Ferry leaves from Buckingham Landing in Bluffton; May River Excursions Water Taxi departs from Old Town Bluffton; Bull River Marina leaves from Savannah; and H2O Sports leaves from Harbour Town Marina. You can also rent a boat from one of Hilton Head's many outfitters and dock at Freeport Marina on Daufuskie. A tightly restricted number of cars on the island are reserved for locals, so nearly all visitors get around on a golf cart. It is highly recommended to rent one in advance so your transportation is ready for you when you arrive.

## 🍴 Restaurants

**Old Daufuskie Crab Company Restaurant**
**$$** | **SEAFOOD** | **FAMILY** | This outpost, with its rough-hewn tables facing the water, serves up Gullah-inspired fare with specialties such as Daufuskie deviled crab and chicken salad on buttery, grilled rolls. Entrées include shrimp and local seafood, while the Lowcountry buffet features pulled pork, fried chicken, and sides like butter beans and potato salad. **Known for:** incredible sunsets; colorful bar; reggae and rock music. ⑤ *Average main: $20* ⊠ *Freeport Marina, 1 Cooper River Landing Rd., Daufuskie Island* ☎ *843/785–6652* ⊕ *www.daufuskiedifference.com/restaurant.*

# Index

# Photo Credits

**Front cover:** Clarence Holmes Photography/Alamy Stock Photo [Descr: The historic Tybee Island Light Station on Tybee Island near Savannah, Georgia.]. **Back cover, from left to right:** Jeffrey Schreier/iStockphoto. Paul Brady/iStockphoto. Sepavo/Dreamstime. Spine: Cvandyke/Dreamstime. **Interior, from left to right:** Sepavo/Dreamstime (1). Ralph Daniel Photography, Inc./Courtesy of Georgia Travel (2-3). **Chapter 1: Experience Savannah:** Sean Pavone/Shutterstock (6-7). Casey Jones (8-9). Geoff L Johnson Photography\Courtesy of Visit Savannah (9). Ferne Arfin/Alamy (9). Master1305/Shutterstock (10). Rose Li/Shutterstock (10). Geoff L Johnson Photography (10). Zuma Wire Service/Alamy (11). Ralph Daniel/Courtesy of Visit Savannah (11). Courtesy of Visit Savannah (12). Courtesy of Visit Savannah (12). Courtesy of Visit Savannah (13). Mary A Roux/Shutterstock (14). Casey Jones/Courtesy of Visit Savannah (14). Scott Anderson/Alamy (14). John W Penney/Courtesy of Visit Savannah (15). Courtesy of Visit Savannah (15). Sean Pavone/Shutterstock (20). James Pintar/iStockphoto (20). Casey Jones Photography (20). Geoff L Johnson Photography (20). Casey Jones Photography (21). Different_Brian/iStockphoto (21). Geoff L Johnson Photography (21). Meunierd/Shutterstock (21). Cotton & Rye (22). Andew Thomas Lee/Pizzeria Vittoria at Starland Yard (23). Rocks on the Roof (24). AJ's (24). Perry Lane Hotel (24). The Cotton Sail Hotel Savannah, Tapestry Collection by Hilton (24). Electric Moon (25). **Chapter 3: Historic District:** F11photo/Shutterstock (55). Nikreates/Alamy Stock Photo (62). Kristi Blokhin/Shutterstock (65). Geoff L Johnson Photography (67). Chia Chong (70). Brianwelker/Dreamstime (72). Meredith Campbell Photography (78). NiKreative/Alamy Stock Photo (85). Sandrafoyt/Dreamstime (89). NiKreative/Alamy (91). Gestalt Imagery/Shutterstock (93). Michael Criswell Photography (105). **Chapter 4: Victorian District and Eastside:** Lazyllama/Shutterstock (113). Ralph Daniel Photography, Inc./Courtesy of Georgia Travel (118). Luke Smith (121). Ryannec/Dreamstime (122). **Chapter 5: Starland District, Thomas Square, and Midtown:** Savannah African Art Museum (125). Daniel Eastwood/Eastwood Photography (134). **Chapter 6: Moon River District, Thunderbolt, and the Islands:** Martina Birnbaum/iStockphoto (139). Edwin Remsberg/Alamy (144). Geoff L Johnson Photography (146). Matthew Rigsby/Shutterstock (148). Xuanren Wang/Shutterstock (150-151). **Chapter 7: Tybee Island:** AppalachianViews/iStockphoto (153). Sframe/Dreamstime (156). Sara Buck Lane (158). Miranda Osborn-Sutphen/iStock (160-161). Amy Murphy (162). Jawijsman/Dreamstime (167). **Chapter 8: Southside, Gateway, and Greater Savannah:** Kelly Verdeck/Flickr (169). Denton Rumsey/Shutterstock (172-173). Bruce Tuten/Flickr (175). **Chapter 9: Hilton Head and the Lowcountry:** William Reagan/iStockphoto (179). Courtesy of Explore Charleston (189). Ddima/Wikimedia commons (193). Chris Allan/Shutterstock (195). Sgoodwin4813/Dreamstime (218). **About Our Writers:** All photos are courtesy of the writers except for the following: Jessica Leigh Lebos, courtesy of Valentin Sivyakov.

*Every effort has been made to trace the copyright holders, and we apologize in advance for any accidental errors. We would be happy to apply the corrections in the following edition of this publication.